WHO'S MINDING YOUR MONEY?

WHO'S MINDING YOUR MONEY?

Financial Intelligence for Canadian Investors

Sandra E. Foster

JOHN WILEY & SONS

TORONTO • NEW YORK • CHICHESTER • WEINHEIM • BRISBANE • SINGAPORE

John Wiley & Sons Canada Ltd
22 Worcester Road
Etobicoke, Ontario
M9W 1L1

Canadian Cataloguing in Publication Data

Foster, Sandra E., 1955-
    Who's minding your money? : financial intelligence for Canadians

Includes index.
ISBN 0-471-64540-0

1. Finance, Personal – Canada. I. Title.

HG179.F67 2000   332.024'00971   C00-932112-8

Production Credits
Cover & text design: Interrobang Graphic Design Inc.
Cover photography: Joseph Marranca
Printer: Tri-Graphic Printing Ltd.

Printed in Canada
10 9 8 7 6 5 4 3 2 1

Contents

Introduction

"No mistakes, no experience; no experience,
no wisdom."

Stanley Goldstein

The stock markets provide the backdrop to one of the greatest real-life soap operas. It is about money—corporate takeovers, job loss, bankruptcy, success, wealth, luck, fame and fortune, rags-to-riches and riches-to-rags, and even, rumours have it, of interesting pillow talk. And everyone is a player in the game, be it through their RRSP, company pension plan, life savings or on-line trading account.

The financial services industry is undergoing a major transformation, moving from a business where the professionals hold all the keys to investment and financial information, to one where consumers have direct access to that very same information. A long-running bull market, price competition, new product developments, regulatory changes, and technological developments that let the consumer trade directly and, last but not least, increased consumer knowledge are fuelling these changes. These changes create both challenges and opportunities: challenges to the consumer to sift through their choices and quickly gain experience; and opportunities for financial professionals to do more for their clients.

Just how big are these changes? Massive.

There are two major investment trends that seem to go in opposite directions: one trend sees individual investors questioning the need for brokers at all and firing them to do their own trading on-line. The other is the growth of professionally managed investment services for those who don't have the time or the inclination to take on the day-to-day responsibility for managing their own portfolios. New investment programs and services are introduced almost daily, and the myriad of new products creates its own problems. The vast array of products and services offered—many with different pricing structures and features—makes them hard to compare.

How is the consumer to make sense of it all?

When it comes to managing your money, to use a restaurant analogy, you have the choice of:

- going to one of the finest (read "expensive") establishments in town
- going to a mid-range restaurant where you can order an all-inclusive package for a set price
- ordering à la carte
- stopping in at the local cafeteria
- cooking at home

To choose your best option, you need to determine what you want *and* what you can afford or are willing to pay for. What you select might change over time; you might even frequent all these places from time to time. You might eat at home most of the time, get a quick lunch in the local cafeteria, but visit a finer restaurant for special occasions. On the other hand, you might be a person who would never eat in the local cafeteria, preferring to dine only at home or somewhere fancy. Or you might eat only at home, preferring to know exactly what goes on in the kitchen.

But regardless of where you eat, it's the quality of the ingredients used, the recipe followed, the experience of the chef, the cost of the food, as well as the presentation and the service that all contribute to your perceived value of the meal. If you're the type who likes to eat mostly in expensive restaurants, you know you have to pay for that experience. Similarly, when you need a lawyer or an accountant, you expect to pay them for their advice and services.

When you eat out, you know there's a bill at the end of the meal. Even if no one would call you "cheap," you still probably look for good value for the dollars you spend. But do you know which investment services are worth paying for on an ongoing basis and which ones, like dessert, you might order only once in a while?

If you like to eat out, you probably like to hear what others are saying about certain establishments. Reviews help you decide if a restaurant is worth your time and money—and sometimes even highlights its speciality. Currently, nothing exists for the wide range of services and advice available in the Canadian financial service industry, although there are some that review parts of the industry, such as mutual funds or pension funds. But mutual funds are just one convenient type of investment product—really a sub-industry within the broader industry. They are not the entire industry. This is comparable to an overview of restaurants that ignores the food and concentrates only on the wine list or the décor of the restaurant. The financial service industry covers a wide range of financial services, products and advice. It includes retail and institutional investing, individual investments, all prepackaged investment products such as mutual funds and segregated funds, as well as the service and advice you receive.

If you go into a McDonald's restaurant for a meal and are in a hurry, you can order a pre-set meal and end up with more on your tray than you really wanted. But you probably placed that order because it simplified the decision of what to eat and how much it was going to cost. Of course, having pre-set meals also helps McDonald's. It defines a set number of meal combinations so that orders can be served more quickly, with fewer errors. Some of the savings are passed on to the customer—there's often a slight price break when you order their pre-set combinations rather than what you might really want. There is also a bundling of investment products and processes occurring. Mutual funds, segregated funds and "wrap" products are pre-set combinations that can help you or your financial advisor to manage your portfolio without having to deal with an infinite combination of investments.

As a backdrop to all these changes, the traditional financial institution is no longer what it used to be. Some of the most revolutionary changes in the world of investing have been brought about by the technology of the Internet. Now you can pay your bills and invest your life's savings with the click of a mouse-button without having to speak with anyone, and access products and services that were once only available to the high net worth investor. This self-service approach has been referred to as "disintermediation" because it makes it possible for you to do your own research and trade without being dependent on intermediaries, such as traditional brokers. Thanks to technology, you no longer need to be "net-worthy," but you do have to know your way around the Internet.

While some Canadians are looking to do it themselves, others are looking for investment advice, related to investing and building their portfolios, or financial planning advice including investment strategies, insurance and tax, retirement and estate planning. Others are looking for both investment and financial planning advice—what I call integrated financial advice or wealth management that used to be available to only the very wealthy. Whether you have $10,000 or over $1 million, there is a financial institution, product or service for your needs.

Every financial institution in Canada and a number of the international ones that have entered Canada want a piece of your banking and investment business. Even non-financial firms have expanded into offering financial products—you can now open a savings account and buy investments along with your groceries. Regardless of the historical roots of the financial firm you choose to deal with, it is likely positioning itself to be able to offer you and the whole world the full range of financial services and products. The bank, traditional broker, discount broker, financial advisor, mutual fund salesperson, insurance advisor, and the investment counsellor, all have services that are designed to make them money for looking after yours. They want you—or at least your money.

If you don't want to go out, on-line trading has brought you the ability to invest from the privacy of your own home. But who's really making the money? Is it the firm that provides the technology to buy and sell securities on-line and charges investors for each transaction? Those firms are finding that it is profitable for them to have you self-serve your financial needs as much as possible. The banks taught us to do our own bank deposits and withdrawals. The oil companies taught us to pump our own gas—it wasn't that long ago that you weren't even allowed near the pump. Now it's the investment industry's turn to "empower" you. While you can save big fees by doing your own banking and commissions by doing your own investing; the principles of personal finance and the disciplines of investment management that can improve your chances of success have not changed. You need to make sure that you don't make costly mistakes or miss opportunities because "you didn't know what you don't know."

Minding your money is more than just studying your investments. There are distinct financial planning disciplines that can help you keep more of what you make. Sometimes the term "financial planning" is used as little more than a come-on for product sales, but it has now evolved to where it is much more than that—provided someone qualified actually does it.

If you are like most people, you've got more money to take care of than you've ever had and are more interested in what is going on in the financial markets. How can you not be, when everywhere you turn, something about finance is being televised or printed? Some people are even making investment decisions based on ideas they get from advertising and the media, rather than doing solid investment research.

According to the Investment Funds Institute of Canada, over $17.7 billion dollars of new money went into mutual funds in 1999. According to the 2000 Canadian Shareowners Study, 49 percent of Canadians now own shares, directly or indirectly. More people are "doing it" in the stock market and, overall, have been fortunate to experience positive markets. Even the dips haven't lasted very long by historical standards. It's easy to underestimate the level of risk you might have in your portfolio—until you have to live through a bad market. If you've only been investing through a bull market with relatively short corrections, how can you know what it's like to live through a long bear market? The events of 1987 seem so long ago. If you're hoping the markets will just take you where you want to go, without focusing on what it really takes to be successful financially, it's time to take a good look. Don't wait. You need to pay attention to who's minding your money and how it's being managed. You've got too much at stake to leave it to chance.

Rising stock market values have left many investors expecting more of the same, believing that it is easy to make money in the stock market and "the sky's the limit." One long-time US professional money manager, Julian Robertson, recently announced that he was winding down his fund, saying, "there is no point subjecting our investors to risk in a market, which I frankly do not understand." Some technology and biotech companies seem to have been fuelling their stock prices with press releases rather than profits and some investors have made money by putting their dollars, or borrowed money, into the stocks of risky companies that, themselves, have no profits. When did investing in companies that actually make money go out of favour? Why are some people mistakenly following the "Seven New Rules of Investing?"

THE SEVEN NEW RULES OF INVESTING (OR RATHER, GAMBLING)

1. Concentrate. Don't worry about having all your eggs in one basket. Let the wheel spin on just a few investments.
2. Don't worry about profits. If a company has a good story to tell, why does it need to make money?
3. If equities are good, then more must be better. Why do you think equities are called growth investments rather than risky investments?
4. Use borrowed money. If they'll lend it to you, why not?
5. Technology and biotech are the only two words you need to know.
6. Access to lots of information is the same as knowledge.
7. Forget the old rules. They make investing just too boring.

Some people behave more like gamblers than investors. One woman told me that her stock investing was a bit like compulsive shoe shopping—except that she didn't even have to explain to her partner what she was doing with their money because there was no "evidence" in the closet. At least not as long as she was making money!

I always have trouble with ads or books that suggest that a firm's investment, technology, or strategy will help control your investments or keep you in control. "Control the stock market" is an oxymoron, like a "family vacation" with small children. Control what? Performance? Emotion? Risk? Regardless of what the ads imply, no one controls the markets! You can manage your portfolio for the long term, but not a short term. You can invest in the "next big thing," but there is no one *sure* thing. But the ads suggest that you should "step right up and give it try." That sounds too much like something you might hear at games at the midway—and just like those games, the odds are against you when you invest if you haven't done your homework.

The financial services industry has a huge marketing machine that markets and advertises its message and products effectively. Do you really want the decisions that affect your financial future to be influenced by the same type of advertising that persuades you to buy a specific dog food or toothpaste? I hope not, but we all know that advertising does have the ability to influence your perception and what you purchase. This book looks beyond the marketing. It looks at what you should pay attention to and gives you some tools to help you find your way through the maze of products, services and people that are out there.

You may be perfectly comfortable educating yourself, reviewing your needs, making your own financial decisions, and embracing the new on-line trading services. On the other hand you may not have the time or are unwilling to invest the time to understand how the financial markets work and the principles of investment management before deciding where to invest your money. If this is you, there are a number of solutions including hiring someone who has the expertise. But don't be tempted to hand off the decisions which will affect your life to the first person with a good, slick sales pitch because it seems like too much work to sort through all the options.

Whether you pay directly for their advice and services through fees or commissions, or indirectly through deferred sales charges and management fees, you need to watch how much you pay so you can figure out if you are getting your money's worth. But much of the cost of investing remains a mystery to many consumers.

Until recently, brokerage firms were rather vague as to the commission you would pay on a stock trade or the spread they kept on fixed income transactions. Mutual funds talked about the costs in terms of percentages rather than dollars.

Now the costs are coming out into the open. On-line brokerages have put the cards on the table regarding commissions. On the Web site of most on-line brokers, the cost of placing a trade through them is clearly spelled out (or you can use their commission calculator). It is often less than $30. A few sites are offering free trades on an introductory basis, and there are some on-line firms that process trades for free, making their money through advertising and other non-investment services. Mutual funds now have to disclose how much you are likely to pay in management fees in dollars, not just percentages.

However, most investment programs don't show on your statement all the fees you pay, let alone project what you will end up paying over the years! It's time you asked the tough question: "How much am I really paying?" Only then can you begin to answer the next question: "Am I getting value for the dollars I'm spending?" And when it comes to investment advice and financial planning: "Am I receiving the advice and management I need?"

Will a $30 trade (or even a free one) help you mind your money? Strong performing stock markets make it look easy to strike it rich by running with a few winning stocks, but even when you find a hot investment prospect, you still have to determine if it's good for *your* portfolio. Minding your money is more than just picking the right investments. We're going to look at some of the tools the pros use that you may want to apply to minding your money—whether you do it yourself or hire a financial advisor or money manager—to help you avoid expensive mistakes. The disciplines and processes of investment management, when combined with strategic personal financial planning, can help you grow and protect your investments *and* keep more of what you make.

It's up to you to decide the level of service and advice that is right for you, how much it costs and make sure you get value for the money you are paying. Even though many of the costs of investing—direct and indirect—are still not fully disclosed to the consumer, it pays to ask for this information.

When I was in university, one of my economics professors was discussing corporate profits and the capitalist system. He said that if we really wanted to know how things worked, all we needed to do was to "follow the money." What he meant was that we needed to figure out who was making the money in any given industry, and how. If you want to understand what is happening in the financial services industry today, you have to follow the money to figure it out.

One of the things we will do in this book is to follow the money to see where it is being made. It is being made in all sorts of ways, but mainly, by charging fees and commissions. There are fees for managing your money, fees for giving advice, fees for processing your transactions, fees for extending you credit, fees to provide you with a guarantee on your capital, commissions for selling you a product. While no one should expect to get something for nothing, you need to make sure you are getting value for the dollars you pay.

You can pay up to 3 or 4 percent a year for investment advice or less than one-half of one percent a year if you can "do it yourself." There's something to suit everyone's needs, and more investment choices are being added to the list. Although attention has focused on the cost of mutual fund investing, anyone using, or considering using, any financial services—ranging from banking to discretionary portfolio management—needs to understand what they pay for those services, both in dollars as well as in time.

If you don't feel you have enough information to make wise choices or you aren't confident about your ability to understand the financial markets, you are not alone. Money management is an important life skill that should be taught in high school. If it had been, you'd feel more confident in your investment decisions, know what to expect from the markets, and know how to build the blueprint for your finances to get from where you are to where you want to go. And you'd know what questions to ask and would be able to state what you want from the firm you chose to deal with. And, finally, you'd pay for only the services and advice that you need.

In my years in the financial services industry, I haven't seen anyone attempt to paint a picture of the people, products, prices, and processes that could be involved in managing your money. Over the past few years, much of the focus has been on the features of specific investments such as stocks or mutual funds. This is the first book that steps back and looks at where the Canadian financial services industry is today, where it is going and what you need to consider to be financially successful. This book looks at the people in the financial services industry and the menu of choices available to investors who want to make the most of their money. It also considers the options you have if you decide to hire or fire professional help. Unfortunately, we see some product sales people being paid on the same basis as full-service advisors, irrespective of the level of service and the value of the advice they actually provide to their clients. You might see some parts of the financial industry with new eyes and become a better investor, and better consumer, because of it.

This book will provide food for thought to those who want to "do it yourself," as well as to those who are looking at full-service options and everyone in between. You don't even have to select one option exclusively. You probably don't do all your grocery shopping in one store, so why should you think that you have to get all your financial services in one place. We'll look at the questions the industry needs to answer as it matures and the questions you need to ask of the industry to ensure that you get good value for your money as well as sound advice.

⌗

The growth of the financial services industry in Canada, the diversity of products available and the competition for your business should be creating a buyer's market for consumers. While some firms would like to have all your business, you can select the options best for you. You don't even have to choose between just the two extremes of doing it yourself or handing it off to a money manager. You can pick some combination of doing it yourself and working with a professional advisor. The future of the financial services industry belongs to those who can provide the mix of financial advice, services and products that Canadians need, at the right price.

⌗

The numbers, examples and illustrations used in this book—including comments regarding tax rates, inflation, interest rates and stock market returns—are all subject to change and reflect the information available at the time of publication.

There is no implied recommendation of any of the investments, strategies or firms offering financial services mentioned in this book for your specific situation. They are included simply to illustrate the points discussed. Your situation is unique and requires a personalized solution. Be sure to contact your financial institution or professional for the current details of the services you may be considering.

Let's follow the money!

The Changing Financial Services Environment

"The most effective way to cope with change is to help create it."

L.W. Lynett

Two key changes are altering the structure of the financial services industry:

1. The changing regulations that govern financial institutions are making the consolidation of firms possible.

2. The technology of the Internet allows individuals to do their own trading on-line.

In this chapter, we'll look at what is happening to financial firms in Canada and then deal with some of the implications of technological change for investors in Chapter 3.

Just over a decade ago, there were four traditional pillars of finance, each designed around a single product or service:

- banks, which processed banking transactions
- insurance companies, which handled insurance
- trust companies, to which you entrusted your assets
- brokerage firms, which handled transactions in the capital markets

Figure 2.1: *The Four Traditional Pillars of Finance*

Banking Services	Trust Services
Investment Products	Life Insurance

You would have had to go to four different financial people to have all your financial needs met: the stockbroker for investments; the trust officer for estate and trust services; the insurance agent for life insurance; and the banker for your banking needs. This meant that you had to give four different financial people all the details of your personal financial situation and attempt to coordinate and balance out what sometimes was conflicting advice.

The financial services industry today is more fully integrated—the products and services these traditional institutions provided are combining in the modern integrated global financial services firm, one that crosses the traditional lines and geographic borders. You'll find banks offering trust and brokerage services and products in addition to their traditional banking products and services. As well, life insurance companies have expanded into the investment and banking business. The independent trust company has all but disappeared, and the traditional stockbroker is rapidly changing to meet the challenges brought about by the Internet and the increased sophistication of the investor. The big are becoming bigger, not just in Canada but around the world. The business vision of many of today's financial institutions is that they can, and will, service all your financial needs. Others prefer to provide you with only the products or services they expect to be most profitable (for them). As the song says, you'd better shop around.

Today, each financial firm wants to provide you with a full range of products and services, all under one roof. You'll find:

- advice and illustrations to support the sale of a particular product
- investment advice in the form of an investment strategy or a managed program
- integrated financial advice, which also includes financial planning or wealth management

There is one notable exception to this trend. Canadians banks cannot use their branch distribution network to offer any insurance products to their banking customers, except for mortgage insurance to their mortgage customers and coverage for loan and credit card balances.

CONVERGENCE AND CONSOLIDATION

While there is consolidation going on in the financial services industry where similar types of firms are merging, combining their client lists or being acquired, the trend is more than just consolidation. There is a convergence of firms, products and services. The traditional financial firms, and some of the newer ones, appear to be heading toward a common goal or point. The banks are not the traditional, conservative banks any more. They are one-stop financial supermarkets offering "more than banking," as the Royal Bank Financial Group ads declare. If you need discount trading, investment advice, trust services, insurance, estate planning or traditional banking, business or trust services, they can provide it for you.

Consider the ads for two insurance companies that underwent demutualization. In 1999, Clarica Life Insurance Company (formerly The Mutual Group) ran an ad that talked about "investments and insurance solutions." In 2000, Sun Life Financial (formerly Sun Life of Canada) ran an ad that read "products and services ranging far beyond individual life insurance…" Need I say more?

• tip Wherever you go, the range of products and services available at any one firm is starting to look very similar to what is available elsewhere, even at firms that traditionally have offered a very different line of products.

Firms seem to be rounding out the financial products and services they offer. Here are a few examples of the scope of these changes:

- Brokerage firms are offering cash management accounts with chequing privileges and phone banking, and have introduced their own proprietary investment products. Brokers now offer life insurance products in addition to their traditional investment products and services.

- Banks are bringing financial planning into the branches, marketing index-linked GICs and the full range of brokerage services.

- Life insurance companies are offering more investments products. They've renewed their line of segregated funds by joining forces with mutual fund companies to offer segregated funds with brand-name mutual funds and have expanded the line of investments they offer within their universal life policies.

- Mutual fund distributors have introduced their own proprietary products and are offering their brand-name mutual funds within a segregated fund wrapper.
- Investment counsellors are managing individual portfolios as well as pension funds.
- The individual investor has on-line access to tools similar to those used by investment professionals.

And it's not just happening in Canada. In Europe, you'll find banking services, insurance and investments under one umbrella. In late 1999, the US Bank Act of 1933 (Glass-Steagall Act) was over-hauled, laying a new legal framework that would enable banks, securities firms and insurance companies to become integrated financial service powerhouses. They could provide their clients with a full range of financial services and products, ranging from traditional banking, loans and mortgages, credit cards and investments, right through to comprehensive wealth management services.

Figure 2.2: *Convergence in the Canadian Financial Services Industry*

The financial services industry is heading toward being made up primarily of global, integrated financial service companies that will:

- manufacture and manage a full range of investment products
- sell direct or through financial advisors
- distribute those products wherever they find interested investors
- package those products alone and as part of other products (e.g., you might find a mutual fund offered by a mutual fund salesperson, or a segregated fund version of it).
- provide services to complement the products, such as asset allocation and financial planning

A trust officer at one major financial institution made an informal comment that "it doesn't matter where you come in. We have the services and products to meet your needs." In other words, it didn't matter if your current need was for discount trading, banking, a loan, full-service investment services or financial planning, life insurance or something else, they had a service or product available. And regardless of what you might need in the future, they have it so you don't ever have to go anywhere else. But as firms get bigger and can "do it all for you," it remains to be seen if they will "do it your way."

Gradually, the regulations that created barriers for Canadian financial services firms will be eliminated, paving the way for the Canadian banks and insurance companies to merge to create our own Canadian-grown global financial services firms which can compete in the global financial marketplace.

And while Canadian firms are going global, international firms are coming to Canada. "The Americans are here! The Americans are here!" And it's not just the Americans. International financial firms based in the United Kingdom, Hong Kong and numerous other countries have set up shop in Canada. The weakness of the Canadian dollar and the fact that Canadians are considered to be relatively good consumers of financial services has provided some firms with the incentive to try and gain a share of the business here.

TREND Size matters. Canadian financial institutions will increasingly go global.

WHY DIDN'T THIS HAPPEN BEFORE?

After the stock market crash in 1929, governments moved to establish barriers between the various types of financial institutions to protect the consumer and reduce the potential for conflicts of interest. The laws governing financial institutions and the securities industry were established to provide a framework that would ensure the integrity of the financial industry—which is one of the reasons we ended up with the four traditional pillars. Three-quarters of a century later, the regulations that govern financial services firms have been loosened in the interests of competition. Time will tell if these changes are in the best interests of the corporations or the consumer.

Up until 1987, banks and securities firms operated separately, but then consolidation of financial firms started when banks were allowed to own brokerage firms and today the banks own almost all of the brokerage firms. Here is a brief summary of these events.

1988	Bank of Nova Scotia acquired McLeod Young Weir. Royal Bank acquired 75 percent of Dominion Securities and renamed it RBC Dominion Securities Inc. CIBC acquired 62 percent of Wood Gundy Corp.
1993	Toronto Dominion Bank formed TD Evergreen Investment Services and acquired First Marathon Securities (not to be confused with First Marathon Inc.), renaming it GreenLine Investor Services.
1994	Bank of Montreal purchased Burns Fry and merged it with Nesbitt Thomson Corp.

| 1996 | Royal Bank acquired Richardson Greenshields of Canada, merging it with RBC Dominion Securities Inc. |
| 1999 | National Bank acquired First Marathon Inc., which was one of the last of the traditional Canadian independent brokerage firms. |

In 1992, the legislation changed again, allowing banks to enter the life and car insurance business as long as they did not solicit their banking clients for insurance sales. If you were a banking client, you had to become a client of the insurance division or call their 1-800 number for information before they could offer you their range of insurance products. Talk about having a great mailing list and not being allowed to use it! But you might have received a mailing that offered you $1,000 of free life insurance—opening the door to turn bank customers into customers of the insurance division.

In 1999, Canadian Imperial Bank of Commerce announced it was getting out of the life insurance business, and closing its doors to new life insurance sales. Maybe they anticipated that they would eventually be able to buy a life insurance company more easily than they could grow one from scratch.

In 1998, Finance Minister Paul Martin disallowed the mergers between Royal Bank of Canada and the Bank of Montreal, and between the Toronto-Dominion Bank and the Canadian Imperial Bank of Commerce, stating that this "reflects the government's commitment to ensuring strong competition in the financial services sector."

In June 2000, he introduced legislation to establish the Financial Consumer Agency of Canada and to amend certain acts in relation to financial institutions in Canada. The legislation contains over 900 pages and includes the setting of a new consumer ombudsman and a new regulatory framework to improve the ability of financial service firms to compete within Canada. This legislation amends the following acts related to financial services: the Bank Act, the Cooperative

Credit Associations Act, the Insurance Companies Act, the Trust and Loan Companies Act, the Office of the Superintendent of Financial Institutions Act, the Canadian Payments Association Act, the Canadian Deposit Insurance Corporation Act, and the Bank of Canada Act. The proposals, when implemented, should provide for some interesting competition among the firms. Some key points from the report that will affect how financial firms operate include the following:

1. Life insurance companies, mutual funds, credit unions, and securities dealers (and their clients) will be able to access the Canadian payments system, which had been controlled by the banks, for clearing cheques and the electronic transfer of funds. Eventually, you'll be able to write cheques and make withdrawals from the ATM or use your debit card for certain types of accounts, regardless of the financial institution that holds the account.

2. Credit unions will be able to build a national presence, and with better economies of scale that come from servicing more clients, be able to provide a broader range of services and products.

3. Banks will have the potential to participate in joint ventures and form strategic alliances with other types of firms, such as insurance companies, to offer their clients a broader range of products and services.

4. Trust companies will be able to provide a broader range of investments to their customers.

To protect Canadian consumers, this legislation restricts certain mergers or acquisitions among Canada's largest financial firms. But around the world, integrated financial firms have created strong viable businesses—that are good for their customers *and* their shareholders. It remains to be seen if this new legislation is enough to enable our largest financial institutions to be players in the global financial marketplace, or whether it inadvertently gives the biggest competitive advantage to the international firm.

TREND It seems the era of regulation for the protection of the consumer is being replaced by an era of maximizing the profitability of the financial institution.

EVERYONE'S CONSOLIDATING

The consolidation trend is now occurring in almost every corner of the financial services industry. Here's a brief summary.

Banking

Who would have predicted these events? The courtship of TD and CIBC and of Bank of Montreal and Royal Bank? Canada Trust and Surrey Credit Union left at the altar? The marriage of TD and Canada Trust and of Royal Bank and Connor Clark? The Canadian banking industry is concentrated among a handful of six large Canadian banks. A number of foreign banks have entered Canada, non-banking firms such as life insurance companies are introducing banking services and now even grocery stores are opening up their own banking operations.

In the fall of 1999, I received a letter from one of the banks I deal with announcing I had been assigned one of their financial advisors. The branch manager had completed the Canadian Securities Course and obtained a financial planning designation. The brochure they sent me introduced "a dedicated highly skilled financial advisor, the latest financial planning tools, advice and solutions tailored to your financial stage of life, a refreshing level of personal service and exclusive benefits worthy of only our most valued clients." Wow.

TREND Expect to see some of the major Canadian banks acquiring other banks or insurance companies, if not in Canada, then abroad.

Credit Unions and Caisses Populaires

The credit unions and caisses populaires have long been local organizations that served the needs of their communities, owned by their members. Caisses populaires are found in Quebec, and credit unions in the rest of Canada. Traditionally, they have represented the needs of their members, not the interests of big business. Some have even taken swipes at the big banks, such as City Savings & Credit Union in 1999 that asked, "Are you satisfied with your big, bigger financial institution?" With relatively small memberships and assets, credit unions and caisses populaires have found it difficult to expand and compete with the bigger financial institutions that are growing even bigger still.

After an attempted takeover by Canada Trust to buy them, the Surrey Metro Savings Credit Union in BC proposed to merge with Richmond Savings Credit Union and Fraser Fishermen's Credit Union, also in BC. In 1999, the Mouvement Desjardins of Montreal and Credit Union Central of Canada announced that they would offer each others' mutual funds to their members.

TREND Expect to see credit unions and caisse populaires build synergies by merging or forming strategic alliances so that they can provide their members with a wider range of services at competitive prices.

Life Insurance Companies

The life insurance industry has been undergoing consolidation for a number of years. Some of the more recent consolidations include:

- Canada Life and Crown Life
- Great-West Lifeco Inc. and London Life
- Maritime Life Assurance Co. and Aetna Inc.
- NN Life Insurance Company of Canada and Transamerica Life Insurance Company of Canada

Five leading Canadian life insurance companies joined the global trend in moving from being structured as mutual companies, owned by their policyholders, to becoming publicly traded companies, owned by their shareholders, in a process known as demutualization. As public companies, they have to pay more attention to their earnings and profitability, but with a share structure, it will also be easier to raise money for, among other things, future acquisitions or mergers. While these life insurance companies have been given protection from hostile takeovers and merging with any other financial firm until after 2001, what's to say they aren't already in discussions?

TREND Some life insurance companies are starting to behave like "stealth" bankers and have introduced financial services and products that look a lot like the ones offered by banks and brokerages. Some have even set up their own "bank." You already can have your chequing account with Manulife, how long will it be before the other life insurance companies follow suit?

Banks and Insurance Companies: Takeovers?

Who stands to be the top Canadian-based global integrated financial services firm? Will the banks buy the life insurance companies or will the life insurance companies buy the banks? A few Canadian banks are selling some real estate holdings to build up their cash, possibly to invest in technology or e-commerce, or to acquire a life insurance company or other financial firm in the future. Canadian banks have already targeted U.S. life insurance companies. Although Finance Minister Paul Martin has indicated that he would not allow the largest banks and the largest insurance companies to merge—unless the federal financial committee finds it to be in the public interest—there is no reason that the largest ones might not swallow up the smaller Canadian ones.

RELATIVE SIZE OF THE TOP SIX CANADIAN BANKS IN CANADIAN DOLLARS	
	Asset Size* **(billions)**
Royal Bank	$280
Toronto-Dominion Bank	$270
CIBC	$267
Scotiabank	$245
Bank of Montreal	$238
National Bank of Canada	$ 74

*2nd quarter 2000

Source: News Releases

It is doubtful that the life insurance companies changed their corporate structure to public companies to let the banks eat them up. Rather, they did it to give themselves the potential to become financial powerhouses, and an interesting battle is developing between the banks and the major life insurance companies.

Mutual Fund Companies

The mutual fund industry in Canada grew rapidly in the 1990s as individual investors embraced that form of investing. Now the industry is maturing. In order to continue to grow and hold on to or increase market share, the biggest mutual fund companies in Canada will continue to get bigger through mergers or acquisitions, leading to an increasingly concentrated mutual fund industry. The following chart shows the concentration that has already developed.

ASSETS IN MUTUAL FUNDS AS OF MAY 2000	
Company	**Assets in $(000)s**
Investors Group	$ 42,619,106
Royal Mutual Funds Inc.	33,548,177
Mackenzie Financial Corporation	32,416,160
Fidelity Investments Canada Limited	31,115,731
TD Asset Management	28,687,617
Trimark Investment Management Inc.	25,034,316
CIBC Securities Inc.	22,738,508
C.I. Mutual Funds	22,534,910
AGF Management Limited	21,792,916
Templeton Management Limited	20,610,283
Assets held in remaining 61 companies	128,941,579
Total Mutual Fund Assets	**$408,283,405***

*includes adjustment of 1,755,897

Source: The Investment Funds Institute of Canada

The top 10 mutual fund companies account for over 68 percent of the mutual fund assets held by Canadian mutual fund companies; the remaining 32 percent is held by the other 61 mutual fund companies. And the smallest 10 mutual fund companies in Canada hold less than 1 percent of the total mutual fund assets.

Mutual fund companies, looking to improve their profitability and market reach, will either:

- merge with others and then combine some of their similar funds to reduce the costs of running them

- form strategic alliances or partnerships to enhance the distribution of their products, as Scudder Canada has with Investors Group Inc. or as many mutual fund companies have with life insurance companies, repackaging some of their mutual funds as segregated funds, as Fidelity and BPI have in the Manulife Financial GIF product

What does the consolidation of Canadian mutual fund companies mean to investors? On one side, it means less choice and price competition. One the other, it may mean lower prices if the mutual fund companies pass some of the cost savings they realize, through improved economies of scale, on to their unit holders. Whether they will or not remains to be seen, but one thing looks clear. As larger foreign and US mutual fund companies enter Canada, Canadian companies will need to provide enough choice and more competitive fees.

Financial Planning Firms

Financial planning firms range in size from the one-person office to firms with a sales force of several hundred people. There are two trends that have been pushing the consolidation in the financial planning or financial advisory business: competition and changing regulations. Financial planning firms need to be large enough to compete and be able to provide their sales force with the necessary resources and professional development. The firms have to have enough advisors and client assets to support the costs of operating the business, including:

- back office systems to process the transactions
- supervision and compliance functions

- investment in technology
- training the sales and advisory force

Regulations for mutual fund dealers are changing. Right now, if you purchase or hold mutual funds with a mutual fund dealer, you only have a minimum amount of investor protection and less than investors who hold the same funds through brokerage firms registered with the Investment Dealers Association (IDA). A goal of the Mutual Fund Dealers Association of Canada (MFDA) is to ensure that investors, regardless of where they purchase or hold their mutual funds, will receive the same levels of protection. This will mean changes for those firms that operate as mutual fund dealers, including new requirements for continuing education for their sales force and minimum capital requirements to ensure the solvency of the firm. Unfortunately, the proposed implementation date of the MFDA was pushed back from mid-2000 to early 2001.

The one-person office, or even an office with a few people, will not likely have enough resources to meet all these qualifications, and many will be forced to join other firms to survive. While the days of the captive sales force that only offers the firm's own products are all but numbered, the days of the independent financial planner is at a crossroad. Some will become niche players, specializing in some area of the business but many will join forces with a larger firm. A few of the consolidators that have been acquiring some of the independent financial planning firms are: AFP, Assante Corporation, BRM Capital Corporation, Dundee Wealth Management Inc., IPC, and First Asset Management.

Stock Exchanges

Many stocks exchanges are "closed clubs," where only members who hold seats are able to use the exchange for trading. They were not open to the public or to others in the industry. Today, these stock exchanges face competition from:

- Other traditional exchanges in North America that have existed for decades. The Toronto Stock Exchange (TSE), Nasdaq and the New York Stock Exchange (NYSE) are competing with each other for companies interested in listing their stock. For example, Canadian technology companies used to have to decide whether to list their company in Canada on the TSE or in the US on the Nasdaq, for the best public exposure and investor support. But the agreement between the Montreal Exchange and Nasdaq to operate Nasdaq Canada, puts the Montreal in competition with the TSE for the same new companies, and maybe even some already listed.

- The alternative trading systems (ATS) and electronic communications networks (ECNs), such as Versus Technologies Inc., Instinet and Island. These trading systems provide an alternative to the traditional stock exchanges and process trades for substantially lower fees. Initially, they processed institutional trades and then became part of the backbone for after-hours trading. It used to be almost unheard of for the markets to open much higher or lower than the level they closed at the previous day, but we now see markets some days opening 100 points higher or lower than they closed just a few hours earlier. The Ontario Securities Commission had banned trading on Instinet for over a decade, but lifted that restriction in 1999 and allowed them to become a member of the TSE. Is this a case of, if you can't beat them, then let them join?

  This competition threatens to put downward pressure on the fees a stock exchange can charge brokerage firms for executing their trades and listing new companies.

  In 1999, the Canadian stocks exchanges were realigned to make them more efficient. What really happened was the business was divided up—the west became the Canadian Venture Exchange (CNDX), the Toronto Stock Exchange (TSE) retained the senior companies and the Montreal Exchange (ME) became the derivative exchange for trading futures and options.

Going Public?

It's not just some life insurance companies that are demutualizing.
Around the world, public stock exchanges are looking to move from
being public, non-profit organizations to corporate structures that
would enable them to more easily raise cash for investments in computer technology to process the growing trading volumes, or to
acquire or merge with other exchanges.

In April 2000, the Toronto Stock Exchange was the first Canadian
stock exchange to move from being a closed club, owned by its member brokerages, to become a "for-profit" corporation held by shareholders. Initially, these shares are to be held by those who previously
held seats in the old structure—mainly brokerage firms. There are
plans to eventually list the TSE as a public company on a major stock
exchange—presumably on the TSE itself—but if it does, controls will
be needed to ensure that the TSE has to meet the same requirements
as any other firm listed on that exchange. The Montreal Exchange
also has discussed demutualizing.

There has been debate as to whether Canada really needs more
than one stock exchange. After all, the US market, which is much
bigger than Canada has only one main exchange—the New York
Stock Exchange. These new share structures may open the doors for
Canada to eventually have one single stock exchange positioned to
compete in the world financial market; something that the political
will has not been able to do.

TREND The demutualization process begins to separate those who
"own" the exchange from those who use it to trade. In the future,
TSE will open up trading privileges to firms that do not hold
shares, and simply charge them fees to process their trades.

Forming Global Alliances

Eventually, you'll be able to trade morning, noon and night, 24-hours
a day, seven days a week. If you can buy a loaf of bread at 3 a.m. on

Saturday night, why not a stock or a mutual fund? With global financial markets, why should Toronto and New York be asleep when Hong Kong and Tokyo are wide awake? In 1999, a number of trading facilities extended their public trading hours beyond 9:30 a.m. and 4 p.m., opening earlier and closing later. The technology needs exchanges and trading networks to operate 24-hours, seven-days a week exists.

What was impossible to imagine is here. International exchanges are joining business alliances to offer round-the-clock trading access, if not to all stocks, certainly for the most actively traded ones. In 2000, the Toronto Stock Exchange and nine major international exchanges created an international trading network—to be called the Global Equity Market—that will allow the stocks of major firms to be traded any time, somewhere in the world.

This development is of particular relevance to Canada, given the importance of the foreign investor to the Canadian markets. However, there are a few issues to work out, such as the fact that the countries report corporate information differently. For example, even Canada and the US have different reporting requirements, even when using generally accepted accounting principles (GAAP).

These global alliances will lead to shorter settlement times. Not so long ago, if you placed an order to buy or sell a security, you had five business days to settle up with your broker and pay cash, if you were buying, or deliver the stock certificate, if you were selling. In 1993, the settlement period was shortened to three business days after the transaction (T+3). As there is wider global access to exchanges and more reliance on electronic processing, the time you have to settle a trade will become shorter, leaving less time for anything to interfere with the order, including a drop in the stock market.

The predicted outcome is that the exchanges of the world will move to one-day settlement (T+1) and eventually to real-time settlement for stocks and bonds to deal with currency exchanges, time zones and investor confidence.

There needs to be enough buyers and sellers in the market while it is open for any market to operate effectively. Consider a farmer's market with all sellers and no buyers, or one with many buyers and only a few sellers. The price for produce would be erratic, to say the least. The same is true for financial markets.

It is expected that there will be fewer trades in after hours trading than during "normal" trading hours, making the market thinner and increasing the trading risk. You might not get as fair a price because of the following:

- There is less liquidity in the market. Just like when the housing market has few buyers, it may be harder to get cash for your asset, let alone the price you are looking for.

- Less liquidity can create greater price volatility and wider spreads between the buy and the sell price.

- There are price changes, up or down, on the release of corporate news after hours.

SO WHERE'S YOUR MONEY, REALLY?

While many financial institutions fantasize about having a cradle-to-grave relationship with their clients and providing one-stop shopping so that you don't have to deal with anyone else for your financial services, it still hasn't been proven that the Canadian consumer has bought into this idea. Most have their money spread among a number of financial institutions.

The Canadian Bankers Association's Web site estimates there are 20 million Canadian retail banking customers, but it was hard to find information on the number of Canadians each bank serves. Although many of these Canadian firms are willing to publicly report the number of clients they have globally in their news releases, they do not report routinely the number of Canadian retail clients they have. What did they tell me over the phone? One has about 9.5 million

Canadian customers, another 6.5 million, another thinks it's about 8 million, another 5.9 million. The other two did not respond to our query, but we're already over 29.9 million customers. Another 9 million Canadians have accounts at credit unions or mouvement des caisses Desjardin. President's Choice Financial and ING Canada combined have deposits for almost 500,000 Canadians. And this doesn't even include your mutual fund accounts or dealings you have with insurance companies.

This supports what many of us already know. We deal with more than one financial firm. If you have money with more than one financial advisor or financial firm, who's really minding your money? When you don't have a consolidated picture of your financial situation and the opportunities available, you're probably missing something. Note that I'm not suggesting that your money should be all in one place, just that someone—it could be you—needs to be paying attention to your goals and financial plan. Managing your money shouldn't be a random act.

SUMMARY

The trend to consolidate is everywhere. Even drugstores are struggling to maintain their client base as grocery stores, discount department stores and mail order services have expanded to offer these types of services, often undercutting the drugstores' own pricing. Similarly, books are being sold in office supply stores, department and grocery stores, as well as over the Internet, in addition to the traditional booksellers. The financial services industry is no different. As companies in this industry continue to look for opportunities to consolidate and converge, the "new" firms will look to earn more profits from the synergies that come from:

- eliminating duplicate processes and functions to cut costs
- laying off employees

- making more money from each existing client by selling them more products
- developing products to attract new clients
- having the resources to develop extensive computer systems so they can compete both within Canada and internationally

Remember that the prize—the profits from managing the money—goes to those with the most assets to manage. Big firms with the cash can buy out smaller firms and acquire their clients' assets, a strategy that may be quicker and cheaper than attracting new clients one at a time. And with size come economics of scale that allow the big ones to cut their costs. Whether or not they will pass on any of their costs savings or higher profits to the consumer in the form of reduced fees or more services for the same dollars remains to be seen. They could simply pass the increased profits on to their shareholders. Will these large firms still have a personal face or will their clients be little more than account numbers and rated according to their profitability to the firm? Time will tell.

Initially, many investors believed that the ability to trade on-line without having to speak with anyone would give them more power. But a full-blown convergence within the financial services industry could concentrate the power in the hands of a few financial firms, leaving consumers with less choice. Over your lifetime, you may need to be able to access a whole continuum of investment products and services. You probably want the lowest cost for straightforward transactions, competitive interest rates on your fixed income investments. You want quality products and services that are tailored to meet your needs. And to know that any price you pay for advice will end up contributing to your own bottom line.

The next chapter will discuss the second key structural change affecting the financial services industry and investors—the technology of the Internet.

The Brave World of On-Line Trading

> "There is nothing wrong with change, if it is in the right direction."
>
> *Winston Churchill*

Even though personal computers have been around for more than two decades, it is only recently that the technology of the Internet has been transforming our world. You can now do almost anything on-line: take courses, buy almost any product you want from books to groceries, do research, complain and communicate around the world in an instant using e-mail. You probably don't even handle as much cash as you used to even though the change you do have in your pocket or purse seems heavier. Your pay might be deposited directly into your bank account and your bills paid automatically. More people are banking on-line and using their debit card to pay for items without touching any cash. You can even transfer money from your saving account and invest it without ever writing a cheque.

Technology has also been a key driver of many changes within the financial industry. Computers initially enabled insurance companies to crunch numbers to study the mortality of large groups of people and banks to track bank transactions. Now, the Internet enables us to do our own banking, access research data and place our own trades on-line—and it continues to open up new possibilities. But is it all good news?

Certainly large structural changes—and computer technology is a major factor in these changes—alter how we do things and what the consumer expects. Alvin Toffler first wrote about the impact of these types of changes in his classic *Future Shock*.

Every brokerage firm seems to be adding some sort of Internet trading facility for their clients, even full-service investment brokers who initially had reservations about whether or not clients would be well served by the do-it-yourself model. For example, in 1998, Merrill Lynch executive John Steffens stated, "the do-it-yourself model of investing, centered on Internet trading, should be regarded as a serious threat to Americans' financial lives." Then, just a few months later, that firm announced it would provide an on-line trading facility for its full-service clients so they could work with a full-service broker *and* place their own trades if they wanted to.

The pressure was on among financial brokerages to offer clients direct access to information for three key reasons: one, in the long run, it's cheaper for them to let you look up the information you want when you want it; two, it frees up the financial advisor to support a larger client base or provide more in-depth advice to clients; and three, it's where the party is.

Today, you can trade through traditional full-service financial advisors who will give you advice and place the trade for you, through to on-line discount brokers, where you don't have to talk to anyone after your account has been set up. Some people have even ventured into the world of day trading.

The number of investors doing their own on-line trading experienced record growth in 1999 due to a combination of factors:

- There were more on-line trading facilities offered even by traditional brokers
- Stocks in the technology sector were hot
- The on-line brokerage firms ran expensive advertising campaigns

In fact, it has been suggested that because of the research and ease-of-access offered by on-line firms, people actually trade more often than they did when they worked with a full-service broker. Not that the on-line discount firms are complaining. If you trade more, they collect more fees from processing your transactions. There are no profits for them if you just hold an account with them. They want you to place trades, and if you've got money in your account and are looking to buy, there is no shortage of ideas to consider.

It almost seems that you don't need advice with all the information that comes at you over the newswire, investment TV and radio shows, investment newsletters, on-line and traditional print—and a rising market. Now, if a stock idea doesn't work out, you don't have to blame a broker for suggesting it. **You're in charge**, or at least you can feel that you are. Remember, no one controls the market. So how do you manage your money responsibly, given all the options you have to choose from?

Trading is the most basic financial service. Whether the brokerage is discount or full-service, the firm makes money by having lots of customers who make lots of trades—or lets them manage their money—and borrows from them to invest when it is appropriate.

TRADING FACILITY OR ADVICE?

The services you can access on-line range from being totally on your own, where you can trade through the facility of on-line discount brokers, to full-service brokerage services that offer advice and access to on-line research and offer, but do not require you to use, their self-serve trading facility.

Full-Service Brokers Who Offer On-line Access

Full-service proprietary research and access to a trading facility used to be only available through stockbrokers for clients who had real money. Brokers would present clients with investment ideas and help their clients sort the good ideas from those that were inappropriate for their situation, and, dare I suggest, offer a sense of moderation. They were called brokers because that's what they did—they brokered investment products such as stocks and bonds to clients. They weren't called investment executives, financial advisors or financial consultants. They functioned strictly as brokers. They helped match those who wanted to buy stocks with those who wanted to sell. But providing trading services today is no longer enough—unless you are a discount broker—and full-service brokers are reinventing themselves to be able to provide you with advice and guidance on a wide range of financial issues, not just stock ideas.

One of the trends with on-line advice is to provide clients of full-service brokers with access to information and research reports. This is as much for the brokerage firm's benefit as it is for yours. When you access this information on-line yourself, you free up the brokers or financial advisors so that they can meet with more clients as well as provide you with higher level financial advice, instead of just servicing your requests for investment data and price quotes.

Some firms have investment programs for clients who want to place their own transactions, but for those who don't want to do it themselves, their advisor/broker is still there to take orders for stocks and other investments that are suitable for your situation. Their advice may be limited to investment advice, or they might provide integrated financial advice (discussed in Chapters 4 and 5.)

Brokers classify orders as either solicited or unsolicited.

- A solicited order is one where the broker recommends an investment that is suitable for your situation. The recommendations are usually based on what the firm's research analyst is saying.

- An unsolicited order is where you tell the broker what you want to buy, not something the firm has recommended for you. In fact, because of the potential risk to firms from unsolicited orders, many brokers will discourage you from buying that investment through them. If you insist on proceeding, they will mark the order as "unsolicited" so that its source is clear right from the time the order is placed.

As we move to the 24-hour trading exchange, anyone who wants help and advice before placing a trade, will have to look for a firm willing to provide phone support around the clock and hires individuals who are willing to work shifts. At 3 a.m., will you be able to talk to a highly trained financial advisor whom you know? You may not have one trusted advisor—no one person can be on call 24 hours a day *and* provide you with coherent advice. There will be a team of people who can access your information on-line when you call. They may not know you personally, but they'll know your file.

On-line Discount Brokers

The on-line discount broker is the younger brother of the discount brokerage firm. In fact, now that Internet access is so widespread, many broker/dealers have moved their discount brokerage operation from being "over the phone" to being on-line. You may find some firms have a different price structure for orders placed on-line and for those placed through a live person. So, if you don't need to speak anyone about your trade, you could save money.

If you get stuck on the mechanics of placing your order, they will provide on-line help, or, in some cases, phone support. What you get is a trading facility and their research, not advice. Even though the term "advice" has many meanings in today's marketplace, just to be clear, you don't get product advice, investment advice and certainly not integrated financial advice. Going forward, you won't even have them checking your order for its suitability for your particular situation.

Suitability Rules

For decades, the suitability rules have been one of the backbones of the securities industry. These rules placed the responsibility on brokers and their firms to ensure that every trade was suitable for the client before filling it. These rules were designed to protect investors from high-pressure sales pitches on highly speculative investments—such as new companies with no profits, companies with limited revenues and no track record, as well as high-risk IPOs or penny stocks—where the investments were clearly inappropriate for the client's financial goals and objectives.

Today, trades placed through a full-service broker are reviewed for suitability to ensure the investment fits within your stated investment objectives. This means, among other things, that the broker must review the investment to make sure it is not too risky for your time horizon, act according to your investment objectives, consider your investment knowledge and understand and monitor changes in your personal and financial situation. Some people consider this to be a valuable service; others feel it just slows down their trading and gets in their way.

Newspaper articles in the early part of 2000 documented the challenges on-line brokers were experiencing: trying to keep up with the growth, training new staff to handle the requests for new accounts and reviewing trades for suitability. Having to review each trade to ensure that it was suitable was blamed for slowing down on-line order fulfilment and straining the resources of on-line brokerage firms. These created very real problems for their investors.

In the interest of speed and reduced cost (and the firm's own profits), the suitability rule was waived for the clients of on-line brokerage firms, provided the firm does not offer them any research or investment advice.

But is this change really in the interests of clients or the brokerage firms? It is good for the brokerage firms because they don't have to hire and train more people, but how is it good for the inexperienced investor, the occasional trader or even those investors who let irrational exuberance get the better of them from time to time? How about first making sure the individual has the first line of protection—enough investment knowledge and experience to know what they are doing?

While the suitability rules may not have kept some people from buying too much Bre-X or over-priced technology stocks for their portfolios, it did give others a point of pause to reflect on the level of risk they were prepared to assume. It may even have stopped some people from acting more out of greed than research. Beware. When you trade on-line, it will be up to you to assess the risk in any investment and determine if it is suitable for you. You'll need to be sure of your own research.

If you are working with a discount trading service (Why should we call it a broker if you only receive trading services?) that does not plan to check your trade for suitability, you will be required to sign a disclaimer statement outlining the risks you will be taking and that you are "on your own." Of course, you'll be reminded that you'll receive speedier trades. (Although slower trades affected investors, they were never really the root problem. The problem lay with the firms that had not hired enough trained staff to support the number of accounts they were opening.) If you've ever gone whitewater rafting, skydiving or bungee-jumping, you'll have signed a disclaimer form that basically says, "there is tremendous risk in what you are about to do, and you are the only one responsible if anything should go wrong." That's basically what you'll be signing with an on-line trading service that does not check for suitability. You might want to get independent legal or financial advice prior to signing. Here's a sample of what the disclaimer might say.

Release of Liability, Waiver of Claims, Assumption of Risks, and Indemnity Agreement

WARNING: By signing this agreement, you give up some important legal rights. When you sign below and use the services of (name of brokerage firm), *you are on your own.* If you make a mistake or lose money, you will have no one to blame but yourself.

In consideration of my using the services of (name of brokerage firm) and all activities related to those services, I acknowledge that I am aware of the possible risks associated with those services and activities, including the risk of losing all my capital, loss due to margin calls and any and all other risks. I could lose all my money.

I am solely responsible for ensuring that I am knowledgeable enough to use the services of (name of brokerage firm) and to select and manage my own investments. The (name of brokerage firm) will provide no supervision of my activities and is not responsible for any costs associated with any problems that may arise.

The (name of brokerage firm) is not responsible for any loss, damage or any liability of any kind sustained by any person while using the services of (name of brokerage firm) and any related activities, including injury, loss or damage that might be caused by the negligence of the (name of brokerage firm).

In return for the (name of brokerage firm) allowing me to voluntarily participate in this service and all related activities, I agree to the following:

1. **I assume and accept all risks** arising out of, associated with or related to my participating in the services.
2. **I am responsible** for ensuring that I have the education, experience and skills needed.
3. **I release (name of brokerage firm) from any and all liability** from any loss, damage, injury or expense that I may suffer, or that my next of kin may suffer as a result of my participating in these services and activities.
4. **I hold harmless and indemnify** (name of brokerage firm) from any and all liability.
5. **I indemnify and hold harmless the** (name of brokerage firm) and its executives and staff from any and all claims, demands, actions and costs that might arise out of my participating in the firm's services.

I understand that I am under no obligation to use the services of (name of brokerage firm). I acknowledge that I have had ample opportunity to seek professional advice prior to signing this release.

I understand that this is a legal agreement that is binding upon myself as well as upon my heirs, executors and representatives, in the event of my death or incapacity. I have read and understand all the terms of this agreement, and by signing this agreement voluntarily, I am agreeing to abide by these terms.

Signature: _____ Date:_____

Even if the wording is different, the meaning will be the same. You'd better know what you are doing. If you don't, you might be safer working with a broker who does. Choose wisely.

If this backbone of the securities industry is broken completely, unsuspecting investors will lose their safety net, which had given them protection not just from themselves, but also from unscrupulous promoters and salespeople. Does the industry then become a free-for-all? One investor might even end up with two or three types of accounts, such as:

1. on-line—no suitability rules applied—and no advice

2. on-line—suitability rules applied for those who want a safety net

3. full-service—suitability rules applied—and advice offered

This could create some issues surrounding where you get an investment idea and where you place your order. Suppose you talk to a financial advisor at a full-service brokerage about a stock idea in general terms. Then you go ahead and buy the stock through the on-line arm of that brokerage firm, or even through a different one where there is no check for suitability? Under the old rules, suitability was the last check done on your behalf before an order was placed. In the brave new world, would you be able to hold a financial advisor liable for discussing the prospects for any company you have heard of, without researching if the stock is suitable for your situation? Financial advisors may eventually be required to discuss all stocks in relation to their potential suitability for you, even if you decide not to buy it through them, in case you place the order with another broker.

TREND Now that on-line brokers don't have to review an order for suitability, full-service brokers may also lobby to have the suitability rules removed. Then they are less likely to be sued if they place an order for you, particularly if it is unsolicited.

WHAT YOU WANT AND WHAT YOU GET

Not all on-line brokers are created equal. In addition to their trading facilities, they offer a wide range of services you'll want to compare with what other firms offer, their costs and, of course, how that fits with what you need. Some key areas to compare are the types of trading they support, their trading facility and its capacity, the research and quoting, and other services.

There is a wide variety in the trading services offered in Canada. Here's a worksheet to help you compare different services side by side to determine which one(s) best matches your needs.

COMPARING ON-LINE TRADING SERVICES

In the first column, check off all the features and services you want from your on-line trading service. Then work through the features in your current program to determine if it matches your most important needs. If there is not a strong match between your current and your ideal, you can use the remaining columns to compare the trading services of on-line brokerages you are most seriously considering. Feel free to add any additional features that you want to compare.

	IDEAL	CURRENT	OPTION 1	OPTION 2	OPTION 3
Trading Services					
Self-directed on-line trading	❏	❏	❏	❏	❏
Broker-advised on-line trading	❏	❏	❏	❏	❏
Trading by touch-tone phone	❏	❏	❏	❏	❏
Wireless trading	❏	❏	❏	❏	❏
Broker-placed trade	❏	❏	❏	❏	❏
Margin accounts	❏	❏	❏	❏	❏
Real-time quotes	❏	❏	❏	❏	❏
Streaming quotes	❏	❏	❏	❏	❏
Real-time account balances	❏	❏	❏	❏	❏
Trading Orders					
Market order	❏	❏	❏	❏	❏
All-or-nothing trades	❏	❏	❏	❏	❏
Minimum quantity trades	❏	❏	❏	❏	❏

	IDEAL	CURRENT	OPTION 1	OPTION 2	OPTION 3
Limit order	❑	❑	❑	❑	❑
Good-till-cancelled	❑	❑	❑	❑	❑
Stop-loss orders on all stock exchanges	❑	❑	❑	❑	❑
Cancel (any order not yet been filled)	❑	❑	❑	❑	❑
Option to have trades reviewed for suitability or stupidity	❑	❑	❑	❑	❑
Options trading	❑	❑	❑	❑	❑
Short sales	❑	❑	❑	❑	❑
24-hour trading					
For all types of trades	❑	❑	❑	❑	❑
Certain types of trades only	❑	❑	❑	❑	❑

Mutual Fund Orders

	IDEAL	CURRENT	OPTION 1	OPTION 2	OPTION 3
No fee front-end mutual fund orders	❑	❑	❑	❑	❑
No redemption fees	❑	❑	❑	❑	❑
No minimum purchase required	❑	❑	❑	❑	❑
No charge switches within fund family	❑	❑	❑	❑	❑
Portion of trailer/service fees rebated	❑	❑	❑	❑	❑
Portion of DSC commissions rebated	❑	❑	❑	❑	❑

Other Services

	IDEAL	CURRENT	OPTION 1	OPTION 2	OPTION 3
Current news headlines and releases	❑	❑	❑	❑	❑
Access to new issues (IPOs)	❑	❑	❑	❑	❑
E-mail or pager alert when price reached	❑	❑	❑	❑	❑
Free pocket PC to connect with Web site	❑	❑	❑	❑	❑
Accuracy in order fulfillment	❑	❑	❑	❑	❑
Errors corrected at no loss/cost to you	❑	❑	❑	❑	❑
Top quality research	❑	❑	❑	❑	❑
Charting/graphing tools	❑	❑	❑	❑	❑
Screening tools	❑	❑	❑	❑	❑
High speed, direct access	❑	❑	❑	❑	❑
Market statistics	❑	❑	❑	❑	❑
Historical data	❑	❑	❑	❑	❑

	IDEAL	CURRENT	OPTION 1	OPTION 2	OPTION 3
Office where you can meet with them	❏	❏	❏	❏	❏
On-line transaction history for 15 months	❏	❏	❏	❏	❏
Facility to print your own statements	❏	❏	❏	❏	❏
Detailed annual tax reporting	❏	❏	❏	❏	❏
Music of your preference when on hold	❏	❏	❏	❏	❏
On-line help	❏	❏	❏	❏	❏
Capacity to process all client orders	❏	❏	❏	❏	❏
100 percent systems reliability	❏	❏	❏	❏	❏
Phone trading when the on-line site is down	❏	❏	❏	❏	❏
24/7 customer service	❏	❏	❏	❏	❏
Adequate staffing levels at all times	❏	❏	❏	❏	❏
Dedicated contact person	❏	❏	❏	❏	❏
Minimum service standard for e-mails or phone calls (such as 95% answered within two minutes)	❏	❏	❏	❏	❏
Priority service for e-mails or phone	❏	❏	❏	❏	❏
Conversations taped	❏	❏	❏	❏	❏
Investor privacy statement	❏	❏	❏	❏	❏
_____	❏	❏	❏	❏	❏
_____	❏	❏	❏	❏	❏

If it doesn't work out

No charge to transfer out your account	❏	❏	❏	❏	❏
Account transferred within 10 days	❏	❏	❏	❏	❏

Are new clients offered:

A signing bonus?	❏	❏	❏	❏	❏
An initial number of trades free?	❏	❏	❏	❏	❏
A free toaster?	❏	❏	❏	❏	❏

	IDEAL	CURRENT	OPTION 1	OPTION 2	OPTION 3
General Considerations					
Minimum account size	$_____	$_____	$_____	$_____	$_____
Average account size	$_____	$_____	$_____	$_____	$_____
Number of accounts each service rep supports	_____	_____	_____	_____	_____
Lot size (orders of multiples of 100)	_____	_____	_____	_____	_____
Minimum order size (such as 100 shares)	_____	_____	_____	_____	_____
Maximum order size (such as 5,000 shares)	_____	_____	_____	_____	_____
Fees					
Flat fee for orders of up to 1000 shares	❑	❑	❑	❑	❑
On-line commission calculator	❑	❑	❑	❑	❑
Trustee fee waived for RRSP/RRIF accounts?	❑	❑	❑	❑	❑
If not, what is the annual fee?	$_____	$_____	$_____	$_____	$_____
No administration fees	❑	❑	❑	❑	❑
Monthly service packages					
Monthly fee	$_____	$_____	$_____	$_____	$_____
What services are included?	_____	_____	_____	_____	_____
	_____	_____	_____	_____	_____
	_____	_____	_____	_____	_____
What will you have to pay for any additional services you need?	$_____	$_____	$_____	$_____	$_____
Clear fee schedule	❑	❑	❑	❑	❑
How much will you be paying each month?	$_____	$_____	$_____	$_____	$_____

Trading Services

The trading services on-line brokers provide range from a facility to place trades from your computer to wireless trading so you can trade from anywhere. You might get real-time quotes, account balances and research, or less timely information.

Some on-line firms are looking to provide all their services on-line. If you have a question, they want you to find the answer yourself using their on-line help. If you have a problem, they want you to send them an e-mail and wait for them to reply. Anything that takes human intervention costs them more money to provide. If the on-line firm is looking to be the lowest cost provider of trading services, don't expect to be able to talk with anyone. Other on-line brokerages offer the services of a broker who will assist you or even place the trade for you.

Types of Trading

Not all types of trades are supported by all on-line brokers. Some process only market orders at the lowest transaction fees or will only accept on-line trades that can be placed without any human interaction which might not include a limit order, a stop-loss order or an all-or-nothing order.

A market order is one where you basically say, "sell my shares at the going price." Of course, before you place a market order to sell, you'd obtain a real-time quote to get some idea of what price the trade might be filled at. But if the market is going up, you could end up paying more than you bargained for. While market orders may be suitable for some, in today's volatile trading market, many investors have found that placing limits on their trading orders helps them minimize their trading exposure.

A limit order basically says, "I'm willing to pay $x for this stock, nothing more." On the other hand, if the market is going down, a stop-loss order automatically triggers a market order so you aren't (hopefully) left holding investments that are plummeting in value. People practice safe sex so they don't end up with more than they bargained for. Certain types of orders help you to have "safe" trading so you don't end up paying more than you bargained for. If you aren't familiar with these types of transactions, you might want to take a course through the Investor's Learning Centre or read the material that comes with the Canadian Securities Course. You don't want to be uninformed if you are trading in the same markets as the pros.

Direct Access to On-line Research

Today's investors have direct access to most of the information and tools which used to "belong" to the broker, trader, and high net worth investors. Anyone who can log on to the Internet can research stocks for free or for a modest monthly fee.

Some investors are taking their "advice" from business shows, such as CNN and ROBtv. Some on-line shows are more like investment newsletters, giving tips on the companies with the breaking news. None of this information really makes investing any easier.

• tip Much of the economic and business news we get is American, with an American perspective. While some of this is relevant to Canadian investors, some is not. Don't just rely on American research. Also look at research offered by Canadian-based firms for the perspective important to Canadian investors.

One of the foundations of a sound stock market is the belief that all investors have equal access to information and that no one should have access to information that could affect the price of a stock before others. But still, not all information is disclosed equally to all investors. Some people, particularly institutional investors and high net worth investors, may still have access to pertinent information before it is generally disclosed to the marketplace. We'll eventually see fewer meetings behind closed doors and more information made available to the investing public via

- Internet broadcasts

- Conference-call facilities or the ability to call in to hear a recording of public announcements

While you can find a lot of research from reliable sources on-line, the Internet is also an easy place for people to post false information. None of these problems are really new, but the Internet, with its e-mail, chatrooms, Web sites and anonymity makes it relatively easy—and certainly quicker—to manipulate investors. You need to make sure you are getting your information from sites that have solid reputations for their research. When you're investing, quality is not a luxury—it's essential.

TREND The regulators will have to be vigilant in dealing with on-line scams.

Real-Time Quotes

Not only do you require timely, reliable research, you also need real-time stock quotes, not price quotes that are 15 minutes old. In today's volatile markets, there could be a dramatic change in the price and even the direction of the stock price in just a few minutes that could be costly.

With the widespread use of the Internet for research, current portfolio values and real-time quotes, the stock and mutual fund listings in the newspaper that report yesterday's prices will become redundant, if they are not already. The more stock and mutual fund data there is to report, the smaller the font the newspaper uses, making it difficult for anyone over a certain age to read without bifocals. It's not just me. I compared today's data with some reports produced just a few years ago. The type has definitely gotten smaller as they try to cram more and more information into a limited amount of space.

TREND All on-line investors will have access to real-time price quotes in the spirit of full disclosure. Brokerage firms that give some investors access to real-time data and others access to delayed pricing quotes, even if there is only a 15-minute delay, makes some investors more informed than others.

Trading Facility

The most basic service would allow you to trade whenever the markets are open. After all, if you're not paying for advice, you're looking for a reliable system that will offer round-the-clock access to the financial markets—one that won't go down or freeze out traders. This commitment requires an investment in dual processing computer systems where one computer system acts as a backup. If the first computer system fails, the backup one takes over, without you even being aware of the problem.

If the entire system happened to go down, would you be able to place a trade over the phone or even in person?

Capacity

Many trading services have already made a significant investment in technology to be able to process high volumes of transactions on a cost-effective basis. You'll also want to know whether or not they have the capacity to process the trading requests of all their current investors and what level of access they guarantee. If the market dropped suddenly and every client wanted to sell out, would their systems have the capacity to process all the orders? When some cell phone companies introduced a flat fee for after-hours services, people found that the lines all jammed and they couldn't get a call through—not even to 911.

Not being able to get through become a common complaint about on-line brokers, particularly when the markets were moving fast. To ensure their orders were filled, some investors went back to their full-service brokers because their systems could get their orders placed. It may have cost more, but getting an order in when you need it could save you money in a falling market, or make you money in a rising one.

Only time will tell if the on-line brokerage firms expect all the people they are signing up to become active users of their trading systems. Let's hope that they don't do as some health clubs did back in the 1970s, and sign up as many people as they could on the assumption that not everyone would make full use of their facilities.

Investor Profile

While the on-line brokers' minimum account size may tell you something about the threshold all their clients have to be able to pass, it doesn't tell you much about who they are really interested in as clients. Are they looking for active traders (from whom they collect transaction fees), mutual fund investors (where they would get paid a trailer fee) or just as many registered clients as they can get so they can sell advertising space on their Web site for a higher price?

You might be interested in knowing something about their other clients: ages, size of the average account as well as their minimum account size, and the percentage of their total assets that their clients hold at the on-line broker. If your account is $200,000 and their average account is $50,000, they may be currently focused on the needs of clients with smaller accounts. Conversely, if your account is $20,000 and their average account size is $100,000, you may find that their pricing structure eventually favours larger accounts.

TREND On-line brokers require their clients to trade to make money. Since on-line firms cannot count on maintaining a high volume of trading activity through not-so-good markets, they may eventually introduce minimum monthly fees or some fee-based services advice for clients who want or need it. We are already beginning to see some blurring of the lines between on-line and full-service firms.

What Is Their Investors Privacy Policy?

Even though you can trade from the privacy of your own home, the technology allows brokerage firms to collect data on what you are doing, how often you trade, the types of research you do and what else you are looking at on-line. They are collecting information about those who visit their sites and what interests them.

There has been much speculation about what firms might do with all this information—both within and outside the financial services industry. They may use this information or "mine" it (which is why it is referred to as data mining) for future marketing activities. For example, when you order a book from Chapters On-Line or Indigo, they know who you are and what you like to read, and they learn more about you with each order you place. And this will allow them to target you for special offers of other books by the same author or on a similar topic, or other types of merchandise related to your interests. Some people will find this intrusive; others will view it as a helpful service.

TREND On-line sites will be required to tell their clients what they intend to do with the information they collect. They will also have to permit you to opt out, even if it means you might miss out on an interesting opportunity.

Other Services

When and if you need it, will the firm be able to provide you with investment education, investment advice, personalized financial planning and/or wealth management services? Eventually, they will. Many discount services already have these services available through their full-service brokerage firms. Two questions remain. One, will you be able to graduate seamlessly to another level of service when and if you need it, or to access additional services as you need them on more of an ad hoc basis? And two, how will you pay for them when you need them?

Lower Costs?

With a traditional, full-service broker, the cost of a trade was difficult to calculate until after they had placed an order. Now, on-line firms post their fee schedules for everyone to see.

The ability to provide on-line trading has driven down commission rates, or rather, transaction fees. What is the value of an investment transaction? Is it $29.95 to trade a stock? $100 to trade a bond? We even have some on-line brokers offering trades for free (mostly in the US) and generating their revenue from ads rather than transactions. So, for now, the pressure is on to keep transaction fees low.

Even bonds and other fixed income investments can be traded at sites where you can see your costs for your order size for good quality fixed income products. Even though you pay no direct commission on these investments, the broker makes money on the difference between the price they paid for the bond and the price they then sell it to you—the spread. The price you see quoted in the newspaper or at some on-line sites is based on large, institutional bond orders, which get better pricing due to their volume.

All this creates challenges for the investment services industry that traditionally has earned revenue by providing trading services and research. When a firm competes solely on price, someone else may come along and offer those services, or a subset of those services for even less. While you don't want to pay more than you have to for what you need, remember that in on-line trading services as in life, you very often get exactly what you pay for.

When the transaction is fully automated, no salaries or commissions have to be paid to a human employee. The computer system has the checks and balances to do everything electronically, so it's a lot cheaper for the financial institution to process your transactions. On the other hand, there are a number of services that still benefit from the skills of a highly trained professional or personal human contact that cannot be replaced—at least not yet—by computer technology. You may get cheap trades, but if you want to work with a qualified financial advisor, you can expect to pay separately for that advice.

In many industries, price cutting has inevitably lead to more price cutting. Cellular phone services, for example, keep dropping in price. You may remember not so long ago when long-distance rates were high and people made personal long-distance calls only on weekends. Now, price competition in long distance has driven the price to as low as 10 cents a minute, even during prime time. Phone companies responded by adding services that come with monthly fees. Those services started to offer monthly service packages free of charge for a trial period, after which it was up to you to let them know if you decided not to continue. Fifty or 75 cents per use, or $10 a month doesn't seem like much but it can add up. As little as $10 a month becomes $1,200 (+ GST) over 10 years, too much to pay for any service you don't need.

While the lower trading costs is one of the attractions of on-line trading, you really have to add up your fees to figure out if it is really cheaper for you than the other alternatives. Your annual costs will depend on the number of transactions you place in a year. When a broker placed these trades for you, they charged you a commission, which was supposed to include investment advice and guidance. When there's no advisor to be paid, the cost is more often referred to as a transaction fee. If you have $10,000 in your account and place 10 trades a year at $30 each, your annual fees total $300 + tax, or 3 percent of your portfolio.

If a broker creates a high level of trading activity in your account, it is called churning, which is considered unethical behaviour. If you do it yourself, it's not smart, but it's not considered unethical. Not long ago, I met someone who told me he had placed over 900 trades last year on-line. This would add up to $27,000 in transaction fees, plus GST. Since his account (at least at one time) was worth $600,000, he would have to earn 4.5 percent a year on his investments *just to break even* before he started to make any money for himself. His costs made the price of investing in a professionally managed investment program look small by comparison. But he'd never totalled up his profits and his annual costs to see how he was really doing. When I asked him if he'd like to share any of his trading secrets, he said, "you don't want to do what I'm doing." I hope his aggressive trading strategies didn't get the better of him when the markets dropped.

In January 2000, one Canadian firm estimated the value of its on-line research to be $300 for three months. Through a series of newspaper ads, it stated that it would make this service available free of charge for three months to new clients who had $20,000 or more to invest.

There are even some sites that offer trades for free. Are they really in the investment business and interested in spending money so that you will become a better investor? Or are they in the business of providing the technology to process transactions, which could be used for almost any type of transaction, including trading or gambling? Or are they mainly interested in gathering enough registered users so they can make money from selling more advertising, or even selling the Web site down the road?

Nothing is really free. We are seeing fee structures related to the size of the account or advice billed on an hourly basis. When you can place a trade for $30 or less and get on-line research free, what is its value? There may come a time when firms will charge a basic monthly fee to those who are primarily "lookers" and not traders, or tie the services they provide to the size of your account. They have monthly fees for banking services, so why not for trading services?

RISKS OF TRADING ON-LINE

While being able to trade on the cheap is attractive, there are the usual investment risks from being in the stock market, in addition to those that being inexperienced or overconfident creates. Some people find the following:

- It is easy to do too much trading.
- The costs, even when the trades are cheap, add up.
- They end up with a lot of tax reporting for their capital gains and/or losses.
- They have to sort out the good research from the bad.
- They don't know enough about investing to place the right order for the right stock.
- They trade when there are not enough buyer and sellers.

As well, there have been complaints by investors using on-line trading facilities regarding the amount of time it takes to set up a new account, unreliable trading facilities, errors, and hours spent on hold, to just name a few. To the credit of those providing these services, they did not anticipate the growth they have been experiencing, and they have been working on improving the situation for their investors. Still, all is not perfect in the Internet world. The

Securities Exchange Commission (SEC) in the US received the following complaints regarding on-line trading in the first nine months of 1999. While the number of claims may not seem significant, this chart shows some of the trouble spots to be addressed as the on-line world grows—not just in the US, but also here in Canada.

ON-LINE TRADING COMPLAINTS RECEIVED BY THE SEC BETWEEN JANUARY 1 TO SEPTEMBER 30, 1999	
Type of Complaint	**Number of Complaints**
Difficulty accessing account	504
Failures/delays in processing orders	393
Errors in processing orders	247
Errors/omissions in account records	116
Transfer of account problems	116
Margin position sellouts	105
Problems with IPO allocations	103
Problems with executing cancellation orders	94
Problems with opening an account	89
Inaccurate quotes/pricing information	62
Problems with depositing/withdrawing funds	57
Use of false/misleading advertising material	47
Inadequate disclosure/understanding of margin	40
Failure to honour limit order	38

Source: *1999 On-Line Brokerage: Keeping Apace of Cyberspace*, SEC

Another risk of access to on-line trading is that some investors have ventured into the world of day trading with their serious money, and are behaving more than like gamblers than investors.

ARE YOU A CLOSET DAY TRADER?

Just for the record, day trading isn't about investing. However, some on-line traders think they are investing when they are really gambling on-line. Day trading is about trading stock symbols on price changes as small as 15 cents a share and selling them within seconds, maybe minutes later and the rush that comes with it. It is not to be confused with on-line investing, which uses the on-line technology to research what companies do and their financial information, and holding those companies in your portfolio for a period of time.

In the fall of 1999, Arthur Levitt, Chairman of the US Securities and Exchange Commission, estimated that about 5 million people were using the Internet for brokerage services. Less than 7,000 of these people were considered day traders, but others using on-line trading facilities may be venturing into the world of day trading without realizing it.

ARE YOU A CLOSET DAY TRADER?

Yes	No	
❏	❏	Have you ever bought or sold a stock because of something reported in the media?
❏	❏	Have you ever decided to stop trading or watching the market for a week or so, only to go back a few days later?
❏	❏	Do you wish people at home or at work would mind their own business about your trading and the time you spend on-line?
❏	❏	Do you place more than 5 trades a week? At $30 a trade, your habit is costing over $150 a week.
❏	❏	Do you envy people who can trade and make money without getting into trouble?
❏	❏	Have you had problems connected with your trading in the past year, such as margin calls, disciplinary action at work, debt counselling or arguments with your partner?
❏	❏	Is your trading more speculative today than it was before?
❏	❏	Have you missed days of work or school because of your trading?

❏ ❏ Have you been physically sick when the market went down?

If you answered yes two or more times, you may be a closet day trader. It's time to get a life.

In the on-line trading world, it still takes about 10 minutes or more for your order to be placed or filled. In the true day trading world, everything happens faster, including order fulfillment, which normally takes just fractions of a second. Day traders use a computer system that gives them high speed, direct access to the market. (When you use an on-line broker, you may think that you are placing your order directly into the market but you may be just sending them an e-mail instruction to place an order on your behalf.) They might use the electronic communications network (ECN), which is one of the trading systems used during the extended trading hours, a system like INSTINET, which was designed initially for money managers and institutional traders, or others. E*Trade Canada now offers high speed, direct access to certain clients.

 TREND As long as we have a bull market, more people will try the day trading game, looking to make "easy money."

These systems provide immediate order confirmation and, in a world where keystroke speed is important, puts day traders just a click away from buying, selling or cancelling an order if it hasn't yet been filled. Some day traders swear that the one "who has the fastest execution, wins." Ten minutes would be too long between placing an order and having it filled, since day traders don't intend to hold the stock for even that long! Some day traders actually place multiple trading orders for the same stock through different systems all at the same time, looking for the best price, and when the first is filled, they quickly cancel the others.

It has been suggested that day trading, and sometimes even on-line trading, gives a person access to the world's largest casino. For the right (or the wrong) person, day trading offers privacy, immediacy, large stakes and (coming soon) a 24-hour playground. When terms like "playing the market," "winning," "playing the news releases," and "keystroke speed" were introduced as part of the day trader's lingo, it hints of Las Vegas. Is it any coincidence that pornography, gambling and on-line trading are among of the fastest growing activities on the Internet?

Strategies for Day Trading

This section was initially titled "Strategies for *Successful* Day Trading," but I changed it because I thought that might be misleading. To get a taste of day trading, I paid $45 and took a three-hour self-promotional course offered by a day trading firm to get a taste of the strategies a day trader might use to try to find an "edge" to beat the markets. (Sounds more and more like Vegas, doesn't it?) Here's five of them:

1. Playing the News

News about a company can cause stock volatility—rising on good news and falling on bad. Day traders look to trade on corporate news before the rest of the world does. They might have a dedicated computer to read the latest news releases direct from the news houses, hear a tip in a chatroom or even just have the TV tuned to the business channel. Hearing about a breaking story five or 10 minutes before everyone else is believed to give a day trader the edge.

Some companies will release their corporate news after the close of the business day to give securities analysts time to assess its impact while the markets are closed. The day trader who has access to after-hours trading may try to take advantage of this news. When the news is good, they might place an order to buy stock at its current price, hoping the price will rise after the general market opens.

TREND As markets move to on a 24/7 basis, corporate news will inevitably have to be released when the market is open. Stock prices will become increasingly volatile as markets react to news, rather than waiting for market analysts and investors to assess it's impact.

2. Trading on Relative Strength

Day traders will look for stocks that are doing better or worse than the market as a whole, or a specific sub-index category, using charting tools or other analytical software. The day trader might buy stocks that have relative market strength and sell short stocks that are weaker than their market (expecting to be able to buy it at a lower price).

3. "Playing the Spreads" of the Market Makers

The price a seller offers to sell a stock at (their asking price) and the price a buyer offers to buy a stock at (the bid price they are willing to pay) are normally different. The day trader tries to make money by playing the spread, the difference between the bid and the ask price of large investors whose trades can affect the price of a stock. Suppose a seller is asking for $23.50 a share and the bid price by someone who wants to buy is $23.30. With only a 20-cent spread between the price, there is not much room to make money by placing an order in between the two prices. Day traders look for stocks with a (relatively) wide spread between the bid and the asking prices and place their order in between.

4. Scalping

Scalping is where day traders look to buy a stock moving up in price that is supported by a significant amount of trading volume. They aim to buy the stock on its way up, and sell it seconds or minutes later when they (hopefully) have made a little money. For example, on a day when Nortel is moving up strongly, the day trader would buy the stock, expecting the price to continue to go up, and then turn around and sell it as soon as it did.

5. Looking for Breakout Stories

A breakout story is a stock, the price of which is hitting a new high or a new low—for the day, the week, the month or even the year. The day trader assumes that a stock hitting a new high will go even higher before the price falls back a bit. A stock that has just hit a new low is expected to fall even further before the price bounces back up.

THREE MUSTS FOR DAY TRADERS

1. Be quick to click. Fatigue and age slow down reaction time.
2. Don't be colour blind. You rely on small arrows on the screen, or colour codes, to tell you if a stock price is moving up or down.
3. Be prepared to lose money. Is this *really* how you'd like to try and make a living?

So Who's Making Money Day Trading?

Many people have tried day trading and given up when they lost some of what they started with. One day trader with a sense of humour said that you could turn $50,000 into $30,000! Before you start, close your eyes and think, "if I lose this money, would I keep going, or would I want to walk away?" If you'd walk away, don't even start. It's an expensive game.

So who is making money in day trading? I wasn't interested in spending my days sitting in front of a computer tracking the smallest movements in stock prices to find out if these strategies work. I'm sure there are some successful day traders around the globe.

As far as I can tell, the successful day trader *owns* the day trading facility (much like the key to success in gambling is to own the casino) and makes money by:

- teaching courses in day trading
- collecting transaction fees from the trades their "graduates" generate (one firm was charging 2.5 cents per share or less depending on the trading volume) or under $30 a trade.

Let's calculate the commissions a day of trading might generate. For this example, let's assume our day trader buys only 10 stock positions and sells them out by the end of the day. That's 20 trades a day, or just four stock trades over five hours. I suspect the average day trader who sits in front of the computer five or more hours actually makes a lot more trades. It's been reported that some serious day traders and their teams trade over a million shares a day.

In our example, if each trade is 1,000 shares, the transaction fee would be $25 (1,000 x 2.5 cents) to buy and another $25 to sell after the price moves or at the end of the day. That adds up to about $500 a day or $10,000 a month in transaction fees. As in Vegas, the house definitely has an advantage.

SPECIAL TAX REPORTING FOR ACTIVE TRADERS

Just a few years ago, the only people who could "play" the markets on a daily basis had significant amounts of money. The more zeros a person had in their account, the more likely their active trading was to be called speculation. Today, anyone with $1,000 or more can open an on-line account somewhere and do their own trading.

Those trading through a day trading firm needed $50,000 or more (or $25,000 and be willing to borrow the other $25,000 on margin) to get started. Most recently, E*Trade Canada announced two direct access packages on which they would charge minimum commissions of $27 a trade. To qualify for the first level, which includes streaming quotes—quotes that are updated on the screen automatically—an investor had to have placed a minimum of 30 trades or spent $1,000 in commissions, in the previous quarter. (To qualify for the second level, which includes seeing what the market makers are doing) an investor had to have placed 75 trades or spent $2,000 in commissions for the previous quarter.)

Just how different is day trading from speculating? Not much, and maybe not at all. Canada Customs and Revenue Agency (formerly Revenue Canada) holds the position that anyone who holds stocks for short periods of time, has special knowledge of the securities market and has a history of active trading could be considered to be in the "business" of speculative trading—and be required to report 100 percent of any money made as business income. If you fit the bill, you could lose the ability to report only two-thirds of the capital gains as income on your personal tax return—and end up paying more tax.

At some time in the future, Revenue Canada may review tax returns, looking for evidence of speculative trading activity or will bring out a rule that states that an investment has to be held for more than 30 days before any profits on it are eligible for the preferred capital gains tax treatment.

HOW MUCH TIME ARE YOU GOING TO SPEND?

How much time are people diverting from their jobs and lives to watch the market and the value of their portfolios on-line? Some people estimate they spend about 20 or 30 minutes a day. To find out, a couple of novice investors on my team conducted an experiment to see how much time is really involved. They followed one tech stock—using my money—and checked on how it was doing and what the markets were up to throughout the day.

The first two days went really well. The stock went up over 30 percent—which really caught their interest. Then the price bounced around, not going really anywhere. Even though their interest seemed to wane a little, they still wanted to know how the money was doing (and so did I, given that it was my money on the line.) We discussed sell strategies. One person wanted to wait until the stock had doubled; the other wanted out once we (the royal We) had made a modest profit. And just in case the stock dropped suddenly, I'd put in a stop-loss order to bail out.

What did we find out? The time varied by person and their interest in the process. One person spent up to an hour a day checking out the stock prices and general market conditions. The other spent less than ten minutes. Even just thirty minutes a day adds up to two and a half hours a week or over 100 hours a year. If this is time you spend working for someone else, you could be robbing them of over two weeks of work a year. If you are working for yourself, figure out if what you might make through your investments is more than the money you might lose by diverting hours from your profession or company. Be honest with yourself.

TREND Productivity will suffer if employees build their on-line research and trading into their workday. While many employees are responsible about the time they spend on "personal business," companies will establish policies on personal use of the Internet at work—playing games, pornography, as well as the time spent trading or watching the markets. There's a bit of fantasy involved in all of them.

SUMMARY

Trading is the most basic service a brokerage can offer. There will always be traders—people who are looking to buy and sell stocks based on a good idea. Just when the financial industry was concerned that the stock market was going to be dominated by institutional traders (the mutual funds and the pension accounts), the Internet has provided a wider range of people with access to investment data and enabled them to trade on-line.

The bottom line of using an on-line discount broker is the physical trade; placing the order to buy or sell a security. The execution of the order is separated from any advice. The primary focus of most on-line traders is stock picking, not on building portfolios and prudent financial management. So, the ideal trading facility for stock trading would give you TRAK:

T-the ability to Trade and Track your investments
R-great Research
A-reliable, on-line Access
K-a Knowledgeable, live person to provide support, if and when you need it

Today's technology gives investors more choice. As with any new tool, it comes with only basic instructions, not what you really need to know to use it well. Suppose you just bought a new power tool. The instructions included would tell you the fundamental things you need to know to operate it—how to turn it on and off and a few tips. But they don't tell you what you need to know to build a dining room table or install new kitchen cabinets. Those things only come from additional training and/or experience.

It's similar for investing. It's not enough to just know how to place an order; you also need to know what you are trying to accomplish and the rules of the game. It's been said that a little learning is a dangerous thing. When on-line trading captures the imagination of investors and a rising market makes it look like picking the right stock is easy, disciplines and processes related to managing money and risk become undervalued. Some novice investors have ended up not just doing it themselves, but doing it *to* themselves, taking on far greater investment risk than they realized, and lost money.

TREND People will use more than one distribution channel for minding their money. They might have a self-service account where they do their own research and trading, an on-line account where they can place their own orders after consulting with a financial advisor, a traditional full-service relationship, or any combination of these options.

Even so, do you really believe that picking the right stocks at the right price and selling them at the right time are the only keys to financial success? While it has been suggested that you can manage your money using on-line services for less than a professional would charge, you are not comparing the same things. Yes, you can trade on-line yourself for less than it would cost you for trading services and advice, but trading and minding your money are not the same thing. Minding your money includes building a solid portfolio, selecting the right investments, managing that portfolio, as well as developing and monitoring a financial plan. Certainly, the investments you select—whether they are individual stocks and bonds, mutual funds or other managed investment products—are important. But so is how you put them together and manage them on an ongoing basis.

Investing can be a risky proposition. The rules of the stock market have not changed. Its temperament sometimes runs like a bull, and sometimes it turns on investors like a bear and mauls them. Whether you have a formal investment plan or manage your portfolio on an ad hoc basis, you will make a series of decisions that will affect your financial success.

Next we're going to consider how to build and manage an investment portfolio, something you can do yourself or hire someone to do for you. Will Rogers said that to be successful, you need to "know what you're doing, love what you're doing and believe in what you're doing."

CHAPTER FOUR

Integrated Financial Advice

PART 1: INVESTMENT MANAGEMENT

"In investing, the return you want should depend on whether you want to eat well or sleep well."

J. Kenfield Morley

The popular notions about managing money have changed over the years. It shifted from building portfolios with individual stocks and bonds to building them with mutual funds and other managed products and services. We now see two trends moving in opposite directions. One trend is more like a rebirth of portfolios made up of individual stocks and bonds and is supported by the growth of on-line trading, which we have just discussed. The other trend is toward a more disciplined approach to managing money for portfolios of all sizes, not just for those who have accumulated significant wealth.

There are two aspects to minding your money. One aspect focuses on the technical issues related to investing, the process of investment selection and building sound portfolios. The other focuses on the strategic financial planning issues, the disciplines of estate and tax planning, retirement planning and more. Both sides are important and are linked by your goals and objectives, target rates of return, and when you need the money.

In this chapter, we'll look at investment management, which is more than picking the hot investments or the right stock; it's a *whole range* of investment processes and disciplines, covering setting your investment objectives, determining your asset allocation, selecting the appropriate investments and more. In the following chapter we'll look at what is involved in strategic financial planning.

Traditionally, there has been a tug-of-war as to which would add more value to your financial well-being: investment management or financial planning. Certainly, they both can. Without a sound investment strategy, you risk not being able to achieve your financial goals and, some argue, would have nothing to plan. On the other hand, achieving good growth means you need to be concerned about tax and estate planning and other important issues. Perhaps we have a bit of a chicken-and-egg situation. Without returns, there isn't much to plan. Without planning, there may not be much to invest.

It's time we think of financial planning and investment management as two sides of the same coin. While it is not always appreciated, the disciplines of investment management and financial planning are highly complementary and lie at the heart of modern wealth management and integrated financial advice. Wealth management is more than just investment management, and it is not just a fancy name for financial planning. And just to confuse things further, you don't have to be wealthy to access wealth management services.

WHAT IS INTEGRATED FINANCIAL ADVICE?

To illustrate the integration of investment management and financial planning, consider the two intersecting circles. The investment performance is the underlying factor in the design of the investment portfolio. It is linked to your asset mix, level of risk, and the rate of return you anticipate needing to create the after-tax income you targeted in your financial plan.

There is both an art and a science to understanding the financial markets. The science lies in the academic models of economists and researchers who report on market activity and analyze market

Figure 4.1: *Key Components of Integrated Financial Advice*

INVESTMENT MANAGEMENT

Performance

Investment Policy Statement

The Law of Economics

STRATEGIC FINANCIAL PLANNING

After-Tax Income

Written Financial Plan

Tax and Other Legal Issues

Investment Selection

Goals and Objectives: What Do I Want?

Tax Planning

Asset Allocation

Return: What Do I Want/Need?

Cash/Debt Management

Risk: How Much Do I Want/Need to Take?

Investment Management

Estate Planning

Investment Philosophy and Process

Liquidity: When Do I Need the Money?

Retirement Planning

The Markets

The Personal Realm

behaviour and trends. There is even an academic discipline called behavioural science that attempts to find some scientific understanding of how people behave. The art lies in tailoring the financial plan and investment policy statement to the needs of the individual.

Since many elements of integrated financial advice are intangible—you cannot see or touch them, only their results—they are sometimes difficult to define, but they can be documented in the following:

- The investment policy statement (IPS) for the investment management process documents how best to build and manage the portfolio to achieve your stated financial objectives.

- The written financial plan documents your personal financial goals, the tax and estate considerations and a wide range of other financial planning objectives you may have. The financial plan may be more personal than the investment policy statement and doesn't have to be linked to the sale of any investment product as long as you are willing to pay for it.

The real power of advice comes when you link strategic personal financial planning with investment management—when you receive integrated financial advice that takes into account your current and future circumstances—that you not only have the potential to make more and keep more of what you make.

THE INVESTMENT MANAGEMENT PROCESS

Investment management is the nuts and bolts of making money in your investments—what investments to select and how to manage your investment risk. It focuses more on investment performance and links the return you might make to your risk profile. Some of the issues related to investment management may seem very academic and analytical; others are much more personal.

The Growth of Professional Investment Management

For many years, investment counsellors and pension fund managers provided professional investment management services to institutional investors and high net worth clients. Those responsible for employee benefit pension plans were willing (and still are) to pay fees for the professional services of money managers to handle the investments on behalf of their employees. Investment counsellors also offered their disciplined approach to investment management to private clients who had substantial assets to invest and were willing to pay fees for their services.

It wasn't long before these types of professional investment services were offered to the individual investors through mutual funds and segregated funds. MFS Investment Management Inc. introduced the earliest mutual fund—an investor trust—in the United States in 1924. Mutual funds were introduced in Canada in the 1950s by names familiar to us today, such as Templeton and AGF. The growth of the mutual funds sub-industry was initially slow until computers created a processing environment where firms could manage money and offer many of the disciplines of investment management to investors with much smaller portfolios.

TREND Formal investment management will continue to evolve as a disciplined approach to managing investments and be available to all interested investors, regardless of the size of the portfolio.

The Investment Policy Statement

An investment policy statement (IPS) is used by investment counsellors and others in the financial services industry who want to add focus and to document the investment management process. If you are working with a financial advisor, the IPS becomes the framework for all the investment decisions for your portfolio and outlines the strategies that will be used when managing your money. When you are hiring a money manager, the IPS becomes the blueprint—the contractual agreement that formalizes the job you want them to do. Whether you will do it yourself or hire someone to do it for you, you need to be clear about the job to be done before it can be done well. It's estimated that less than 20 percent of investors have an investment policy statement.

While the format of the investment policy statement (IPS) varies from firm to firm, it generally includes the following information that will be used when building and managing the portfolio:

- the investment philosophy
- the asset mix
- guidelines for selecting, monitoring and managing the investments
- your investment objectives (including the rate of return you expect, your risk profile, when you need any money from the portfolio and any constraints you have placed on the portfolio)
- the costs
- review and reporting
- any other details pertaining to the job you are hiring the money manager to do

To be successful when minding your money, you need to understand what you want to achieve and how you plan to do it. If you really want to *manage* your own investments (as opposed to just trading to make a quick buck), you might do what investment counsellors, pension plan managers, trustees and professional money managers do: develop a personal investment policy statement to provide a framework for making decisions. Here's an investment policy statement worksheet to help you get started.

INVESTMENT POLICY WORKSHEET

Complete this investment policy worksheet to build a framework for your investment portfolio and a better understanding of your investment objectives and needs. Complete all the information that applies.

Investment Philosophy

_____

_____

_____

Investment Goals

What are you hoping to achieve from your investments?

❑ Low volatility   ❑ Balance

❑ Conservative return   ❑ Growth

❑ Solid performance   ❑ Aggressive growth

❑ Income   ❑ Capital preservation

Guidelines for Investment Selection

Range of investments for the portfolio:

❑ Individual stocks   ❑ Mutual funds

❑ Stock indexes   ❑ Segregated funds

❑ Individual bonds   ❑ Index funds

❑ Other managed money *(pools, wrap accounts)*

❑ Other _____

Any exclusions? _____

Investment Objectives

What's the money for?

❑ Security   ❑ Buy real estate

❑ Retirement   ❑ Educate children/grandchildren
❑ To leave an inheritance   ❑ Other _____
❑ Buy a business

Return Expectations

What return do you need to make each year?

❑ Return equal to GICs   ❑ 10-12%
❑ 6-7%   ❑ 12-15%
❑ 8-9%   ❑ 15% +

How does this tie in with the return you need to make (according to your financial plan)?

❑ Same   ❑ Higher   ❑ Lower

Risk Profile

To help assess the investment risk you're prepared to accept, how much money would you be prepared to lose?

❑ None   ❑ 20% of capital
❑ 5% of capital   ❑ 25% of capital
❑ 10% of capital

Time Horizon

When will you need to use some of the money in your portfolio? All of the money?

I need some money in: I need all the money back in:
❑ Less than 1 year   ❑ Less than 1 year
❑ 1—3 years   ❑ 1—3 years
❑ 3—5 years   ❑ 3—5 years
❑ 5—10 years   ❑ 5—10 years
❑ more than 10 years   ❑ more than 10 years

How much money might you need from your portfolio within the:

Next 12 months? $_____

1—3 years   _____

3—5 years   _____

5—10 years   _____

More than 10 years   _____

Investment Constraints

❑ Foreign content rules to be followed for RRSP/RRIF

❑ Investments that should not be included for ethical or moral reasons

_____   _____

❑ Investments to be limited to publicly traded securities

❑ Limits on the maximum amount to be held in any one stock or sector

Percentage _____   Investment/Sector _____

Costs

Estimated cost of maintaining your portfolio

In the first year   ___% $_____

After 5 years   ___% $_____

After 10 years   ___% $_____

Review and Reporting

How often will you review the following?

Investment performance

❑ Monthly ❑ Quarterly ❑ Annually ❑ Other____

Investment selection

❑ Monthly ❑ Quarterly ❑ Annually ❑ Other____

Economic outlook

❑ Monthly ❑ Quarterly ❑ Annually ❑ Other____

Costs for managing the portfolio.

(Factor in your time.)

❑ Monthly ❑ Quarterly ❑ Annually ❑ Other____

Changes in your personal situation

❑ Monthly ❑ Quarterly ❑ Annually ❑ Other____

What will you compare your performance to?

❑ Benchmarks. If so, which one(s) _____ _____ _____

❑ A mutual fund

❑ The target return you need to achieve your goals

❑ Other _____

Investment Philosophy

The investment philosophy sets the tone for the investment portfolio. You might be interested primarily in capital preservation, growth or risk management, among other things. Here's a sampling of different investment philosophies used by various members of the Investment Counsel Association of Canada.

"Three main objectives guide our investment decisions:

1. preservation of capital

2. consistent asset growth

3. solid performance in all types of markets"
—*GrowthQuest Capital Inc.*

"prudent balance between risk control and return enhancement"
—*Guardian Capital Inc.*

"blended philosophy of value and growth"
—*Hutton Investment Counsel Inc.*

"unbiased judgement and highly personal investment management"
—*Priority Capital Management Inc.*

Asset Mix

Your asset mix, the percentage of fixed income or equity investments held in your portfolio will be guided by the outlook for the various financial markets, your risk profile, and the rate of return you've targeted to achieve your financial objectives.

This mix determines the amount of risk in the portfolio. Some investors have taken the approach that if some equities are good for a portfolio, then more must be better; and so they have pushed their equity holdings into the highly aggressive range. It's only when markets stop going up that they are reminded of the risk they have taken on. The higher the percentage invested in equities, the higher the portfolio risk. The riskier your portfolio, the higher the long-term potential investment returns and short-term losses.

Hypothetically, in 1999, if your portfolio was concentrated in two stocks, say Nortel and Qualcomm, your return would have been better than someone's whose portfolio was split 50/50 between fixed income and equity investments. That is until early 2000 when technology investors were hit hard.

 To help you determine your risk profile and an optimal asset mix for your portfolio, you might be asked to complete an investor questionnaire to determine if you are a relatively conservative investor or more on the aggressive side.

It is commonly accepted that diversification is the key to minimizing risk and optimizing return, but a well-diversified portfolio is not designed to make you the top return in any year. Its goal is to protect you from huge losses, by diversifying away some of the market risk. Even an equity mutual fund, which invests in many stocks, can diversify away some of the risk that comes from investing in only a few stocks.

No financial advisor working in the best interests of his or her client would have recommended a portfolio made up of only one or two stocks. Such a limited strategy would have had too much portfolio risk and the potential to lose money. Hindsight is always 20/20. The role of the financial advisor is to consider what *might* happen and plan accordingly. If you are managing your own portfolio, the only person you are accountable to is yourself—and your spouse.

Some firms use computer software to recommend an "ideal asset mix" based on the investor's goals, risk tolerance and assumptions regarding the relationship among the returns of different asset classes. Some of these portfolio optimizers are very simple; others are complex, but even the most respected models are "proven" using historical data. While these optimizers attempt to provide a scientific basis for portfolio design, there is no certainty that past performance will be repeated. Only time will tell if the "ideal" asset mix is better or worse than a diversified portfolio designed by an experienced advisor.

Guidelines for Investment Selection

Determining what types of investments will be in your portfolio— setting investment selection guidelines—adds discipline to your investing. The portfolio could be built using individual securities, index investments, managed money investments, an investment management program or some combination. Each investment, or investment product would be reviewed to determine whether or not it was suitable.

The portfolio would be built according to the asset mix looking for investment opportunities. If your portfolio is to include individual stock holdings, the characteristics of the investments selected would complement each other: passive index investing, management style, active investing for growth or value, industry sector, currency, and geographic region. As well, expectations for the financial markets (based on an assessment of economic and political issues) and for particular industry sectors and companies are considered. Some portfolios focus 60 or 70 percent of the equity holdings in about 30 core companies and round out the portfolio with other investments. Sometimes investors will focus on a particular investing approach, such as value or momentum investing. Some portfolios try to market time; others take a buy-and-hold approach.

A stock's price-earnings ratio and price momentum are traditional measures of the stock price. The price-earnings ratio looks at the corporate earnings expected for each share. A stock trades at a multiple of its earnings, such as 10 times earnings—a P/E multiple of 10—or 120 times earnings. Analysts assess the earnings potential of a company but their research has been known to be influenced by their own biases, or to just be wrong, which is not uncommon among people who are trying to predict the future. Consider Microsoft in the spring of 2000. There were analysts suggesting that the stock "might just be a buy," just before its price fell another 25 percent.

Some investors confuse the "value" of an investment with its current price. Consider two houses up for sale in the same neighbourhood, which are comparable in every way except for their list price. The first house is listed for $250,000 and the owner has been unexpectedly transferred overseas. He paid $225,000 for the house and his company is paying all his costs related to the sale, including the real estate commission and legal fees. The other house is listed for three months at $290,000. Its current owner paid $280,000 a few years ago and now wants to downsize.

You've just been through both houses and could see yourself calling either one of them home. What is the value of each house? The price the current owner paid? The asking price? Is one really worth $40,000 more? It boils down to whatever the seller can get for the house and whatever a buyer is willing to pay.

Similarly, when buying investments, it can be hard to comparison shop, even to evaluate companies in the same industrial sector. Investors sometimes get emotionally attached to certain companies, particularly if the stock price is going up, which can drive the price up even further. The value of the company ultimately lies in what it does, its profits and its outlook for the future—and what investors believe it will do in the future.

The price-earning ratio is only one factor used when assessing the value of a company's stock and whether or not it is suitable for the portfolio. The traditional disciplines of investment selection seemed out of fashion in 1999 and early 2000 when the only criteria seemed to be the amount of visibility a company achieved, not whether or not the company actually earned any profits for its investors. It seemed that the more frequently a company issued news releases, the more its price went up, even if all it had to sell was an idea. But traditional investment analysis considers the company's outlook and their financial information and is designed to:

- filter out the companies that are dogs
- find companies that are doing well

Unfortunately, this analysis is often discussed in investment terminology.

TRANSLATING INVESTMENT-SPEAK

INVESTMENT-BABBLE	TRANSLATED
Earnings surprises	Are they making/losing good money faster than people thought they would?
Financial strength	Do they owe more than they can pay?
Global expansion	Are they moving into new markets where they might make money?
Market share gains	Are they stealing customers from their competitors?

INVESTMENT-BABBLE	TRANSLATED
New products	Are they innovators?
Price increases	Can they raise prices without losing customers?
Positive cash flows	Are they making money or going into debt?
Profit-margin improvements	Are they laying off people?
Quality management	Is management doing its job and not about to be fired?
Reasonable valuations	Can I buy this stock without paying too much?
Share repurchase	Do they have cash they don't know what else to do with?
Stable shareholder base	Do other investors like the company?
Sustainable earnings	Can they keep making this kind of money?

Why do some people select a stock for their portfolio? Often it's because they like the story of the stock (and the company) and have assessed that the story is likely to come true.

Some stocks are harder to assess than others. For instance, It may be hard to determine the underlying value of a new company raising money through an initial public offering (IPO). IPOs come with higher risk than the stock of an established company. Although it now seems relatively easy to raise money in the capital markets, it wasn't so long ago that a company in the early stages of development had to go to a venture capitalist—or even to family and friends. Today, companies with no track record or revenues are trying to raise the money. Investors beware. It can be difficult to separate the companies with great prospects from those that don't.

Some former mutual fund investors are using the portfolio holdings disclosed by the fund company (even though it is out-dated by the time it is disclosed) to shortlist the investments they might purchase for their own portfolios through their on-line brokers. Their reasoning is that if the pros like a company, it must be good, so they use their lists as a starting point for their own research. Investors attempting this need to realize that they are not working with all the information. Portfolio managers do not have to disclose which companies they might be in the process of buying or selling.

There's been a sense of optimism that's kept consumers spending, which in turn feeds the corporate earnings that gives investors the optimism to put their faith in the stock market. While public companies have always had to report their financial information, the Ontario Securities Commission has introduced rules that will require them to report their revenues and earnings on a quarterly basis, not just year-to-date figures, so investors may better spot trends that may be occurring.

Investment advice narrows the selection of investments or investment products to those most appropriate for your situation. Some people do it themselves; others hire professional money managers or mutual fund managers to select the individual investments. These professionals might be right only about two-thirds of the time. The other third of the time, well, they'd rather not talk about that. How would you like a job where your performance is publicly reported every business day? Not just every day when there's a pro-sporting event, not just after a major performance, but every day the markets are open? That's what money managers whose numbers are published every day have to deal with.

Your Investment Objectives or "What's the Money For?"

Defining your investment objectives and goals helps you be clear on what you are trying to achieve. Are you looking for long-term growth so you can retire? Looking to build a portfolio that will provide you with regular income? Looking to preserve your capital? Your objectives, in turn, tie in with your return expectations, time horizon, how much risk you might have to take on and any restrictions you want placed on the investments.

Return Expectations or "What Do You Need to Make?"

No one really wants to take on more risk than they have to. The questions are: "How much would you like to make?" and "How much do you need to make?" When the market is going up, investors tend to expect to earn the returns of the top performing market index, and when the market is going down, they expect to make what they could have made if they'd held their money in a GIC.

Your IPS would link the return you need to earn, or expect to need, to your target returns in your financial plan. Suppose two 40-year-olds with the same size portfolio expect to retire comfortably at age 65. If one wants to retire at age 60 without saving any additional money, that person would have more in equities to try to grow the portfolio faster.

The flip side of return is risk. In some years you will earn less than you expected or even lose money.

Risk Profile or "How to Build a Portfolio So You Don't Lose Sleep"

Your risk profile attempts to measure your attitude toward risk and how much the value of your portfolio could drop before you would panic. However, no one knows what investment risk feels like until they have to live through a tough market for an extended period of time. Most investors today didn't experience the crash of October '87 for themselves. But if you bought a house in Toronto in the late '80s, Montreal in the early '90s, or Vancouver in the late '90s, you know what it feels like to have an asset drop in value.

While a risk profile questionnaire may be helpful, it is not a substitute for a financial plan that would indicate the target returns and the related risk you need to achieve your financial goals.

A conservative investor who would prefer a low-risk portfolio but needs higher returns (that might be possible through a more aggressive portfolio) has to reconcile these differences. If you have enough assets and the target return you require is low, you have the luxury of building a low-risk portfolio, or not. Completing a risk profile questionnaire can help you understand your risk tolerance, but if your portfolio in constructed with only the amount of risk you are comfortable with, it may not provide enough return for you to retire comfortably. I've always been amazed with the phrase "are comfortable with." How many people are comfortable knowing they could lose money in the markets? However, if you find yourself losing sleep over the ups and downs in your portfolio, you may need to reassess your financial goals so you can reduce the risk in your portfolio.

Time Horizon or "When Do You Need the Money?"

How many people put their down payment into technology stocks—and had to put off the purchase of a house when the market dropped? Time horizon considers when you need money out of your portfolio so that it will be there. It provides a discipline so you don't have money you need soon, in stocks.

Suppose your money in your portfolio has two purposes: some is for a down payment within the year and some is for retirement. The money for the house would have a time horizon of less than a year and would be safer kept out of the stock market. The money for retirement would have a long-term time horizon and be able to weather the short-term ups and downs of the stock market.

Investment Constraints or
"Are There Any Restrictions on Your Investments?"

You might have some restrictions or constraints on the investments for your portfolio. Here are the more common ones:

- Foreign content inside your RRSP and RRIF must be kept within the government limit.

- Religious or ethical restrictions, such as no tobacco companies or polluters.

- Restrictions on how much your portfolio will hold in any one stock or sector, such as technology or biotech, so that your portfolio is not overexposed to what happens to the stock price of any one company. Professional money managers and index funds often limit the amount they will hold in the stock of any one company or any one sector to no more than 10 or 15 percent of the portfolio. This restriction might also reflect investments you hold elsewhere. For example, if you like to study and invest in high-tech companies in your on-line account, you might want your professionally managed portfolio to exclude all technology stocks.

- No privately owned companies allowed in the portfolio.

Costs

In addition to how the money will be managed, the investment policy statement should also indicate the fees you will pay. These costs would include the percentage charged for investment management and related services, such as custody and transaction costs, as well as a calculation estimating how much you will be paying annually in dollars and cents.

TREND More consumers will look for money managers and financial advisors who will put in writing how their investments are to be managed. The IPS will formalize the relationship and clearly define the job they are hiring them to do.

Review and Reporting

Investment management is an ongoing process. The review section of the investment policy statement will specify how often you will review your investment program and its performance. It should also be reviewed if there are changes in your personal financial situation, such as your employment or marital status. The review process indicates if everything is on track or if modifications are required as a result of changes in your situation or objectives, or in the tax rules or other regulations that may affect your planning.

If you are working with an money manager or financial advisor, the review and reporting section of the IPS would document how often you can expect to hear from them and in what form (phone, e-mail, in person, etc.) It should also outline what to do to rectify any problems that might occur.

• tip The review is an opportunity for you to ask your financial advisor questions and make sure what you expected to happen is happening.

OTHER INVESTMENT MANAGEMENT SERVICES

While the investment policy statement is a starting point for your investment program because it adds focus to your investment process, there are other investment management services that can help you mind your money. These include the following five:

- Balancing your asset mix
- Comprehensive reporting and personalized rate of return
- Optimize your pre- and after-tax returns
- Capital gains and dividends for your personal holding period
- Personal financial planning advice.

Balancing Your Asset Mix

Balancing the asset mix in your portfolio helps manage its risk level. *Passive* asset management balances the portfolio back to the weightings that were targeted when the portfolio was set up and assumes the original mix is still the most appropriate for your situation.

Dynamic asset management balances your asset mix back to the original target mix only when the market outlook appears to warrant it, or on the frequency or conditions indicated in the IPS. Suppose your original asset mix called for 50 percent fixed income and 50 percent equity and your equity investments grow faster than your fixed income ones. Over time, the asset mix might end up being 40/60, which has significantly more risk than the 50/50 mix. The IPS might indicate that the portfolio is to be rebalanced quarterly, or it might allow the investment manager to maintain the higher level of equity when the market outlook was favourable. On the other hand, if it appeared a time to be cautious, your portfolio could be balanced back and even end up with a lower percentage in equities. So, the asset mix in a dynamically managed portfolio could differ significantly from the original target.

• tip Watch out for rebalancing that generates unwarranted fees or commissions. Sometimes it's hard to know if you are being sold a good story or a good change for your portfolio. Unfortunately, some commission- or transaction-based advisors have used rebalancing to increase their own bottom line. If you have any doubts or suspicions, ask "will this change create additional fees or commissions," or get a second opinion.

Comprehensive Reporting and Personalized Rate of Return

Ideally, statements report more than the market value of your investments and the details of all the activity that has occurred in your account. Good statements provide the information you need to make good executive decisions, including:

- the current market value of each investment in your portfolio.

- the amount you originally invested

- details of all the activity in your account, contributions, withdrawals, reinvestments

- your personal rate of return, which lets you tie what you *actually* make to your objectives or to the target return in your financial plan. Of course, this would also highlight poor performance, which may be one reason many statements don't report it

- how your rate of return compares to the appropriate benchmarks and the targets you set

- a detailed report of fees, commissions and other expenses charged to your account

- detailed tax reporting showing the total interest and dividend income, capital gains and losses for the year, as well as the current adjusted cost base for each investment in your portfolio, making it easier to plan for the current tax year and less time-consuming to prepare your annual income tax return

• tip If your accounts are not consolidated at one firm or your investment statement doesn't report this information, you'll have to calculate these numbers yourself or hire someone to do it for you. Your accountant would calculate the tax details, but it'll cost you.

If you don't know how you are doing, how can you learn from your experience and modify your strategy so you can improve? Or how can you compare how well your money manager (even if it's you) is doing compared to others with the same investment objectives and constraints, or the appropriate benchmark(s)?

There are many indexes that could be used as a benchmark. The key is to use the one(s) that would provide an appropriate comparison for your portfolio. Since most portfolios are made up of a number of different asset groups, the most appropriate benchmark is probably one that is made up of a number of different indexes, with weightings similar to your portfolio. Suppose your portfolio was made up of 50 percent Canadian fixed income, 30 percent Canadian stock and 20 percent US stocks. You might compare your personal portfolio to the returns from a benchmark portfolio made up of 50 percent of the ScotiaMcLeod Capital Bond Index, 30 percent of the TSE300 Index and 20 percent of the Dow Jones Industrial Average.

TREND Your investment statement will report what you actually earned and your target returns so you can make any needed changes to your plan, such as adjusting your asset mix, increasing your savings rate or working for more years.

Optimize Your Pre- and After-Tax Returns

Recognize it's not just what you make; it's how much you get to keep that matters. Holding your investments in the appropriate account can maximize your after-tax return and some investment management programs provide this service. Here are three of the more common strategies.

1. Dividend and capital gains income receive tax preferred treatment when held outside your registered plans. Dividends receive the benefit of the dividend tax credit; only two-thirds of capital gains income are taxable. All other things being equal, holding investments that attract capital gains and/or dividends outside your RRSP or RRIF can maximize your after-tax income.

2. Use the tax brackets of family members to your advantage. If you have a spouse who is in a lower tax bracket than you are, the investments that generate the most income annually could be held in his or her account, and your account would hold the investments that let you defer the tax for as long as possible, such as those that earn capital gains income.

3. Consider holding your foreign fixed income and equity investments outside your registered accounts so you can claim the foreign tax credit for any tax that was withheld at source.

Capital Gains and Dividends for Your Personal Holding Period

A large number of managed money programs in Canada, including most mutual funds, distribute taxable capital gains and dividend income based on your ownership as of a certain date, not on when you made the investment. Each unit holder receives a distribution based on the number of units they hold, not when they invested. Who wants to pay a tax bill for income that was earned by someone else before you even made your investment?

If you didn't hold the investment for the full reporting period, you could end up paying tax on income the investment earned, but *you* didn't. Suppose you bought a mutual fund on October 1 for your investment account. Even though you only held the investment for just three months, you could end up paying tax on capital gains earned over the full year!

TREND So unit holders don't have to pay tax on income they didn't "earn," managed money programs, including mutual funds, will develop software to calculate the income investors earn for their personal holding period.

Index investments, individual stocks and certain managed money programs allot the income earned according to your personal holding period.

Personal Financial Planning Advice

A financial plan should not be tool to sell you more financial products or services. Personal financial planning can help you maximize the effectiveness of your overall financial life, not just your investment portfolio and help you achieve your life goals as effectively as possible. This is discussed in the next chapter.

Financial advice could be included in the fees you pay or billed as an additional service. Some firms have experts on staff that you can hire or will recommend experts within your community. A few firms provide their investment clients with an annual credit of up to $500 to obtain independent tax and/or legal advice with the person of their own choosing.

TREND Financial advisors will offer comprehensive financial planning to their investment clients.

SUMMARY

Investors often make investment mistakes because they get emotionally attached to their stocks, particularly when they go up in value and when they don't. Sometimes people make mistakes because they are too cautious with their investment strategy; others make mistakes because they are overly confident and start to think they are smarter than they really are. A defined investment management process takes much of the emotion out of managing money and can contribute to your financial success.

Next, we'll look at the flip side of investment management, strategic financial planning.

Integrated Financial Advice

PART 2: FINANCIAL PLANNING

"The use of money is all the advantage there is in having it."

Benjamin Franklin

The International Certified Financial Planning Council, an organization made up of financial planning organizations from over 11 countries, adopted the following definition of financial planning to provide a common framework for their global discussions:

Financial planning is a process to provide a client with impartial assistance in analyzing and organizing personal financial affairs in order to achieve financial and lifestyle goals.

Financial planning is not a product you can see and touch. It is a process of thinking about the future and figuring out what you really want to do with your money and how you will do it. A financial plan should consider your financial needs today and project them into the future, taking into account your goals, your current financial situation, your resources, your family circumstances, your investment profile and preferences, and the issues of tax and estate planning.

Strategic financial planning is more than just the amount you need to save and the return you need to have enough income in the future. It lays out strategies you can implement so you can mind and keep your money. While financial planning has often been tied to selling investment and insurance products, it is really a separate process with its own disciplines and can be independent of any product recommendations.

The result of the planning process is a written financial plan that outlines recommendations of specific strategies to achieve your goals. Written plans used to be 30 or 40 pages long and contained a lot of general boilerplate educational material, such as how investments and the tax system worked. Today, they are usually much shorter, and more focused on your particular situation and needs. Having a plan in writing adds structure to anything you are trying to do. Businesses have business plans; architects have blueprints; and pilots chart their course. Investors have investment policy statements to document their investment management program and financial plans to help them achieve their financial and lifestyle goals.

COMPREHENSIVE FINANCIAL PLANNING

Strategic financial planning advice can be either modular or comprehensive. A modular financial plan would concentrate on one or two areas important to you, while a comprehensive financial plan is, well, comprehensive and considers all aspects of your personal and financial situation, including:

- developing your investment strategy
- retirement planning, including projections that help you determine how much you should save for retirement, what you need to do to prepare for retirement and how to manage your income throughout your retirement
- estate planning to provide for your dependants and reduce your final tax bill. Your financial planner can help ensure your estate plan is well integrated, but they cannot give you a legal opinion on your estate planning documents, unless they are also a lawyer
- how to minimize the impact of taxes
- the risks you should manage and an analysis of the amount of insurance you should have (life, property and casualty, disability, critical illness)
- debt management and cash flow
- issues related to family law and more.

"Life transition" events often involve a high level of emotion and uncertainty, and getting an outside expert opinion and a financial plan could give you some perspective—and advice—to help you make the appropriate choices and decisions. These events include:

- getting married
- the death of a spouse or loved one
- losing a job
- retirement
- birth of a child
- divorce and separation
- leaving the country

- disability
- buying or selling a house

This chapter includes a checklist that will give you an idea of some of the issues covered in a financial plan. You can use it to assess the depth of the financial planning advice you're currently receiving.

Modular Financial Planning

A modular financial plan addresses only one or two of the areas that would be covered in a comprehensive financial plan, such as tax or estate planning or dealing with a major life change. For example, it might look at the financial impact an event such as getting married, losing your job or buying a house has on your financial health. A modular plan might be called a retirement plan when it focuses on retirement planning issues, or an estate plan when it focuses on estate planning issues. Because a modular plan takes less time to prepare, it costs less than a comprehensive financial plan but it may not tell you everything you should need. If you hire a financial planner to do a modular financial plan to review the income you will need in retirement, they would not ensure that you have the proper estate planning documents in place, since estate planning would be outside the scope of the engagement.

THE FINANCIAL PLANNING PROCESS

According to the Canadian Association of Financial Planners, there are six steps to any financial plan:

1. Clarify Your Current Situation
2. Identify Your Financial and Personal Goals
3. Identify Financial Problems or Obstacles
4. Get Written Recommendations and Solutions

5. Implement Your Financial Plan

6. Review Your Financial Plan to Stay on Track

We'll discuss each of these steps below in more detail.

Step 1. Clarify Your Current Situation

Before you can determine what planning can be done, you need to take a snapshot of your current financial and personal situation. All the information related to your finances needs to be considered, including (if you have them):

- your sources of income and list of your expenses
- your liabilities (loans, mortgages, lines of credit, credit cards, family loans, margin, etc.)
- investment and RRSP/RRIF statements
- details of your government benefits
- copies of your latest tax returns
- life and disability insurance policies
- details of your property, casualty and car insurance
- details of your company pension plan and the latest pension benefits statement
- copies of your will and power of attorney (mandate in Quebec) documents
- copies of any marriage or cohabitation agreement
- any trusts or companies you may have
- details of any other financial asset(s) you have
- any other documents that are pertinent to your financial situation

You'll be asked to provide details regarding your personal situation, including your age, marital status and dependants, and some information about your values and what makes you tick.

Step 2. Identify Your Financial and Personal Goals

In order to get where you want to go it helps to articulate what you want to accomplish. You might have many things you want to do, such as securing your retirement, providing your children with a post-secondary education, reducing your taxes, eliminating debts or increasing your net worth. Some investors just want to make sure they are making the most of what they've got.

Rather than thinking about your goals in general terms, you will start to get specific about what you want to do. As examples, wanting to help your children or grandchildren through school might become a specific goal of paying for their first year of post-secondary education by establishing a RESP. Wanting to retire early might become a specific goal of retiring at age 60 by saving a set amount of money each year.

Sometimes, it is hard to articulate your goals but once you do, those goals provide you with a framework for assessing any strategy and/or recommendation. The formal financial plan will look at strategies to make your goals happen. Or if your goals are not very realistic, a financial plan can help you make them more realistic. But it will not provide any instant solutions nor will it set your priorities for you.

Step 3. Identify Problems or Obstacles

You need to know what stands between you and financial success, if anything. Issues might include not having the necessary financial documents, paying too much to have your investments managed, having too much or too little insurance coverage, missing opportunities to reduce your tax bill, and so on. It might also include some personal obstacles such as spending too much because "you're worth it!" or some particularly high expenses that you don't have much control over at this particular time, such as daycare or caring for an elderly relative. Unfortunately, some obstacles are difficult to overcome without making major changes.

Step 4. Get Written Recommendations and Solutions

The next step in the financial planning process is to outline what needs to be done. The financial planner will analyze your information and identify any opportunities and realistic options, as well as their recommendations for further discussion. Some present the financial plan as a discussion paper where they expect you to ask questions and help you find ways to commit to your financial plan. Although the financial planner will make recommendations, it's your plan, not theirs, and the decisions are ultimately yours. After all, you're the one that has to live with the consequences. Even the best financial planner will not tell you what to do.

Here's one small example of some solutions taken from a comprehensive financial plan. Suppose you are a conservative investor who wants to retire at age 60. To achieve this goal, you have to decide among the following options:

- increasing the percentage of stocks you hold in your portfolio— and taking on more investment risk
- saving more each year—and having less to live on now
- retiring later
- some combination of taking on some more investment risk and saving some more than you currently are.

Making choices and trade-offs are a normal part of the planning process. For example, you might find a strategy that would enable you to defer the maximum amount of tax for as long as possible, but find that this would require you to compromise the level of risk in your investment strategy. In fact, there may be no "best" financial plan. You are looking for strategies that marry your personal objectives with the ones that make the most of all the rules.

If your situation requires it, your advisor may recommend bringing in the expertise of other professionals or specialists, such as accountants, lawyers or even other financial planners who specialize in a particular area.

Step 5. Implement Your Financial Plan

Once you have your financial plan, you should be able to implement it wherever you want. There should be no requirement that you implement the plan with the person or firm that prepared the plan, whether or not you paid for it.

However, most financial planners who sell products are willing to help you implement your financial plan—particularly where they will be paid commissions or receive ongoing fees from the investments. This leads to concerns over the potential for conflicts of interest. However, if you're looking for a financial advisor to help you manage your investments and you like what you've seen and heard up to this point, the plan could become the road map for how you would work together.

 More people will be paying for a financial plan and using it as the blueprint to implement it themselves. Today, with more discount brokerage and no-load options, this is more feasible than it was just a few years ago.

Step 6. Review Your Financial Plan

Financial planning is a dynamic process. Regular reviews mean that adjustments can be made as they are needed—nips and tucks along the way—particularly when things are just not quite what was expected or what they used to be. Market conditions, the legislation related to tax and other issues, and your personal situation can all change over time and affect your planning. Just as the cruise ship that has the sonar on may be able to avoid an iceberg more successfully than by looking out the window, the earlier you identify changes that are needed, the easier it is to deal with them.

If you were running a company, you'd compare your projections with your results on a regular basis and make any adjustments that were necessary along the way. Similarly, in piloting a plane, you'd make adjustments after takeoff to deal with what you find on route. Since none of the information in your financial plan is guaranteed, reviewing your financial projections, including your retirement independence calculation and insurance needs will let you see if you are on the right track and make adjustments as necessary. If you earned more or less than you assumed you might, you'll want to know this and refine your financial plan. If you make less, your options would include: increasing the amount you save each year, topping up your retirement plan with a lump sum, or resigning yourself to the fact that you'll have to work longer.

Professional pension plans are required to do a major review every three years to see how they are doing and make adjustments if they are needed. Your personal goals and financial plan are just as important. You probably don't need a full review more than every few years unless there have been major changes in your financial or personal situation, but you should monitor your financial plan and strategies to make sure you stay on track.

• tip Review the numbers in your financial plan annually to make sure you're on the right track and determine if there are any legislative changes that would affect your planning. If there is a significant change in your personal or financial situation, you might even need a new plan.

ASSESSING YOUR FINANCIAL PLAN

A comprehensive financial plan is more than a retirement plan or an investment plan. You can use this checklist to assess the depth of issues your financial planning advice currently covers. Check the appropriate box for any statement that could be relevant to your situation. Any *"No"*s or *"Unsure"*s may require special attention.

Pre-Retirement Planning

Yes No Unsure

❑ ❑ ❑ My retirement independence calculation was updated less than a year ago.

❑ ❑ ❑ My actual rate of return is equal to or better than the target rate of return used in my retirement calculation.

❑ ❑ ❑ I know what to do to achieve my retirement objectives.

❑ ❑ ❑ My retirement savings are on track.

❑ ❑ ❑ I don't need the stock market to do all my savings for me.

❑ ❑ ❑ I understand how my CPP and OAS benefits work.

❑ ❑ ❑ I understand how my employer's pension plan will work when I don't.

❑ ❑ ❑ I know what I'm going to do with my time in retirement.

❑ ❑ ❑ My spouse and I have coordinated our planning.

❑ ❑ ❑ I'm working on maximizing my RRSP.

❑ ❑ ❑ I have a plan to use up my unused RRSP contribution room before I'm 69.

Retirement Planning (if you are retired or close to it)

❑ ❑ ❑ I can honestly say I planned to move from saving for retirement to enjoying my money in retirement.

❑ ❑ ❑ I have determined my best option for maturing my RRSP.

❑ ❑ ❑ I plan to withdraw regular income from my portfolio.

❑ ❑ ❑ I understand all the options available to me under my company pension plan.

❑ ❑ ❑ I have a plan to maximize my after-tax retirement income.

Yes No Unsure

❏ ❏ ❏ I'm a snowbird. My financial plan reflects how that could affect my health care and any US estate tax problem.

❏ ❏ ❏ I have explored the ins and outs of the reverse mortgage.

❏ ❏ ❏ I have obtained an estimate of amount of CPP I'll be eligible for.

❏ ❏ ❏ I've calculated how much income my spouse will have after my death and vice versa.

Tax Planning

❏ ❏ ❏ I have reviewed the tax planning opportunities available for my situation.

❏ ❏ ❏ I have a plan to *defer* tax: RRSP contributions, pension plan, capital gains investments outside your registered plans, etc.

❏ ❏ ❏ I have a plan to *divide* income: spousal RRSPs, spousal loans, salaries to children, splitting CPP benefits, testamentary trusts, RESPs.

❏ ❏ ❏ I have a plan to *deduct* income: RRSP contributions, charitable donations, etc.

❏ ❏ ❏ My plan will minimize the amount of tax I pay over my lifetime and on death.

❏ ❏ ❏ I have used all reasonable strategies to reduce my tax bill.

❏ ❏ ❏ I do tax planning before December 24th.

❏ ❏ ❏ My tax plan is integrated with my other financial planning strategies.

❏ ❏ ❏ I consider the tax costs before selling my investments, including any stock options.

Education Planning

❏ ❏ ❏ I have considered the most tax-effective way to save for post-secondary education for myself, my children and/or my grandchildren.

❏ ❏ ❏ I know about the $400 grant that is part of the RESP.

Yes No Unsure

❏ ❏ ❏ I've researched the RRSP lifelong learning program.

Investment Planning

❏ ❏ ❏ My investments have a 90 percent probability of giving me the long-term returns I need.

❏ ❏ ❏ I have an investment strategy and a target asset mix.

❏ ❏ ❏ The ownership of my investments, home and other assets have been carefully considered and coordinated with my estate planning and tax rules.

❏ ❏ ❏ My portfolio and investments are being managed the way I want them to be.

❏ ❏ ❏ I have a written investment policy statement.

❏ ❏ ❏ I know my personal rate of return my portfolio has earned.

❏ ❏ ❏ I know how much I am paying for my investments, directly and indirectly, each year.

❏ ❏ ❏ I've done a comparative analysis of the features I need in my investment program.

❏ ❏ ❏ I've assessed the cost-benefits of my investment program.

❏ ❏ ❏ My portfolio is tax efficient.

❏ ❏ ❏ I know the adjusted cost basis (ACB) for tax purposes for my investments held outside my RRSP/RRIF.

❏ ❏ ❏ I periodically review my investment(s) to make sure I have what's right for me.

❏ ❏ ❏ My investment program/products are working for me.

❏ ❏ ❏ My portfolio currently reflects my target asset mix.

❏ ❏ ❏ My investment program compares favourably with other options appropriate for someone in my situation.

Estate Planning

❏ ❏ ❏ My will reflects my wishes and current laws.

❏ ❏ ❏ My power of attorney/mandate/proxy reflect my wishes and current legislation.

❏ ❏ ❏ I've put a plan in place to make sure I don't pay more in probate tax and other fees than necessary.

Yes No Unsure

❑ ❑ ❑ I've estimated my final tax bill and I won't have to pay any more tax than necessary.

❑ ❑ ❑ My beneficiary designations are coordinated with the instructions in my will.

❑ ❑ ❑ I've set up a tax-effective charitable donation program.

❑ ❑ ❑ I've assessed if a testamentary trust would be an effective estate planning tool for my situation.

❑ ❑ ❑ My personal objectives, estate planning documents and tax planning are all integrated.

❑ ❑ ❑ I've made arrangements so the cottage/business/property can stay in the family.

❑ ❑ ❑ My estate has enough cash to pay the tax bill on death.

❑ ❑ ❑ I've dealt with any US estate tax issues I might have.

❑ ❑ ❑ I've considered the needs of my beneficiaries.

❑ ❑ ❑ I've taken care of my family obligations under family law and dependants' support.

Debt and Cash Management

❑ ❑ ❑ I've done a cash-flow analysis and a net worth statement.

❑ ❑ ❑ I've a plan in place to eliminate all non-deductible debt.

❑ ❑ ❑ I've negotiated the best interest rates and terms available on my credit cards, lines of credit, mortgages, and personal loans.

❑ ❑ ❑ I can carry my debts comfortably.

❑ ❑ ❑ My expenses are less than my income.

❑ ❑ ❑ My surviving spouse will have quick access to cash.

❑ ❑ ❑ My deductible debt is working out as planned.

❑ ❑ ❑ I've reviewed the amount I spend on banking service fees.

❑ ❑ ❑ I've negotiated my bank service package.

❑ ❑ ❑ I've made sure I'm paying no more in bank transaction fees than I have to.

❑ ❑ ❑ My cash is earning a competitive rate of interest.

❑ ❑ ❑ My emergency fund is in place.

Yes No Unsure

Risk Management

❑ ❑ ❑ I have adequate disability income coverage.

❑ ❑ ❑ I have enough life insurance and so does my spouse.

❑ ❑ ❑ I've done some comparison shopping for my insurance.

❑ ❑ ❑ My home/tenant insurance policy covers replacement costs.

❑ ❑ ❑ I've inventoried my possessions.

❑ ❑ ❑ I have all the liability insurance I need.

❑ ❑ ❑ My car insurance premiums are competitive.

❑ ❑ ❑ I've done a needs analysis for health care insurance (extended health, long-term care, outside Canada, etc.)

For Business Owners

❑ ❑ ❑ My business has the right structure (franchise, sole proprietorship, consultancy, partnership, corporation, trust or joint venture).

❑ ❑ ❑ I've got a working business plan and marketing plan.

❑ ❑ ❑ My business and personal financial planning are integrated.

❑ ❑ ❑ I've introduced a benefits program for my employees.

❑ ❑ ❑ I've reviewed the pros and cons of an estate freeze and family trust.

❑ ❑ ❑ I've developed a workable business succession plan.

❑ ❑ ❑ My key employees are protected.

❑ ❑ ❑ I've got buy/sell agreements with my business associates.

❑ ❑ ❑ I've got adequate lines of credit.

❑ ❑ ❑ My company will be eligible for the $500,000 capital gains exemption.

Other

❑ ❑ ❑ I have a written financial planning agreement.

❑ ❑ ❑ I have a written financial plan.

❑ ❑ ❑ I've reviewed my entire financial plan in the last 12 months and made any updates that were needed.

Every *no* or *unsure* could be costing you money or creating a situation where you could end up paying more than necessary. A financial plan could help you maximize your financial opportunities.

WHAT WILL THE FINANCIAL PLAN COST?

You could do a basic financial plan yourself, but if you work with a qualified financial planner for a customized plan, the cost should be related to the amount of work involved and the complexity of your personal financial situation. Although the prices vary from region to region and the time involved, if the plan is being prepared on a fee-for-service basis, prices will range from around $1,000 to more than $5,000 (plus GST/HST). If you have a business or professional practice, your plan will likely cost more than someone whose income comes primarily from employment. A more experienced financial planner may charge more.

From start to finish, the process might take five to 10 hours or more—some of spent it in meeting between you and the financial planner and some working on the plan itself. This would include an initial meeting of one to two hours and another meeting of about the same length to discuss the financial plan.

Some people will charge less to do a financial plan—sometimes nothing—assuming that if you like what you see, you will invest through them and the commissions and/or fees generated from those investments will more than compensate them for the time they spent preparing the financial plan. This is why it's not always safe to assume that your financial plan is objective. To some advisors the financial plan is the best sales tool that exists. After you tell them what it is you want to accomplish and what all your assets are, they can then customize your financial plan so that it provides "solutions." Suppose you have a "plan" prepared and then invest $100,000 in DSC mutual funds where the financial planner will be paid a 5 percent commission by the mutual fund or insurance company. The $5,000 commission is more than you would have paid for an average financial plan on a fee-for-service basis.

One prominent financial planner will do all the work for your financial plan for a fee, without any obligation that you implement any of the solutions with him. But if you do, he will refund the cost of the financial plan back to you. Is he telling you the plan isn't that important to him because of the products he can then sell? Is the financial plan then your solution or his? Why should financial planners be different from other professionals? For example, dentists get paid for their consultation and knowledge, regardless of whether or not you need to have any expensive dental work done. They don't offset the cost of the consultation because they get to do more on your mouth. They are separate jobs and expect to be paid for both.

There is increasing interest in the services offered by fee-for-service financial planners who are perceived to be neutral and more objective. Trust companies used to have lawyers on staff to prepare wills for their trust clients, but they no longer do this because they recognized that clients needed to be sure they were receiving advice that was independent of the firm that would be handling their money. Today, clients are encouraged to have their wills prepared by lawyers who are not associated with the trust company—that independence is important. Similarly, there will be more interest in financial advice that is independent of financial products.

TREND Financial planning will be seen as a separate service, not just an adjunct to investing. More financial institutions will start to outsource their clients' financial plans to independent financial planners.

SETTING STANDARDS
FOR THE FINANCIAL PLAN

You could go to three different financial advisors and get three completely different financial plans depending on the assumptions they use in their calculations. Not too long ago, a number of financial planners were asked their opinions on what a particular couple would have to do to achieve their retirement objectives. The amount the couple would have to save ranged from nothing more than they were already putting aside, to increasing their savings by over $10,000 a year. The two key assumptions that resulted in the wide variation in recommendations were the rate of return and the income the couple needed to support their lifestyle in retirement.

Suppose Joan Richardson, who is 52 years old and earns $65,000 a year, has squirrelled away $150,000 in her RRSP and $50,000 into her investment account. Joan has just paid off her house and now wants to focus on her retirement goals. She would like to retire at age 65 estimates that she is going to need 70 percent of her pre-retirement income ($45,000 in today's dollars, plus inflation).

Let's look at two retirement illustrations, each with a half a dozen assumptions that are the same, with one exception. In one, the rate of return assumed is 6.5 percent and in the other, 8 percent return. The other assumptions are:

Rate of inflation   2%
Marginal tax rate   50%
Life expectancy   age 90
CPP and OAS will still be there as we know them today

When we assume an 8 percent rate of return on the $200,000 she currently has, Joan would need to save $354 a month or $4,248 a year. If we assume a 6.5 percent rate of return, she would need to save $1,192 a month or $14,316 a year—$10,068 more. While she might not be comfortable investing aggressively in stocks to try to get higher returns, she might be able to achieve her goals if she was able to save more then $4,248 a year and tilt her portfolio more in favour of equities. If Joan selects too conservative a portfolio and can only save a modest amount, she will not achieve her original target retirement income.

Rates of Return

Assumptions are key to the quality of the financial plan but there are few financial planning standards or rules as to what assumptions should be used. So can you know if your plan is based on realistic assumptions, or numbers that have been pulled out of thin air? Let's look at what actuaries have to consider when they do calculations regarding company pension plans. They have to link the rates of return they use in their projections to the current long-term bond yield and the asset mix in the portfolio.

The 1999 Annual Report for Sears Canada used an actuarial projection of 7 percent for its employee pension that had a balanced asset allocation. CIBC's Annual Report for 1999 indicated that it assumed the expected long-term rate of return on plan assets would be 7.5 percent. The investment policy for Ontario Municipal Employees Retirement System pension plan indicates that the minimum inflation-adjusted investment return required over 20 years is 4 percent. These all seem like conservative assumptions.

The 2000 Investors Group/Gallup Canada Survey that indicated that 43 percent of investors expect to earn returns of less than 10 percent over the long term; almost one-third expect between 10 and 15 percent; and about one-fifth expect 15 percent or more.

While you may want to hear from your financial advisor about double-digit returns, no one can guarantee what the financial markets will earn for investors. Sometimes the market can deliver higher returns for a while but there's an investment industry saying: "All returns eventually return to the mean." In other words, even though there are highs and lows, it all seems to average out over time. So what rate of return should be used in your financial plan? It should be one your financial advisor could prove in court was prudent—and not a sales pitch.

The rate of return used in your personal financial plan should be linked to the economic outlook, your personal asset mix, the inflation rate and the long-term historical rates of return for those assets, less management fees. Here's a simple illustration that considers just two asset categories. Suppose the long-term rates of return and your annual fees for these assets are:

	Long-Term Return	Annual Fees	Net Return
Bonds	8%	2%	6%
Equities	10%	2%	8%

Based on the above long-term rates of return, if your asset mix is 50 percent fixed income and 50 percent equity, your financial plan might assume a long-term return of 7 percent calculated as:

	Asset Weighting	Net Return	Weighted Return
Bonds	50%	6%	3%
Equities	50%	8%	4%
Total Target Return			7%

None of the numbers used in the financial plan are guaranteed and may not accurately represent the future. Even a "realistic" rate of return that is assumed could be widely off since the rate is not constant each year. The numbers show you what *might* happen but nowhere does a financial plan say this is what *will* happen. In fact, your financial plan should be accompanied by a disclaimer that would look something like this:

> The numbers in this financial projection are based on information provided by the client and a number of assumptions. There is no guarantee that the future will bear any relationship to the numbers in this financial projection. The numbers are provided to assist in making your financial decisions and shouldn't be relied on to be accurate.

So why bother doing a plan if everything is so uncertain? Because it can help you determine if you are on the right track, assess the impact of different choices and decide what you need to do. In fact, most financial planners will do more than one financial projection so you can see the impact your decisions will have on your ability to reach your financial goals. One financial projection is not enough, not when preparing a business plan and not when doing a personal financial plan.

We should have standards, or at least working guidelines for setting the assumptions for returns, inflation and how to determine the retirement income needed in a financial plan, to protect:

- the client who is making personal financial decisions based on the financial plan
- the planner from professional malpractice

Regulations in the financial advice-giving arena will likely increase. Standards will be set for training individuals before they can provide you with advice. Also, working guidelines will be established for the assumptions used in financial projections, not unlike the framework that actuaries are required to use when calculating the commuted value under a pension plan.

Watch Those Other Assumptions Too

Other assumptions used in a financial plan include:

- how long you will live. Some financial planners use the average life expectancy, but if you live longer than the average, you could run the risk of outliving your money.

- your future marginal tax bracket. Most plans assume that the tax rates will be similar to what they are today. The good news is that it looks like we will see tax rates fall, even if only slightly.

- your tolerance for investment risk, which could be based on an investor profile quiz. These tests do not necessarily reflect how you will really react when there are negative returns, or nor do they link your risk preference to the return you might need to earn

- inflation and its impact on your future purchasing power.

- how much money you will need and the costs of items in the future, like medical expenses and nursing care. The closer you get to retirement, the more accurate you can be. There is a rule of thumb that suggests that a person will need about 70 percent of their pre-retirement income. But what you need could be more or less. You need to consider the cost of the lifestyle you would like to have—and plan accordingly.

• tip Some of the financial planning calculators you'll find on the Internet give very different results. Take a look at the assumptions they use and decide if they are appropriate for your situation.

Is Your Retirement Projection Realistic?

Some retirement projections done in the last few years have been based on unrealistically high rates of return. Some advisors and authors discuss retirement income scenarios using rates of return that would be hard to achieve, unless the consumer was an aggressive investor and not everyone needs, or is willing to assume, that much risk. If the potential return for your investments seems too good to be true, it probably is. Assuming 7 or 14 percent will give you two completely different outlooks on your future. Assuming too high a return might suggest you could live on easy street; too low a return might indicate you have to work part-time in retirement.

TREND You may be presented with a "Monte Carlo" computer simulation, to show you the probability you have of achieving your financial goals, which runs hundreds of multiple illustrations. The highest probability for one achieving their financial goal is 90 percent—the future is never 100 percent certain.

THE PROFICIENCY EXAM

Over the years, a number of educational programs and financial planning designations have evolved in Canada related to financial planning, which may confuse consumers as much as they may help, since they do not indicate if the person is also licensed to sell product. Here are some of the professional designations and accreditations that individuals practicing as financial planners might hold across the country:

ACFP	Associate Certificate in Financial Planning
CA	Chartered Accountant
CFA	Certified Financial Analyst
CGA	Certified General Accountant
ChFC	Chartered Financial Consultant
CIM	Certified Investment Manager
CLU	Chartered Life Underwriter

CMA	Certified Management Accountant
CFP	Certified Financial Planner
FCSI	Fellow, Canadian Securities Institute
FCA	Fellow, Chartered Accountant
FCIA	Fellow of the Canadian Institute of Actuaries
FIIC	Fellow of the Insurance Institute of Canada
FMA	Financial Management Advisor
PFC	Planificateur Financier Certifie
PFP	Personal Financial Planner
PRP	Professional Retirement Planner
RFP	Registered Financial Planner
SFC	Specialist in Financial Counselling

In December 1999, the Canadian Securities Administrators (CSA) published their requirements for the Financial Planning Proficiency Examination (FPPE) for those who are licensed to sell and distribute investment products in Canada (referred to as registrants). In October of the same year, Quebec introduced its own set of comprehensive regulations governing financial planning in that province which requires all new financial planners to complete a one-year course and successfully pass an examination.

As early as in 2004, individuals who want to act as a financial planner *and* are licensed to sell investment products (including stocks, bonds, mutual funds, segregated funds, and life insurance) will be required to pass the Financial Planning Proficiency Examination, or its equivalent, and have two or more years as a registrant (to sell products), before they will be able to hold themselves out as providing financial planning advice to investors.

These proficiency requirements do not apply to financial planners who do not work for a firm that sells products, since they are more likely to provide objective advice and less likely to have conflicts of interest when providing financial planning. This does not imply they are unqualified or inexperienced. Many have completed one of a number of programs that are not part of these proposed regulations.

In the past, the training of people to sell products, such as life insurance, stocks and mutual funds focused primarily on the products themselves rather than on financial advice. These new requirements are an attempt to protect the public from product salespeople who call themselves financial planners but do not offer financial planning advice—like a wolf in sheep's clothing.

PROPOSED EQUIVALENCIES FOR FPPE

An individual registered to provide investments who has successfully completed a recognized course of study or received a designation will be deemed to have completed the equivalent (or better) to the proposed Financial Planning Proficiency Exam (in effect 2004):

- Personal Financial Planner (PFP) designation (issued by the Institute of Canadian Bankers)
- Specialist in Financial Counselling (SFC) issued by the Institute of Canadian Bankers) indicates someone has passed its insurance and estate planning course as well as the taxation and investment course.
- Professional Financial Planning Course and exam (offered by the Canadian Securities Institute)
- the comprehensive financial planning program offered by the Canadian Institute of Financial Planning
- the Registered Financial Planner (RFP) designation (issued by the Canadian Association of Financial Planners)
- exams offered in the Chartered Financial Consultant program (offered by the Canadian Association of Insurance and Financial Advisors)
- Professional Proficiency Exam (offered by the Financial Planners Standards Council)

Before individuals licensed to sell product will be able to call themselves financial planners, financial advisors, financial consultants, investment counsellors, or investment advisors (among others) they'll have to demonstrate their proficiency in financial planning, the idea being, if it calls itself a duck, it better look like a duck and be able to quack.

RESTRICTED USE OF FINANCIAL PLANNING TITLES

What people do is implied, in part, by the title they use and the services they provide. Outside of Quebec, the securities regulators have introduced legislation that "restricts the use of titles by individuals who are licensed or registered to sell financial products that would convey to customers the impression that objective, comprehensive, integrated financial advice tailored to their present and future financial circumstances is being offered." (Notice of Proposed Multilateral Instrument 33-105, December 1, 1999). Financial planners who are not registered to sell investment products have no restrictions on the title they can use.

Only registrants who have passed the proficiency exam or its equivalent will be able to use a title on their business card that implies they are a financial planner. The restricted titles are expected to include almost any combination of the words related to financial planning including:

Financial	Planning	Money
Mutual fund	Planner	Asset
Securities	Wealth	Expert
Insurance	Advisor/Adviser	Manager
Retirement	Consultant	Counsellor
Security	Specialist	

The Quebec government has set in place the following minimum provincial standards for all new financial planners, except those who are members of another profession (accountant, lawyer, notary, etc.), before they can call themselves financial planners:

- complete a 450-hour financial planning certificate course. Prerequisite is a university bachelor degree or two certificates.
- 60 hours of continuing education every two years
- only one designation can be used—financial planner

There are a variety of titles that are being used in the financial services industry. For the rest of this book, let's use the term "financial advisor" from the concept of integrated, objective financial advice.

TREND Consumers will look for higher standards in financial planning. To be widely recognized as a profession, financial planning could look at what other professions do, including a formalized post-secondary education program, an internship, and rigorous examinations. Remember, we are still in the early days of financial planning advice.

BUYER BEWARE

While the regulators have taken a step in the right direction, the new rules do not include:

- any prerequisites for the proficiency exam
- standards for providing financial planning advice

Consumers will still need to assess whether or not the individual they are working with has the experience and knows how to apply the material that the exam covers. Some people are very good at preparing for, and writing exams. They may or may not be good financial planners.

No Prerequisites for the Proficiency Exam

There is no set course of study required nor are there any prerequisites a person must have before they can attempt the Financial Planning Proficiency Exam. Thus, people could pass the exam and call themselves financial planners without having any depth of training or actually having done any financial planning. (Although they have to have complete two years as a registrant, they may have spent their time manning the phones at an on-line broker, not actually doing financial planning.)

This is not dissimilar to the rite of passage an individual used to go through to become registered to sell securities in this country. As recently as 1992, an individual did not have to take any preparation course (self-study was sufficient) before writing the Canadian Securities Course (CSC) examination. Now a person is required to take a course and complete a series of assignments before they can even attempt that exam and after they pass it, they have to complete a 90-day training program with their employer.

Eventually, individuals who want to be licensed to provide product *and* financial planning advice will have to complete a prep course, with assignments and case studies, before they can attempt the Financial Planning Proficiency Examination.

Don't Assume You'll Get A Financial Plan

When the new rules are implemented, financial advisors will have to pass the basic Financial Planning Proficiency exam to be able to call themselves a financial planner or a related title, but will not *have* to provide any objective integrated financial planning advice.

So how will you know if you are really getting integrated financial planning advice, not just product-related advice? You have to look beyond the title on the business card and focus on what you actually get and know what you should expect—starting with a financial planning agreement or letter of engagement.

TREND You'll see more written agreements outlining the scope of the financial planning engagement, the costs and the advice you are hiring the financial advisor to provide. If you don't have a financial planning agreement, you may not be getting objective financial planning advice.

LETTER OF ENGAGEMENT

A financial plan might start with a financial planning agreement or letter of engagement, even if the fees for the plan are built-in to your investments. Starting in 2001, all practicing financial planners who hold the R.F.P. designation through the Canadian Association of Financial Planners will be required to provide their clients with a financial planning engagement letter.

This letter or agreement should outline, in writing:

- the services the financial advisor and their firm will provide
- the type of plan and service—comprehensive or modular
- the scope of the financial plan
- the areas that will be reviewed
- the fee (if it is a flat fee) for the plan or the basis on which the fee will be calculated (such as an hourly rate)
- any potential conflicts of interest the financial planner may have, such as being licensed to sell products
- that there is no requirement to implement any aspect of the financial plan with the person or firm that prepared it

TREND Financial planning agreements will become more popular, partly as a competitive difference and partly as the standards of the financial planning profession evolve.

Here's a sample agreement.

Sample Financial Planning Agreement

Scope

I/we will prepare a comprehensive/modular personal financial plan for you by analyzing your current financial situation and making written recommendations to assist you in achieving your financial goals.

We will focus on opportunities in the following areas:

❑ goal setting

❑ investment portfolio design and risk reduction

❑ estate planning

❑ retirement income planning

❑ saving for retirement to achieve financial independence

❑ tax planning strategies

❑ cash flow and debt management

❑ education savings

❑ insurance (life and disability) and risk management (property and casualty, professional liability)

We will address the following life transition situations:

❑ death

❑ divorce

❑ marriage/remarriage

❑ retirement

❑ inheritance

❑ job loss with or without a severance settlement

❑ job transfer/relocation

❑ birth or adoption

❑ serious illness

❑ cashing stock options

❑ major expense or anticipated purchase of _____

❑ selling your business

❑ winning the lottery!

Limitations of the Financial Plan

The financial plan will be based on commonly accepted financial planning principles and the detailed financial and personal information provided by you or your other advisors. This data will be treated as confidential information and we will not disclose it, except to your other advisors to assist in this engagement. This information will not be reviewed or audited for accuracy.

The illustrations and calculations in the financial plan will be based on assumptions about the future. There is no guarantee that these assumptions accurately reflect the future and there may be material differences between the anticipated and the actual results.

This plan does not include accounting services, preparation of any legal documents, or any other services not specifically outlined in this letter.

Compensation

The following fee method will be charged for the financial planning:

(a) a one-time fee of $_____ (+ GST/HST) for the preparation of the financial plan

(b) an annual fee of _____% of the assets under administration (+ GST/HST)

(c) a financial consulting fee of $_____ per hour (+ GST/HST) will be charged for the fee-for-service financial planning services provided. We expect your fees to be no less than _____ but not to exceed _____.

(d) the cost is paid for indirectly through the assets you hold.

A deposit of $_____ will be required before the financial planning begins. The balance will be due on presentation of the invoice. Fees for managing your assets and investments, if needed, will be billed separately. You will not be billed for any additional services unless you agree to them in advance.

Implementation

You are not required to follow any of the recommendations in the written plan, nor do you need to implement any of them with us. You are free to take the plan, or portions of it, to any person or firm you wish. We will be available to assist you or your other advisors with any of the recommendations in the plan and will bill you for these additional services for the time spent, based on our standard hourly rate of $_____.

Limitation of Scope of Services

These services should not be considered a substitute for your own judgment. The financial plan is designed to supplement your own personal planning and analysis and to assist you in fulfilling your financial objectives. These services are not designed to discover fraud, irregularities or misrepresentations made in the materials provided to use concerning existing or potential investments.

Review

It is recommended that the financial plan be reviewed every three years or when there is a material change in your circumstances, tax and other legislation, or in the economic conditions. The review would assess your progress and recommend any adjustments needed to stay on track.

Disclosure

We are/are not registered stockbrokers, insurance or mutual fund representatives and will/will not give advice on specific investments. We are qualified to prepare the financial plan.

Signed and dated:

Financial Planner _____ Client _____

SUMMARY

There is a difference between advice related to the sale of an investment product or program and objective personal financial planning. Product-related advice focuses on the features and benefits of the product, and while it might include financial illustrations or projections, those could be just sales tools masquerading as financial advice. For an idea of the range of information that could be included in the estate or retirement component, you might want to take a look at my first two books, *You Can't Take It With You: The Common-Sense Guide to Estate Planning for Canadians* and *Make the Most of What You've Got: The Canadian Guide to Managing Retirement Income*.

Less than 40 percent of Canadians say they have any sort of financial plan (Hart Study) although 72 percent of the same people say that having a written plan is somewhat to very important. Good financial advice can help you make the most of what you've got as well as help you plan for major life events.

A financial plan should help you feel that you have more control over your financial future and provide you with a yardstick against which you can measure whether or not you are on track. By putting all your cards on the table and going through the financial planning process, you should end up with a coordinated plan that helps you visualize where you want to go and plan how you can get there— and know whether or not you are on the right track. You don't have to try to make sense of seeing four different people, each regarding a specific issue. A plan should pull it all together for you. Many of the services provided by the financial services industry are intangible— a written financial plan is one of the few tangibles.

There is a subjective element to integrated financial planning advice that makes it hard to regulate. In some ways, the financial industry was easier to oversee when it focused on trading activity and the suitability of investments.

The Cost of Minding Your Money

"A cynic knows the cost of everything, and the value of nothing."

Oscar Wilde

Think of the financial services industry as one big shopping mall and the services and products they sell as just goods, like breakfast cereal or toothpaste on the shelves. Banking products and investment products can be found packaged in a generic form— the house brand—or under a premium label, with varying prices to match.

There is a wide range of prices among the different types of products, and even among similar ones from different financial institutions. Some items are priced just right, some are on sale and some are premium priced.

On the banking side, you could have a no-fee credit card or a premium loyalty card, with interest rates ranging from 9.5 percent to more than 18 percent. On the investment side, the fees for an index mutual fund might range from almost as low as a pure stock index or as much as an actively managed mutual fund. You'll find some investment products charging what the market will bear, rather than what's fair and reasonable.

In this chapter, we're going to look at some of the costs the consumer is faced with for banking services. Transaction fees, service and interest charges on the banking side of the financial services industry parallels the evolution of transaction and service fees now occurring on the investment side of the industry.

If I take my car in for repairs, I get a quote outlining what needs to be done, how much it costs and a detailed bill. But when shopping for banking service and/or financial advice, most people don't ask for a quote or even a statement itemizing their annual costs. With my car, I can easily shop around and get competitive quotes.

In Canada, it is not easy to compare the cost of various financial services and advice you might need. If you were shopping for a house, you'd probably make a list of all the features you'd like to have—maybe three bedrooms, a fireplace, large yard, whatever. You'd go house hunting to see what you could find that fits the bill and how much it would cost—and figure out what you were really willing to pay. You either put in an offer, or keep looking. Or you might be more like the people who just stopped by an open house, bought it, and then made the list of the features they wished it had.

Buying services from the financial services industry doesn't need to be all that different from buying a house. Sooner or later, you'll look at what you want or what you've got and compare it to what you need. However, financial services are harder to evaluate because they are intangible, and since you can't see or touch them, it's harder to know what you are buying. And to make matters more difficult, if you go to several different firms, they may have similar but slightly different products to offer you. Since they have different features, you end up comparing apples with oranges, making an informed decision difficult. And there are few guarantees and you can't return it if you are not happy.

The best starting place is to determine what investment services you might need and then decide whether you need the generic or the name-brand product. Refer to the "Managed Money Shopping List" in Chapter 10 if you want to go "shopping" prepared.

The financial services industry is very profitable, in part because consumers do not always understand how much they are paying. It is time investors paid attention to the cost side of managing money, not just the return side. If you don't think Canada's financial institutions are making money on the financial services they provide, take a look at the net income some of them earned in the second quarter of 2000.

NET INCOME FOR CANADA'S SIX BANKS* AND FOUR LIFE INSURANCE** COMPANIES

Financial Institution	Net Income
CIBC	$676 million
Royal Bank	$578 million
TD	$537 million
Bank of Montreal	$497 million
Scotiabank	$465 million
Manulife Financial	$225 million
Sun Life Financial Services of Canada	$197 million
National Bank	$138 million
Canada Life Assurance Company	$ 70 million
Clarica Life Insurance Company	$ 70 million

* For the three months ending in 2nd Quarter 2000
**For the three months ending in 1st Quarter 2000

Source: News releases

THE COST OF BANKING SERVICES— FEES, FEES, EVERYWHERE FEES

Everywhere you go, there is some sort of fee or cost involved—service charges, transaction fees, monthly packages, interest, and opportunity costs. Every dollar you pay is money you don't get to keep.

The Opportunity Cost

Whether you realize it or not, the low return you might be settling for on your bank account is a cost. In technical terms, it is called an opportunity cost because you and your money are missing out on the opportunity to earn a higher return elsewhere. In this case, accepting a low interest rate when your money could be making more, represents a lost opportunity.

However, Canadians appear to be a loyal lot, staying with financial firms that don't pay a competitive interest rate. Why else would people forgo the opportunity to earn more? What type of service are you receiving if your financial institution leaves you earning around one-half of 1 percent a year without even pointing out that there are ways to earn more with them, including redeemable GICs and money market investments. Whose interests (no pun intended) are they serving?

So how much might this be costing you? Suppose you have $10,000 sitting in a chequing account earning one-half of 1 percent (or next to nothing), $50 a year. Over 10 years, that $10,000 compounds slowly to $10,511. Compare that with what you might earn if you moved the $10,000 to an account where it earned 5 percent. Over 10 years, it would grow to $16,288 or $5,777 more without any added risk. Leaving money sitting in a low-earning account costs you!

	Interest Income		Opportunity Cost
Rate	Over 1 year	Over 10 years	Over 10 years*
3%	$300	$3,439	$2,928
4%	$400	$4,802	$4,291
5%	$500	$6,288	$5,777

*10 years compounded growth

Does anyone other than me wonder why we still have to have both a personal savings and a chequing account? Why can't we combine them into one and still receive a competitive rate of interest? Or would they prefer you to move your money into a money market account where they can collect annual management fees?

Service Charges

If you're anything like me, you're probably tired of financial institutions calling their fees "service" charges. Why don't they just call them what they are—fees?

Recently, I went into a major bank—it doesn't matter which one—to deposit a cheque for US$1,125 from a major corporation into my Canadian dollar chequing account. They made me pay for the "service" three different ways:

1. The "service" charge was $2.75.

2. The exchange rate was not very competitive.

3. They placed a 21-day hold on the money, during which time I could not even move it to a money market account where it might have earned at least some interest—an opportunity cost. Financial institutions can clear cheques electronically across borders with the speed of light, so how long do they really need to hold a cheque from a recognized corporation?

Some financial institutions are now offering free phone and Internet banking, free cheques with no minimum balance required, free Interac debits, and more—but not necessarily with a full range of services.

 TREND You will be able to negotiate not just the rate for your mortgage, but also the price you pay for your banking services. Financial institutions will have to demonstrate that they want your business.

Using Your Debit and ATM Card

Did your bank tell you how to use your debit or ATM card when you received it? Did they point out ways you could reduce the charges you pay? You need to take a good look at your bank statement or passbook to make sure you're not paying more than you have to. If you make withdrawals at a machine that belongs to a financial institution other than your own bank, you will notice that you have to pay an additional $1 or more for each withdrawal. Even just one withdrawal a week from a machine belonging to a bank other than your own adds up to over $50 a year in transaction fees you wouldn't have to pay if you planned accordingly.

• tip Make cash withdrawals from your bank's machine so that you don't have to pay interbank service charges for each withdrawal in addition to the fees your bank may charge you.

Store merchants are required to pay a fee for every transaction they place using your debit card. This is not to suggest that there are no benefits to the merchant. There are. Because they no longer accept as many personal cheques, they have to deal with fewer NSF cheques and have fewer trips to the bank to physically deposit them.

TREND You will eventually be able to use your debit card to access cash from your mutual funds, life insurance policies and other investments, not just your bank account.

Service Plans

To get the right banking package, you need to determine which services you need, the minimum balance you will keep and the number and type of transactions you do in a month. The Canadian Bankers Association also has put out a booklet called "Getting Value for Your Service Fees." I guess they've had a few complaints, and they're trying to address them with this information. (Take another look at their profits.) You might also want to look at Industry Canada's fee calculator at www.strategis.ic.gc.ca where you can enter the details of your own situation and get suggestions on the type of package that would be appropriate.

Since the financial institutions are actively competing for your business, be sure to review your needs periodically to ensure your current package is still the best one for you. You might even take a look at the newer entrants into the banking business such as ING Direct and President's Choice Financial. Their interest rates on savings accounts are currently better than the traditional banks—and they don't charge fees.

TREND You'll be seeing more on-line banking programs, or virtual banks, to encourage you to bank from home instead of coming into the branch.

Banks should put the "personal" back in personal banking. While you need to have a level of service you can count on, you also want to deal with someone who knows what kind of customer you are. For example, if you've dealt with the same branch for 20 years, you want to be treated as a long-term customer, not like someone who just showed up on their doorstep. You can be known in your own branch but be treated like a complete stranger through the automated banking system. If you've never deposited a bad cheque, why do they treat you as if the next one you deposit will be?

THE COST OF BORROWING

Not only are there more ways for you to spend your money, you can even spend or invest money you don't have. These include personal loans, lines of credit, credit cards, home equity loans, margin accounts, reverse mortgages, personal mortgages… the list goes on. If your credit is good, every financial institution—from the local credit union, national bank, trust company, and insurance company—will be willing to loan you money. What we can do with borrowed money seems more exciting than eliminating a debt or even staying out of debt in the first place.

There are many valid reasons for taking on personal debt, such as buying a home or a car. However, many people agree that taking on debt to live a lifestyle you can't really afford will eventually get you into trouble or put you on a debt treadmill that only profits the lender.

How Much Debt Can You Afford?

The banks and trust companies have always been willing to loan money according to their own formula. But "how much will they loan you?" is not the same question as "how much debt can you comfortably afford?" Even though being told you qualify for $100,000 might make you feel worthy, you still have to decide if it is really in your own best interest to take a loan for that amount. You will have to be able to handle the loan payments over the life of the loan, and consider what other financial goals you might have.

When you take on debt, you should lay out a plan to pay it off. Disclosure rules for conventional loans with a fixed rate of interest require the financial institution to tell you the total amount of interest you will be paying over the life of the loan. The rate of interest charged for a secured line of credit—one where you guarantee the loan with security such as your home or investments—varies according to market conditions, and the dollar amount of interest you will end up paying is not known when you secure the loan.

The problem with debt is that it can turn into a continuous cycle that keeps some people from getting ahead. Suppose you take out a three-year loan to buy your first car and the payments are $500 a month. While you're making those payments, you probably won't be able to save much for your next car, so when the time comes, you could end up with another loan or a lease.

When my grandparents bought their first house, the bank would only allow them to finance 50 percent of it. The generation that survived the Great Depression and World War II firmly believed that one should not borrow or lease things on time. Over the decades, that attitude toward debt has become much looser, encouraged by employment stability and rising incomes as well as the profits financial institutions which could make by extending credit. In the 1980s, when inflation was double digit and salaries kept more or less in step, the reasoning of the day was that a person could take on as much debt as possible since their incomes would go up, making it easier to make the payments in the future. Today, with inflation low and salaries relatively stable, this strategy no longer works.

Credit Cards

Do the credit card companies (many are subsidiaries of the banks and trust companies) offer frequent buyer points because they really want to give you free flights and gifts? Why are these so popular? I suspect it's because we like to feel that we have the opportunity to get something back. Today's credit card "programs" range from the no-frills, no-fee option where you focus on what the card really is (a credit card), through to those that combine credit with a loyalty program.

The interest rates credit cards charge vary greatly, from under 9 percent to over 18 percent. If you can't afford to pay off the balance every month, a lower interest rate does cost less. Suppose you have an outstanding balance of $5,000. A credit card charging interest of 9 percent a year would cost you $450 less than a card charging 18 percent—$450 that could be put toward paying down the debt or toward your own personal loyalty program, where you do what you want with the money.

Don't forget how credit cards work. The credit card company collects somewhere between 2 and 4 percent from the store merchant for every dollar you put on the card. If you buy something for $200 where the store merchant is required to pay 2 percent, the credit card company would collect $4 from the store. The more you use your credit card, the more the credit card company makes. They also collect interest from cardholders who don't pay off their account every month.

• tip Check your credit card statement and agreement. Some programs charge interest from the day you bought the merchandise with the card even if you pay it off every month. Other programs don't charge any interest if you pay the balance in full before the due date. Why pay interest if you don't have to?

Mortgages

The financial world is always changing. You may or may not remember that just 25 years ago, the financial institutions were in the driver's seat when you wanted a mortgage. You could take a mortgage for 25 years with no prepayment privileges. That was it. There was no negotiating. All you got to do was sign on the bottom line.

Compare that to mortgages today. You want to pay less than prime? Sure. You want the rate guaranteed for six months? No problem. Seven years? OK. You want to skip the principal payment and only pay the interest for a few months? Why not? The competition for mortgage business has opened up a wide range of terms, conditions and privileges. Today, the qualified consumer looking for a mortgage is in the driver's seat. What's to prevent this type of competition from occurring in the investment business?

Line of Credit

It used to be consumers took a loan to buy their cars and a mortgage to buy their homes. As interest rates have drifted lower and lower with little threat of rising rapidly, some people have opted for a secured line of credit rather than a mortgage—in order to get a lower rate of interest and greater flexibility in repaying it. However, a secured line of credit requires more discipline to pay it off than a mortgage. If you pay only the amount required to cover the interest charge, your monthly payment is lower but you aren't paying anything towards the principal, you aren't securing the roof over your head.

Compare $100,000 secured line of credit with a traditional mortgage to be paid off over 20 years. The interest rate on the mortgage is 7 percent for annual payments of $9,529. The interest rate on the secured line of credit is 6.25 percent and if you pay only the interest, the annual payments are $6,250:

	Traditional Mortgage		vs	Interest Only on Line of Credit	
After	Interest paid,	Balance outstanding		Interest paid,	Balance outstanding
5 years	$33,771	$86,125		$ 31,250	$100,000
10 years	$61,846	$66,552		$ 62,500	$100,000
20 years	$90,487	0		$125,000	$100,000

After just five years, the person with the traditional mortgage has paid $33,771 in interest and has approximately $86,125 outstanding. The person paying only the interest required on a secured line of credit has paid not much less in interest—$31,250—and still owes the original balance of $100,000. After 10 years, the person paying interest only will have paid $62,500 in interest and still owe $100,000. The person with the mortgage will have paid $61,836 in interest and owe only $66,552. Who would you rather be? The financial institution has no incentive to encourage you to pay off the line of credit since it will collect more interest if you don't.

> **• tip** If you have a secured line of credit and paying off the amount of the loan is important to you, try making your monthly payments equal to the amount you would be required to pay for a conventional loan or mortgage, rather than just paying the interest. Then you'd be using the lower interest rate on the line of credit to your own advantage.

For your convenience, at least one bank is marketing the concept of a "credit portfolio" so you can better track your debts. Another has a "total equity plan," which combines your mortgage, line of credit, personal loan, credit card, and overdraft protection into a "single comprehensive borrowing program." I hope their statements total up the interest you pay each year and include suggestions on how you could eliminate your non-deductible debt faster. A credit portfolio or a total equity plan makes it sound as if you have something when you don't, but it's really just financial obligations that reduce your personal net worth. It may be part of the financial firm's asset portfolio—but it certainly isn't a part of yours!

Manulife Financial has introduced an all-in-one program that combines banking and debts into one account whereby you can have your paycheque deposited into your "mortgage" account (to reduce the principal) and then write your household cheques from this mortgage/line of credit for one annual fee. With the right amount of discipline, this type of program could reduce the interest you pay on your mortgage. If you're not careful, it may condition you into believing you have easy access to credit whenever you want, since you just have to write a cheque, and the money will be there, whether you really have it, or not.

Investing on Margin

A margin account is a type of investment account held with a brokerage firm that permits you to borrow money (and pay interest) from the broker to buy additional securities. Since most brokerage firms in Canada are owned by banks, we will briefly discuss investing on margin in this section.

Borrowing to invest—whether it is on margin, using your line of credit or a home equity loan—increases your investment risk, and securities regulations require that the risk of borrowing to invest be disclosed to investors. Here's a sample of the type of letter you'll be asked to sign.

Sample Disclosure Letter Regarding the Risk of Using Borrowed Money to Invest

Mutual funds, stocks and other securities may be purchased using cash, borrowed money or some combination. Some clients borrow money to invest from their bank, trust company, credit union, or brokerage firm. Some use a line of credit, a margin account or may secure the loan using their home or the investment itself. The use of borrowed money magnifies the gain or loss on your investment.

When cash is used to pay for the investment, the gain or loss will equal the amount the investment increases or decreases in value. The return on the investment equals the return on your money. For example, if you pay $10,000 in cash for the investment and its value increases to $11,000, your return is 10 percent. If the value decreases from $10,000 to $9,000, your loss is –10 percent.

When money is borrowed to invest, it magnifies, or leverages, the gain or loss on the money invested. If you invest $7,500 using

$2,500 of your own cash and $5,000 of borrowed money and the value of the investment falls from $7,500 to $6,750 (a decline of 10 percent), the value of the cash you put up has fallen from $2,500 to $1,750, for a loss of 30 percent.

Because leveraging magnifies the potential gains or losses of investing, an investment program that uses borrowed money has greater risk than one that does not. If your investments go down in value, the risk is magnified because you are using "other people's money."

When the borrowed funds are secured by the investments themselves, such as in a margin account or other loan arrangement, the lender may require that the ratio of the market value of the investment and the amount loaned be maintained below a certain level. If the market value of the investment falls below that level, you will be required to add additional cash or securities to your account. Otherwise, investments may be sold at a loss to bring the ratio back in line with the agreed-upon level.

Interest charged on the borrowed money is your financial obligation. You should have enough income to make the interest payments and additional resources to add to your account if the market value of the account falls below the agreed-upon level.

Client Signature _____ Date _____

Borrowing to invest makes sense for some investors. The financial advisor and brokerage firm could have some inherent conflicts of interest when they recommend you borrow to invest. After all, when they loan you money on margin, they earn interest on the amount they extend you as well as additional fees or commissions from the additional dollars you then have to invest. The Investment Dealers Association reports that the amount of margin debt as of April 2000 was $10.3 billion at IDA member firms. If they charge 5 percent on these margin loans, the brokerages collects a cool $515 million in interest from their clients. These figures only include the amount of debt in margin accounts—they do not include any money clients may have borrowed against their home, line of credit or through mutual fund dealers.

• **tip** Watch out for strategies that recommend you borrow to invest, unless this is suitable for your situation. Investing with borrowed money increases your investment risk, as well as the fees you might pay and/or commission paid to the financial advisor.

The amount they will extend on margin varies from 50 or 70 percent of the value of the investments in your account, to as low as 20 or 30 percent, depending on its quality. As long as the value of your securities remains stable or increases, your account remains in good standing. However, if the market drops and takes the value of your securities down with it, or you just pick a losing stock, the brokerage firm will give you a margin call (and may notify you by phone, e-mail or letter) which is not at all like a social call. The financial institution will expect you to add more cash or securities quickly to your account, or they will sell enough of your stocks—at the lower prices—to cover the outstanding margin position.

Sample Margin Call Letter

Dear Investor:

The market value of your account no longer supports the loan/margin in your account. To avoid having investments sold in your account, you have the following options:

1) Add $(amount) of cash to your investment account or

2) Add additional securities valued at no less than $(amount) to your investment account

If you wish to deposit additional cash or investments in your account, please courier a cheque payable to (name of financial firm) or call to make arrangements to transfer funds to (name of financial firm) or securities to your investment account no later than 3:00 p.m. on (date).

If you do not make arrangements to increase the market value of your account by (date), we will exercise the redemption of assets in your account to bring your account back into good standing according to your loan/margin agreement.

Since margin calls happen when stocks are down in value, you could end up violating one of the basic rules of investing: "buy low, sell high." On the more volatile stocks—such as some in the technology, biotech or resource sectors—the brokerage firm may not extend any credit. This has not stopped some investors from using their home as collateral or taking out a personal loan. If the brokerage firm considers these stocks too risky, maybe that should tell you something about those stocks. Maybe they really don't have much security.

 TREND Brokerage firms will be required to make public their list of stocks that are not eligible for margin.

SUMMARY

Fees, fees, everywhere you look, there are fees for financial services traditionally offered by the banks, trust companies and credit unions. While many investment products and services are still offered on a commission basis, many investors are now paying fees—fees to have their money managed through mutual funds and other managed money investments, transaction fees for orders they place on-line and annual fees based on the size of their account, to name just a few. In the next chapter, we'll be examining the fees and other costs that investors pay to acquire and maintain their investments.

The Cost of Investing

"Speculation is an effort, probably unsuccessful,
to turn a little money into a lot.
Investment is an effort, which should be successful,
to prevent a lot of money from becoming a little."

Fred Schwed, Jr.

Did you ever fall in love with a car but not buy it because it would cost more to insure and maintain than another one with the same sticker price? As with a car, there are two types of costs you need to consider when investing. One is the cost to acquire your investments, and the other is the cost of maintaining them over time. You need to ask:

1. What does it cost to *become* an investor? Are there any initial fees or commissions?

2. How much will it cost to *be* an investor? Are there any ongoing fees?

Some investments cost nothing to acquire—they have no sales fee or commission, but could turn out to be among the most expensive over the years. Others charge on-going annual fees that may not be fully disclosed when you invest.

Some of the "cheapest" investments are the ones that are the "purest" in form, such as an individual stock and some index-based mutual funds. But be careful what you are comparing. An index mutual fund that you can buy yourself should have a lower cost than a mutual fund you might buy through a financial advisor since most Canadians currently pay for financial advice—whether they need it or not—through their investments. If you don't need this advice, or some of the features the more expensive products may offer, then you will not receive any added value for the higher price.

YOU PAY FOR CONVENIENCE

Some investments are available in raw form, such as a stock or a bond. Others come partially assembled or "ready to serve" and packaged as investment management products such as mutual funds. Here's a basic rule of thumb when shopping for investments and investment products. The more layers (of people and companies) that handle the money, the more services are bundled together, and the more processes involved, the more likely you are to pay on an ongoing basis. Think of coffee. It costs just pennies to grow the coffee beans, more to buy them roasted, ground, and ready to take home, and even more to buy them as a hot cappuccino or latte. Similarly, a segregated fund usually costs more than a mutual fund, which in turn costs more than a stock index.

THE PACKAGING OF EQUITY INVESTMENTS

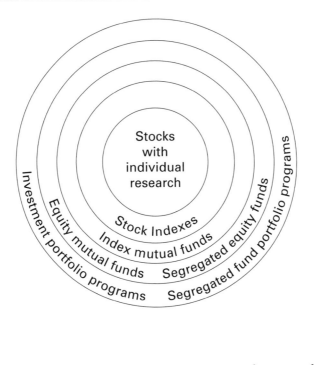

With all fee-based investment programs and managed money products, you pay to have your money managed. The management services may range from investment selection to portfolio rebalancing and customized asset allocation. The fees may also include the services of a financial advisor or planner.

Compare the people and the processes involved in managing a stock index with a segregated fund. Suppose you buy 100 units of the TIPS index yourself, an investment that simply mirrors the value of that index—no one is deciding which investments to buy or sell. Alternatively, if you buy an actively managed segregated fund product, such as ManuLife Financial's GIF (Guaranteed Investment Fund), you have to deal with someone licensed to sell life insurance products (who will want to be paid) and the investment is made up of:

- brand-name mutual funds, which are managed by a team of the professional money managers from those mutual fund companies, who also want to be paid for their services
- a segregated fund wrapper (which provides the segregated fund guarantee) administered by the life insurance company

COSTS OF ACQUIRING YOUR INVESTMENTS

Let's focus on the costs related to acquiring investments for your portfolio. There are different commission and fee structures to acquire stocks, mutual funds, life insurance, and bonds. We'll start with the products that are the simplest and cheapest to acquire and then look at the ongoing costs of investment and insurance products and programs. In Chapter 9 we will consider whether or not you are getting value for your money.

Stocks

Traditionally, brokers were able to charge healthy commissions for stock trades, when the minimum commission to buy or sell started at $75 and went up depending on the size of your order. Now, if you are doing your own trading, the cost to buy a stock can be less than $30 if you don't want any advice. But as we have already discussed, you need to monitor the level of trading you do to make sure you're not spending too much on transaction fees.

• tip How much are you paying in commissions for trading stocks with your broker? If you don't know, then you need to get a straight answer. The commission charged is based on the firm's internal schedule, the number of shares being traded, the dollar value of the transaction, the number of trades you place a year, and the value of your account. In other words, the more business you do with them, the more likely you will be able to shave dollars off the commission. In today's marketplace, the full-service commission may be negotiable.

Bonds and Other Fixed Income Investments

Brokers who buy and sell bonds and other fixed income investments make their money on the difference, or spread, between the price at which they buy the bond and the price at which they then sell it. Usually this spread is not disclosed, but you now can see it on some of the Internet sites that trade fixed income investments.

If you hold the bond in your portfolio until its maturity date— the end of its natural life—you don't have to pay any other commissions or fees, unless it is held in a managed money portfolio or one of the newer fee-based brokerage accounts.

Stock Indexes

Stock indexes let you invest in a basket of stocks in key markets without having to research individual companies and have become synonymous with low cost. There is an index option for every major market in the world, as well as for a variety of sectors, such a technology and biotechnology. These include stock index participation units (IPUs) such as Toronto Index Participation Units (TIPS) and the i60 (S & P/TSE 60), SPDRs (pronounced spiders) in the US and the international World Equity Benchmark Shares (WEBS). Index participation units trade like stocks. If you buy them yourself through a discount broker, the transaction fee could be less than $30.

There are administrative costs to match the index to the movements of the stocks that make it up, but you don't pay for professional money management or research, because there isn't any. The on-going costs are generally less than one-half of 1 percent for Canadian indexes; 1 percent or more for international indexes.

But there is another "cost" related to the risk that could be inherent in the index, particularly when it is not broadly diversified. That's the added investment risk from investing in an index that is concentrated in a handful of companies. Here's a sampling of the stock concentration that existed in three Canadian stock indexes as of April 2000.

TSE 300 INDEX: TOP SIX HOLDINGS	
Nortel Networks	18.57%
BCE Inc.	13.16
Seagram Co. Ltd.	3.12
Royal Bank Canada	2.59
Toronto-Dominion Bank	2.56
Bombardier Inc. B	2.34
Remaining 294 stocks in index	57.66
	100.00%

Source: © 2000 Bloomberg L.P.

TSE 35 INDEX: TOP EIGHT HOLDINGS	
BCE Inc.	10.12%
Nortel Networks	10.11
Bombardier Inc. B	8.04
Celestica Inc.	7.39
Research in Motion	4.52
Toronto-Dominion Bank	4.30
BCT.Telus Comm	4.21
Seagram Co. Ltd.	4.18
Remaining 27 stocks in index	47.13
	100.00%

Source: © 2000 Bloomberg L.P.

S & P/TSE 60 INDEX: TOP SIX HOLDINGS	
Nortel Networks	25.55%
BCE Inc.	10.08
Seagram Co. Ltd.	4.28
Royal Bank Canada	3.55
Bombardier Inc B	3.21
Toronto-Dominion Bank	3.05
Remaining 54 stocks in index	50.28
	100.00%

Source: © 2000 Bloomberg L.P.

As an example, two companies made up almost 25 percent of the TSE 300, even though this major index represents over 300 of the largest companies listed on the Toronto Stock Exchange. In the newest Canadian index—the i60 index—Nortel Networks and BCE Inc., just two companies out of 60, made up over 35 percent. Whatever happens to these companies, irrespective of whether they are good companies or not, will have a major impact on the performance of these indexes just because they make up so much of it. If you think this is an issue for Canada, consider Finland's situation. Nokia Corporation makes up about 70 percent of their major stock index.

If you had $1 million to invest, would you put $255,500 in Nortel and $100,800 into BCE? This would concentrate your future in the future of two companies. If you were a mutual fund manager or pension manager you wouldn't, because their regulations require that they hold not more than 10 or 15 percent in any one company—25 percent for index fund managers who now have to disclose the added risk this concentration brings to the portfolio. But today's investors may be underestimating this risk, preferring to pay attention only to recent performance.

You might want to consider why index investing has only recently become popular. Costs and performance are the two key reasons. When the index holds a stock that is going up in value, the index must buy more of it. If the value of a stock in the index falls, the index must sell some. As long as an index has more money coming in than going out, it continues to buy more, pushing up the price of the stocks in the index. This is the demand side of the supply and demand theory pushing up the price, which in turn can create a self-fulfilling prophecy when investor preference is tipped toward index investing or the stocks that make up the index. (This is an oversimplification, but it might give you food for thought.)

One investor who put money into the i60 index in early 2000 said he "was having trouble riding out the dips" that resulted primarily from the two top companies. Remember that one of the cornerstones of investing is to not place your future on any one investment or investment style. But if you believe that no one can successfully outperform the market over the long term—even you—the indexes might be a core holding in your Canadian and international equity portion of your portfolio.

One index supporter suggests holding 70 percent of your Canadian equity investments in indexes or index funds and the rest in actively managed funds. If you used the i60 index and had 40 percent of your portfolio in Canadian equities, you'd have 28 percent of your portfolio in the i60 fund or about 7 percent in Nortel and almost 3 percent in BCE. This itself wouldn't be considered too concentrated unless the actively managed mutual funds in your portfolio also hold significant percentages of these companies.

Stock indexes may be simple to trade but they do not have some of the ease-of-use features that are found in mutual funds, such as pre-authorized investment programs (PACs), automatic dividend reinvestment and systematic withdrawal programs (SWIPs). If you don't need any of these features and don't believe active money management adds any real value, index investing may be the simplest, cheapest investment option.

You'll also find mutual funds and segregated funds that invest in stock indexes.

Funds that Invest in Stock Indexes

A number of mutual funds and segregated funds now invest in the underlying stock indexes. The also have the added risk from concentration, just a many stock indexes have. But you also get features that are not available with a stock index, such as reinvestment of dividends, systematic savings and withdrawal plans and, with segregated funds, a guarantee of your capital in certain situations.

However, since there is no active management of the portfolio, the on-going management fees should be very low compared to actively managed funds. In fact, it's not even really accurate to call them management fees—they're more like additional administrative charges or transaction fees to maintain and service your investments.

Here's a table comparing some of the features of stock indexes, mutual funds that invest in stock indexes and other mutual funds.

COMPARISON OF FEATURES			
	Stock Index	Index Mutual Funds	Managed Mutual Funds
Individual holding limit	none	15%	10%
Management Expense Ratios (MERs)			
Canadian	less than .5%	29% and up*	less than 3%*
International	less than 1%*		less then 3%*
Commissions	to buy/sell	depends	depends
Currency management	no	no	maybe
Management style	passive	passive	active

	Stock Index	Index Mutual Funds	Managed Mutual Funds
Cash in portfolio	no	limited	usually
PACs	no	yes	yes
SWIPs	no	yes	yes
Located/managed	listed on exchanges	fund company	fund company
Broker advised	yes/no	yes/no	yes/no
Purchased through	brokerages	brokerages and mutual fund planners	
Place limit order	yes	no	no
Sell short	yes	no	no
Stop loss order	yes	no	no
Company research	no	no	yes
Automatic reinvestment of dividends	no	yes	yes
Free redemptions	no	maybe	maybe
Ethical restrictions on investments	no	no	maybe
Foreign funds RRSP-eligible	25%**	maybe	maybe
Fees fall as account size grows	no	no	maybe
Outperform comparable investments			
In up markets	sometimes	sometimes	sometimes
In down markets	not expected to for the same reasons they may outperform in up-markets		maybe
Investment management tailored			
to your personal situation	no	maybe	maybe
Financial advice included	no	maybe	maybe

*some are higher than this

**rising to 30% in 2001

Mutual Funds

Mutual funds are investment products that pool the money of a number of investors and manage their money according to the investment objectives stated in the simplified prospectus. The mutual fund could manage money passively and invest in stock indexes, as we have just discussed, or actively where a money manager researches and manages a portfolio of individual securities. Mutual funds have built-in features not found with individual stocks and bonds, or stock indexes including automatic reinvestment of interest and dividend payments, daily redemptions and systematic savings and withdrawal plans.

Mutual funds can be purchased on:

- a no-load, no fee, no commission, basis
- a front-end load basis, where a fee or commission is deducted from your initial investment. If you purchase $10,000 of a fund with a 4 percent front-end commission, $9,600 would go into your account and $400 to the firm your advisor works for. The front-end commission or acquisition fee ranges from 0 to 5 percent or more. In the early 1980s, some were as high as 9 percent.
- a deferred-sales-charge (DSC) basis, where you don't pay any commission personally. However, the mutual fund company pays a commission or 4 or 5 percent to the financial advisor on your behalf and you are bound by the terms of the redemption fee schedule—locked into that family of funds for a set period of time, such as six years. If you want out earlier, you actually have to pay the sales charge—that's why it is called "deferred"—which would be deducted when you redeem your investment.

Some DSC mutual funds pay out a higher commission than other funds. How can financial advisors recommend them without the client thinking that they are being self-serving? They can't. As an example, in 2000, Spectrum United Mutual Funds cut the commission it paid on its DSC equity mutual funds from 6 to 5 percent, to bring them in line with the industry norms.

The amount of the redemption fee depends on how long you have held your units and the mutual fund company's declining fee schedule. The redemption schedule lasts for up to six or nine years (although a few are shorter), depending on when you purchased the investment. The fee may be based on the amount you invested or its value at the time of the redemption. The schedule that applies to your mutual funds is found in the simplified prospectus. Here's a sample redemption fee schedule:

Period Redemption Made	Redemption Charge
During the 1st year	6.0%
During the 2nd year	5.5%
During the 3rd year	5.0%
During the 4th year	4.5%
During the 5th year	3.0%
During the 6th year	1.5%
Thereafter	nil

All mutual fund investors pay annual management expenses to the fund company, even for no-load mutual funds.

Segregated Funds

Segregated funds and mutual funds share many of the same benefits and features—some people say they look a lot like cousins. Segregated funds pool the money they receive from investors and manage it according to a particular investment objective or set of objectives. Now that some mutual funds are available in a segregated fund version, the line between mutual funds and segregated funds is even more blurred. The key difference is that a segregated fund is an insurance product that comes with a guarantee that will pay 75 percent (and sometimes up to 100 percent) of the amount you originally invested after a 10-year holding period, or death. The guarantees vary among life insurance companies so read your segregated fund's information folder to find out how yours works.

Similar to mutual funds, segregated funds can be purchased on a no-load basis, front-end load or on a deferred-sales-charge basis (with a redemption fee schedule). The DSC sales option is still popular for segregated funds and those who sell them. After all, since you are planning to hold the investment for 10 years, you can probably be convinced that a six-year redemption schedule doesn't look like it will be much of a problem.

Life Insurance

When you buy a life insurance policy, the life insurance company pays the representative a first-year commission that could be as much as 100 percent or more of the first year premium, depending on the type of policy and the agent's agreement with the life insurance company. After the first year, the agent receives a renewal commission, which is generally much more modest than the initial premium.

There is no requirement that any sales commission or selling incentives related to life insurance policies be disclosed to the Canadian consumer, even though these costs have an impact on the policies that have a savings or investment component, particularly in the early years of that investment. (In the US, it is expected that full disclosure of insurance commissions will soon be required.) For now, if you want to know what the financial advisor is being paid, you have to ask them.

TREND Now that many financial advisors are licensed to provide both traditional investments and insurance products, eventually there will be regulations that require financial advisors to disclose the dollar value of the commissions and fees for life insurance policies, as well as the impact these costs have on any cash values or investments it might have.

THE ONGOING COST OF MAINTAINING YOUR INVESTMENTS

"Sometimes one pays the most for things one gets for nothing."
—Albert Einstein

Annual management fees for managed money investments and annual fees for fee-based investment accounts are something like the maintenance fees condo owners pay. If you live in a condominium, you pay annual fees to hire a property manager and to maintain the common property so that you don't have to do it yourself. In all probability, you get a better rate by hiring as a group than you could if you hired individually.

It doesn't matter how much or how little you pay upfront to acquire these investments; *you* still pay ongoing fees, either directly or indirectly to participate in any managed money or fee-based investment programs. The fees you pay may cover more then just the investments; they often include the services of a financial advisor.

Managed Money Programs

All managed money programs, including mutual funds, segregated funds, pooled accounts, and wrap accounts, collect fees each and every year, regardless of whether or not the professional money manager actually makes any money for you. Suppose the total annual fees are 2 percent. If the investment earned 10 percent before expenses, you would earn a net return of 8 percent (10 percent less the 2 percent fee). If the money manager "earned" a return of 0 percent, the fees would be taken from your capital, and your return would be -2 percent. You get the idea. A 2 percent annual fee over five years becomes 10 percent of your initial investment, higher than any investment commission being charged today.

Mutual Funds

Even though we are going to explore management expense ratios for mutual funds here, no managed money product escapes this discussion. It's just that the ongoing costs of mutual funds have been in the spotlight more than those other managed money products lately.

The management expense ratio (MER) of a mutual fund reflects the actual expenses of running the fund and is usually expressed as a percentage of the value of the fund ranging from less than 1 percent to over 3 percent depending on the fund.

The MER includes:

- management fees paid to the money managers, who get paid for overseeing and managing the portfolio, based on their contract or employment agreement
- money for ongoing marketing and promotion of the fund
- trailer or service fees paid to the firm the advisor works for
- legal and audit fees
- custodial and safekeeping fees
- registrar and transfer agency fees
- taxes, interest, operating, and administrative costs
- the costs to file financial and other reports to comply with securities laws

- trading costs or brokerage commissions
- servicing the needs and answering the questions of clients and the financial advisors
- other operating and administrative costs
- GST or HST (Harmonized Sales Tax)

TREND Currently, Canadian mutual fund orders are processed and valued at the close of each trading day. But, if the "normal" business day becomes extended or never closes, we might find mutual funds being traded like stocks or indexes, priced to the market throughout the day. This could result in higher expenses due to increased operating costs and transaction fees, as well as more audits to ensure there are no reporting irregularities.

As of February 2000, mutual fund MERs must include any taxes and any other charges that are paid by the fund, which means that, all things being equal, the MERs reported for many mutual funds will be higher in the future. In the same month, Canadian mutual fund investors started to receive "plain language" mutual fund disclosure documents that provide:

- educational information about mutual funds, their tax implications and costs

- specific information regarding each fund, including its top 10 holdings, even though these will change over time

- an annual information form (AIF) reporting the fund's performance and information about the mutual fund company, including any penalties or sanctions imposed on the key personnel of the fund, if they are relevant to unit holders.

It is important to look beyond the name of any mutual fund to determine if the manager is really actively managing the fund or simply following the top funds in the index as much as possible.

Take a look at the simplified prospectus and the stocks in the manager's top 10 list, information that must accompany the initial purchase of a mutual fund investment. There is at least one simplified prospectus in Canada that clearly states the portfolio is "not actively managed" and charges a management fee of 2.25 percent plus GST.

TREND Expect to see the regulators monitoring the performance reporting practices of all managed money portfolios to ensure they are not being pumped up to make the performance look better than it really is.

The fund company is also required to show the amount it collects in fees and what it pays to dealers for the following:

- selling its products
- trailer or service fees
- marketing or education

You'd have to pore over the annual financial statements of the mutual fund to figure out how it is spending the money it collects. You might be interested in knowing how much of it is being used to maximize your potential returns to help you get richer and how much is being used to attract new investors to help the fund company get richer. Now, this issue isn't isolated to the investment industry. Consumers of most products pay for the marketing and advertising of that product—whether it is breakfast cereal, computers or cars.

Some investors do not realize they pay ongoing fees on their investments because they don't show up on any statement. But these fees impact performance over time: positively if these investments outperform other investments you might have held, and negatively if you pay too much. While low fees are desirable, so is a good track record and management style. A managed money investment earning a rate of return of 12 percent with annual expense of 2 percent is preferable to one earning a return of 7 percent with expenses of 1 percent.

Here's a chart showing the range of MERs that are charged for publicly available mutual funds offered in Canada.

RANGE OF MERS OF CANADIAN MUTUAL FUNDS AS OF MAY 31, 2000				
Fund Type	Fund Sub-Type	Low	High	Average
Cash				
	Canadian Money Market	0.25	1.77	0.89
	Foreign Money Market	0.52	2.11	1.09
Fixed Income				
	Canadian Bonds	0.66	2.55	1.61
	Canadian Short Term	0.57	2.34	1.45
	Canadian Mortgage	1.44	2.00	1.68
	Foreign Bond	0.92	2.78	1.96
	High Yield Bond	1.30	2.50	2.11
Balanced Funds				
	Canadian Balanced	0.88	3.21	2.13
	Canadian Tactical Asset Alloc	0.95	2.95	2.25
	Canadian High Income Bal	1.24	2.36	1.65
	Global Bal & Asset Allocation	2.00	2.94	2.52
	Global Balanced	2.00	2.94	2.51
	Global Allocation	2.38	2.80	2.56
Canadian Equity				
	Equity	1.07	3.49	2.30
	Large Cap Equity	1.20	3.00	2.30
	Small/Mid Equity	1.45	2.96	2.45
	Dividend	1.13	2.88	1.94
	Labour Sponsor Venture	2.40	7.00	4.45

Fund Type	Fund Sub-Type	Low	High	Average
Foreign Equity				
	US Equity	1.11	3.06	2.35
	US Small & Mid Equity	1.88	2.99	2.54
	Global Equity	1.63	3.64	2.52
	International Equity	1.39	2.92	2.40
	North American Equity	1.16	2.90	2.23
	Latin American Equity	2.40	3.24	2.87
	European Equity	2.00	3.00	2.55
	Asia/Pacific Rim Equity	2.00	3.16	2.67
	Asia ex-Japan Equity	2.55	3.49	2.86
	Japanese Equity	2.37	3.12	2.61
	Emerging Markets	2.25	3.83	2.90
Sector				
	Country	2.50	5.08	3.48
	Natural Resources	2.00	4.91	2.63
	Precious Metals	2.14	5.68	2.95
	Science & Technology	2.00	2.97	2.57
	Real Estate	2.25	2.82	2.57
	Specialty/Miscellaneous	1.65	2.67	2.41

Source: Morningstar Canada

So let's add them up. Suppose you invest $100,000 in a mutual fund that collects an all-inclusive annual management fee of 2 percent. Here's a table showing the fees that would be deducted from your returns if the fund earned 7 percent over 20 years or 10 percent over 20 years.

| | 7% Return Before Fee | | 10% Return Before Fee | |
Year	Management Fees Paid	Value of Your Account	Management Fees Paid	Value of Your Account
1	$ 2,140	$104,860	$ 2,240	$107,800
5	11,792	126,780	12,855	145,577
10	26,741	160,731	31,569	211,928
15	45,695	203,774	58,813	308,519
20	69,723	258,723	98,473	449,133

If the mutual fund was able to earn 7 percent before fees, after 20 years your account would have grown to $258,723 and the mutual fund company would have collected $69,723 to manage your money. If your return was 10 percent before fees, after 20 years, your account would have grown to $449,133, and the fund company would have collected $98,473, an amount almost equal to the amount you originally invested.

Industry Canada and the Ontario Securities Commission also have a Mutual Fund Fee Impact Calculator in the investor resources section on their Web site at www.osc.gov.on.ca that you might find interesting. The calculator will add up what you might pay in fees over the years, based on the value of your investment, the rate of return you expect to earn, the number of years you plan to hold the investment, and the MER of your mutual fund.

Certain investors may face additional costs, such as redemption fees or fees for switching from one mutual fund to another within the same company. Although the simplified prospectus allows the financial advisor to charge up to 2 percent for switching, many charge nothing or only a low administrative charge.

Mutual funds have done so well bringing professionally managed money investments to the Canadian public and they now face competition from other types of managed money products and services, including equity-linked GICs, wrap accounts, segregated funds, and pooled accounts. As well, do-it-yourself trading and index investing offer added competition.

Segregated Funds

Although they have not received as much publicity, segregated funds also charge their investors ongoing fees, that include costs similar to mutual funds, as well as the costs of the guarantee. Here's a chart showing the range of the fees that are charged for segregated funds offered in Canada.

EXPENSE RATIOS FOR CANADIAN SEGREGATED FUNDS AS OF MAY 31, 2000				
Fund Type	Fund Sub-Type	Low	High	Average
Canadian Money Market		0.64	2.25	1.36
Fixed Income				
	Canadian Bonds	0.96	2.65	2.06
	Canadian Short Term	1.52	2.25	1.96
	Canadian Mortgage	1.67	2.40	2.06
	Foreign Bond	1.63	2.40	2.12
Balanced				
	Canadian Balanced	1.63	3.38	2.57
	Canadian Tactical Asset Alloc	2.06	3.32	2.71
	Global Bal & Asset Allocation	2.37	3.44	2.87
Canadian Equity				
	Equity	1.04	3.87	2.61
	Large Cap Equity	0.96	3.05	2.49
	Small/Mid Equity	1.00	3.43	2.71
	Dividend	1.73	3.02	2.32

Fund Type	Fund Sub-Type	Low	High	Average
Foreign Equity				
	US Equity	1.63	3.54	2.79
	Global Equity	2.11	3.63	2.83
	International Equity	1.63	3.76	2.91
	North American Equity	3.09	3.76	2.91
	European Equity	2.13	3.73	3.00
	Asia/Pacific Rim Equity	2.40	4.02	3.01
	Emerging Markets	2.65	3.97	3.65
Sector				
	Natural Resources	2.65	3.43	3.07
	Science & Technology	2.50	3.73	3.11
	Specialty/Miscellaneous	2.70	3.75	3.53

Source: Morningstar Canada

In additional to passing the costs of managing and operating the investment, segregated funds also pass on the cost of the guarantee to the investor. But the dirty little secret about segregated funds is that although your capital has a guarantee—the costs don't. Currently, the guarantee adds another 1/4 and 3/4 of 1 percent more than most mutual funds. For an investment of $100,000, this would increase the costs by an extra $500 to $750 a year. Let's compare the MERs for some segregated funds that are managed by the same managers as the mutual version, only inside a segregated fund wrapper. Here's an example from just one company.

Fund	Mutual Fund	Segregated Fund	Difference
Trimark Select Canadian Growth	2.35%	2.8%	.45%
Trimark Select Growth	2.36%	2.81%	.45%
Trimark Select Balanced	2.25%	2.7%	.45%

Source: www.trimark.com

For the guarantee, the stock market would have to go down in value and stay down *and* you would have to hold your investments until the guarantee period is up, or until you die. Of course, you would have to continue to pay ongoing management fees of the investments, as well as the cost for the guarantee.

A version of the modern segregated fund allows an investor to lock in (or reset) the guaranteed amount, the death benefit or both. Some allow you to do this once or twice a year, and at least one will automatically reset the guaranteed amount for you every day your investment increases in value, giving an investor all the upside of the market, less expenses. While this reset option enhances the amount of capital that is guaranteed, it also means the 10-year holding period is restarted with each reset and pushed further into the future. It also means you are likely to hold your assets with the insurance company and your financial advisor for longer.

Suppose you invested $10,000 in a segregated fund in 2001. If the value of your investment had increased to $12,000 in 2001 and you wanted to guarantee (or lock in) your $2,000 profit, you could reset the guaranteed amount to $12,000 (provided you were comfortable with the 10-year holding period that would now end in 2012).

Suppose you invest $100,000 in a segregated fund that collects all-inclusive annual fees of 2.5 percent. Here's a table showing the fees that would be deducted from your returns if the fund earned 7 percent and 10 percent over a number of years.

Year	7% Return Before Fee		10% Return Before Fee	
	Management Fees Paid	Value of Your Account	Management Fees Paid	Value of Your Account
1	$ 2,675	$104,325	$ 2,750	$107,250
5	14,583	123,578	15,895	141,901
10	32,605	152,716	38,477	201,360
20	82,397	233,221	115,86	405,458

If the segregated fund earned 7 percent before fees, in 10 years when the guarantee period expired, your account would have grown to $152,716 and the life insurance company would have collected $32,605. If your investment earned 10 percent before fees, your account would have grown to $201,360 after 10 years and the life insurance company would have collected $38,477 in fees, more than one-third of your original investment. (You might want to compare these numbers with the earlier table for mutual funds.)

What might the fees be if you reset the guarantee every year for the first 10 years and held the investment for 20 years? If your segregated fund made 7 percent, the value would have grown to $233,221 and the fees collected would be $82,397. At 10 percent, the value would have grown to $405,458 and the fees to $115,863—more than the amount you invested originally.

Adequate Disclosure?

Mutual fund prospectuses are now required to disclose the fund expenses that are paid indirectly by investors and to provide an illustration of the dollar value of these expenses over time. In one simplified prospectus, the illustration used an assumed rate of return of 5 percent for both a money market fund and an international equity fund. The dollar value of the expenses over five and 10 years for an initial investment of $1,000 were as follows:

	Money Market	International Equity
5 years	$ 34.38	$ 73.40
10 years	$ 76.95	$161.14

While a step in the right direction, this disclosure underestimates the expenses the investor would pay. Long-term historical returns for international equity funds are over 10 percent, more than double the return used in the illustration, which would mean higher expenses. Are they trying to hide what the expenses might be?

Segregated funds do not even have to supply as much information as mutual funds, which does not provide the potential investor with as much protection. As I see it, the points of difference between mutual funds and segregated funds would suggest that segregated funds should have to disclose at least as much, if not more, regarding their terms and costs, than mutual funds—not less. Their costs are generally higher, they are more complex and they might end up being a longer-term investment, particularly if the investor needs the benefit of the guarantee.

Fund of Funds Programs

A fund of funds program packages together a number of mutual or segregated funds in predetermined combinations or "customized portfolios" tailored to a variety of investor profiles or needs—ranging from ultra-conservative to highly aggressive. Some people use them to construct and manage their entire portfolio; others use them to complement their existing investments or not at all. Some of these programs have been successful, providing value for the costs, and others have just not taken off.

The ongoing costs for this type of investment program start with the management expense fees of the funds, plus an *additional* fee for overseeing the program. This additional fee may be as low as $100 a year, as for the STAR program through Mackenzie Financial Corp, or as much as 1.5 percent a year of the value of the account.

Wrap Programs

In 1995, the Wrap Fee Subcommittee of the Association for Investment Management and Research (AIMR) in the United States coined the following definition of a wrap fee program:

a program (account) under which any client is charged a specified fee or fees not based directly upon transactions in the client's account for investment advisory services (which may include portfolio management or advice concerning the selection of other investment advisers) and execution of client transactions.

There are a wide range of products and services offered under a wrap umbrella. Some are more like a package of mutual funds; others are more like the fee-based investment management programs offered by investment counsellors. Some are like a "private" mutual fund, put together by a brokerage firm for their investors. At other firms, wrap programs invest primarily in individual stocks and bonds.

There's no standard definition of what you can expect when the term "wrap" is used. It's a bit of a grab bag—you don't know what's inside until you look under the wrapper. The common denominator of wrap programs is that the ongoing fees are not based directly on transactions, advice or activity in the account, but on the account, ranging from around 1 to 3 percent or more a year. You'll find wrap fees based on:

- a percentage of the value of your account, which might decrease as its value passes certain dollar thresholds
- percentages tied to the types of assets you have in your account and their value (e.g., the percentage charged for a fixed income investment is lower than that charged for equities)
- a flat annual fee

In December 1999, RBC Dominion Securities announced the following wrap fee schedule:

- Fixed income pool   1.25%
- Conservative portfolio   1.9%
- Moderate growth portfolio 2.04%

Based on this schedule, an investor with $100,000 in a conservative portfolio would pay $1,900 a year in fees.

These fees may be charged indirectly (where you never see them on your investment statement), or they may be charged directly to your account and itemized on your statement. Where performance and the level of advice are comparable, look for the wrap with the lower cost, just as you would if you were taking out a mortgage.

TREND Wrap fees will be based on the types of investments you have in your portfolio—lower for fixed income investments than for aggressive growth ones—better reflecting the value the money manager can potentially add by managing those investments.

Fee-Based Accounts

Rather than nickle-and-diming clients for transactions, a number of firms have introduced fee-based accounts. These accounts are meant to provide a range of financial services and advice for an annual fee based on the value of their account.

 The all-inclusive fees may not include the costs of other types of investments you make with the financial advisor, such as segregated funds or investments done inside a universal life policy.

As an example, one full-service firm charged annual fees of 1.5 percent of assets under administration, with an annual minimum fee of $1,500 per year and no maximum. This implies that the financial firm felt it needed to collect at least $1,500 a year to provide their clients with a full-service package, including access to a financial advisor and the firm's resources, including:

■ unlimited trading on-line or trading with broker assistance

■ proprietary research done by the firm's research analysts

> **• tip** If you have mutual funds in a fee-based portfolio, you might want to ask if the firm collects service or trailer fees from the mutual fund companies in addition to the percentage they charge you.

Some managed money programs require you to invest a minimum dollar value in their managed program or in their fee-based account before you are eligible to open an account with them. The minimum account size could be $500 or less for some mutual funds or more than $1 million for some private investment accounts. Other programs have both a minimum account size and a minimum annual fee. It's important to consider the minimum annual fee and how it is calculated. Some investors might qualify under the minimum account size, but find they end up paying more in fees than they expected to because of their investment mix.

Some fee schedules are further divided by the type of assets in the account. Here's one example:

- one-half of 1% for cash and money market investments
- 1% on fixed income investments
- 1.5% on equities

Here's some sample fee calculations for a couple of asset mixes using the above fee schedule.

A portfolio holding 100% individual stocks charged 1.5% would pay $1,500, enough to satisfy the annual minimum fee as follows.

Asset mix	Market Value		Annual fee
100% stock portfolio	$100,000	at 1.5%	= $1,500

If you like to place your own orders, compare this to the cost of trading direct. If each trade cost $30, that $1,500 would buy you 50 trades a year—just over four a month. The service that works best for you will depend on the type of trader you are, the level of service you require and whether or not you think two heads are better than one.

Investors who are not active traders might wonder why they have to pay the same fee as someone who is active, simply to hold equities in their account. Clients holding cash may wonder why they have to pay any fees at all for these assets. In the long run, they may save money if they could find an account where they pay a flat fee for a basic set of services and limited number of transactions, forking out additional fees for any services they need only occasionally.

In early 2000, many investors switched to fee-based accounts and found value related to the number of trades they were placing in the hot market at that time. By late spring, some of these same investors had been shaken by the downward trend of the stock market and cut back on their trading activity but continued to pay the same fees based on the size of their account, even though they were using fewer services. Eventually, investors will want their fees to be tied to the resources they actually use and the advice they receive.

However, someone with a balanced portfolio of $100,000 using the above schedule, might end up paying the minimum fee based on the following calculation.

Asset mix	Market Value			Annual fee
10% in cash	$ 10,000	at	0.5% =	$ 50
40% in fixed income	40,000	at	1.0% =	400
50% in stocks	50,000	at	1.5% =	750
				$1,200*

*Minimum fee of $1,500 would be charged

TREND Expect to see the introduction of more products and services that charge separate fees for investment management and financial planning advice, as well as a wider range of investment service packages.

The larger your account, the higher your annual fee, regardless of the level of service and advice you are really using. Suppose your neighbour had an account worth $200,000 and was paying an annual fee of 1.5 percent, or $3,000. If your account were $400,000 and your fee was also 1.5 percent, you would be paying twice as much, or $6,000. If you are not getting twice the service, you might want to look at a program where the fee schedule declines for assets over various thresholds. You may find you can reduce your costs if you consolidate your portfolio at one firm rather than spreading it among two or three firms.

Here's an example. Suppose your accounts total $600,000 and you have $200,000 at three firms (each with a different fee schedule). Since you haven't reached any threshold for reduced fees, your costs might be:

Firm 1	$200,000 at 2%	=	$ 4,000
Firm 2	$200,000 at 2.1%	=	4,200
Firm 3	$200,000 at 1.8%	=	3,600
Total Cost			$11,800

Now that your portfolio has grown, you are considering consolidating your accounts at one firm with the following all-inclusive fee structure of:

First	$500,000	1.5%
Over	$500,000	0.75%

Your annual costs would then be:

First	$500,000	at 1.5%	=	$7,500
Balance	$100,000	at 0.75%	=	750
Total				$8,250

(or $3,550 less than before consolidating)

Not only is the total cost lower each year, these lower fees add up to significant savings over the years as your account grows.

Other Fee-Based Investment Programs

In the past, investment counsellors received most of their business through referrals, almost like a private club. They generally work with larger accounts of $500,000 or more, although some are now managing accounts starting at $100,000. But you don't have to be part of that private club any more to access this type of investment management. It is now available as one of the product lines in the traditional brokerage environment, so you may not have to leave them if you are looking for a different level of advice and service.

The services of an investment counsellor are generally provided on a no-load basis, that is, there are no acquisition fees or commissions to become a client and make the initial investments. Fees are charged on a pay-as-you-go basis as a percentage of the value of your account or as an annual professional advisory fee. They may be collected in advance, at the beginning of each quarter, or in arrears, at the end of the quarter. Fees for brokerage transactions and custodial costs are extra.

Let's look at a sample fee schedule for an investment portfolio program held at a trust company. The fees may be subject to negotiation, particularly for larger accounts.

Size of Portfolio	Percentage Charged
First $250,000	1.25
Next $250,000	0.75
Next $500,000	0.5
Next $4 million	0.375

In addition to a minimum annual fee of $3,000 for investment management, annual administration fees are as follows:

First $500,000	.55%
Next $500,000	.44%
Next $4 million	.18%

Based on this fee schedule, the annual fee for a portfolio of $1 million would be calculated as:

Management fee	250,000 at 1.25%	$3,125
	250,000 at 0.75%	1,875
	500,000 at 0.5%	2,500
		$7,500
plus		
Administration fees	$500,000 at .55%	$2,750
	$500,000 at .44%	2,200
		$4,950

For a total of $12,450 or 1.24% a year.

• tip Since the financial firm may not be able to give you an exact dollar amount (because of changing market values) of your costs, get in writing:

- the fee schedule listing the percentage charged as well as an estimate of the dollar amount you would pay
- an example illustrating how all the costs will be calculated for an account similar to yours in size and asset mix
- any additional costs that will be charged to your account, directly or indirectly.

You don't want to be surprised 12 months from now with costs that are much more than you thought they would be.

Universal Life Policies

When you purchase a universal life policy, you contract for a certain amount of life insurance coverage, pay the basic premiums for the insurance and additional premiums to "invest" in a portfolio within the life insurance policy.

A universal life policy has a term insurance component and an investment component (sometimes referred to as a tax shelter). Although the minimum death benefit is normally guaranteed, the value of the investments depends on investment performance.

The insurance salesperson is paid an insurance commission upfront by the insurance company. That and ongoing costs keeps the investment values in your account low in the early years. Here are some cost considerations:

- Is the cost of insurance fixed or variable and how does the monthly mortality charge (the cost of the insurance) compare with the other types of life insurance policies?

- How much is the annual policy fee?

- Are there any administration charges?

- Do you have to pay fees for any or all transactions?

- What are the ongoing costs (like MERs) on the investments? Are they actively or passively managed?

- Is there an annual maximum fee once the portfolio reaches a certain size?

- Do the costs decrease as your investment portfolio passes certain thresholds, such as $200,000, $500,000, or $1,000,000 in value?

- Is there a good trade-off between the cost you pay and the tax you defer?

While there can be major differences among the features and the costs of universal life policies, the sales battle was often based on which financial advisors provided the better looking financial illustration—a sort of "my policy's better than your policy." As with a financial plan, an illustration is no better than the assumptions that went into it. A financial illustration that projects a target return of 10 percent might make the policy look better, but it may not be realistic.

There might be additional costs to consider, particularly if you end up cancelling your policy. You should ask:

1. What surrender charge would be levied if you cancelled the policy during the first 10 years? In the early years, the surrender charges can significantly reduce the cash value.

2. If you have any guaranteed investment annuities inside the policy (the life insurance industry's version of GICs), what market value adjustment (MVA) would be charged, if you cancel it before the maturity date?

Eventually, the statement you receive for your universal insurance policy will itemize all the direct costs and indirect charges you pay for, including management fees for the investments, such as segregated funds.

Annual Trustee Fees

The firm you deal with may charge trustee fees for RRSP, RRIF and RESP accounts, ranging from $25 to $150 plus GST a year. While this may not sound like much, even these fees add up over time. Over 10 years, $100 becomes $1,000, and when the annual fee is reinvested at 5 percent, compounds to $1,258. After 20 years, it compounds to $3,307. At $100 per year (not including GST), look at how much these fees add up to over time.

COST OF THE TRUSTEE FEES*

Long-Term Average Return	10 years	20 years	30 years
5%	$1,258	$3,307	$6,644
7%	1,382	4,100	9,446
9%	1,519	5,116	13,531

*assuming the $100 annually stays in your RRSP and is able to earn the average long-term annual return.

AN INCREASING VARIETY OF INVESTMENT OPTIONS—THEY WANT YOU!

Make no mistake about it—the financial services industry is big business in Canada and the rest of North America and continues to grow. If you doubt that, just look at the value of the industry's corporate stocks and profits. The benefits of marketing efforts by mutual fund companies are not reflected in the unit value of a mutual fund, only the price of that company's stock. This is also true for the firms that provide other managed money products.

Financial firms want to sell more investment products and services, either to existing customers or to new ones, to be able to generate ongoing fees for managing and processing trades and/or commissions. They are adding more investment programs with numerous variations on a theme, that all generate on-going fees for them, including:

- putting brand-name mutual funds in a segregated fund wrapper (e.g., a number of mutual fund companies have teamed up with insurance companies to offer a segregated version of their own mutual funds)

- mutual fund companies expanding their line of mutual funds and adding more specialty funds
- participating in mutual fund fund-of-funds programs, such as Artisan and Keystone
- managing pension funds in addition to their retail investments, such as Bissett and PH&N
- building an institutional, or pooled, fund class of their own mutual funds, such as the Mackenzie private trust accounts
- creating their own in-house money management programs
- building private-label versions of successful products
- developing fee-based asset management or wrap programs

ADD UP YOUR FEES

Are the fees for these programs too high? Some of them are, but unless they are itemized on your statement, you might not even be aware that you're paying them, let alone how much they are. Mutual funds were the first managed money product required by the securities regulators to provide better disclosure of their fees to investors at the time of purchase.

But there is no industry-wide requirement for all managed money and fee-based programs to disclose the dollar amount investors pay to participate in their investments.

 TREND To give the public more protection, segregated funds, wrap accounts, and other managed money products, as well as fee-based accounts and investments inside life insurance policies, will be required to provide better fee disclosure. They will have to clearly state what an investor will pay in dollars and cents, rather than just percentages, similar to what mutual funds are now required to do.

This disclosure statement will help investors compare the costs and features of similar, but different, types of investment products. Don't be afraid to ask for a written estimate of what your costs will be and how they are calculated. Ask "how much?" and assess the impact those fees have on your investment returns. Don't take the attitude that if you have to ask, you can't afford it. Being a good consumer means knowing the costs and how they are calculated so that you can comparison shop and determine if you have the right products and services.

Anyone who has ever taken out a mortgage knows the difference a half a percent in the rate can make to their bottom line. If you know the percentage that is charged annually (or can estimate it), on a mutual fund, segregated fund, wrap account, fund-of-funds account, investment counselling service, universal life policy or fee-based investment account, you can use the Cost Tables in the Appendix to estimate how much you could actually be paying over the years. Find the table for the long-term rate of return, before fees, you assume your portfolio will earn. The tables go up to 15 percent. Then find the column for the annual percent you are being charged in fees or expenses. Go down to the row for the number of years you expect to hold that investment to get your personal cost factor. Then multiply the market value of your account today by this cost factor. The result is approximately the amount you can expect to pay to have your money managed and reflects your increasing market value as your portfolio grows. When the cost factor is greater than 1, the fees you will have paid will greater than the amount you originally invested.

Costs will not remain one of the great secrets of investing. Eventually, your year-end statement will itemize all the costs of your investment program.

SUMMARY

As we've discussed, there may be costs to acquire an investment as well as on-going fees to maintain it. Do these fees make managed money products bad investments? Not necessarily. Managed investments have given many investors access to the stock markets here and around the world. They also provide investors with the benefits of professional money management. But all other things being equal, higher fees leave less in your pocket. And unlike the interest payments on a mortgage, which lasts only 20 or 25 years, you pay these fees as long as you hold your investments—which could be much longer. Regardless of how much or how little you pay up front, you need to pay attention to the ongoing costs and what you get for your money.

One of the industry's great debates is the performance and costs of actively managed mutual funds vs. index-based investing. Index-based investing is cheaper—it is closer to pure product than actively managed ones. But if you want advice, you have to pay for it, either through higher annual management or investment-based fees, or an hourly rate for the time you spend with a financial advisor. The next chapter looks at the pivotal role financial advisors can play in minding your money and how you can best work with them.

Working with Financial Advisors

"If the time comes when you can't manage money on your own anymore and you need more exper-tise, don't think of it as an admission of failure but rather as a sign of success."

Based on a Salomon Smith Barney ad

Let's be frank. Not everyone needs to work with a financial advi-sor or money manager, and not every financial advisor is some-one you'd want to work with. But if you are looking for assistance with your investments, help in developing a financial plan or a second opinion on what you are doing yourself, an experienced financial advisor can provide you with their expertise, guidance and level-headed advice. They can help you sort through the opportunities that are available, keep you focused on what's most important to you, help you avoid costly mistakes, and provide recommendations that are tailored to your personal situation.

A recent estimate put the number of individuals registered to provide financial products in Canada at over 70,000. That's about one licensed person for every 428 Canadians or approximately one financial advisor for every 171 households (assuming 2.5 people per household), if they were all looking to work with a financial advisor.

In this chapter, we'll take the whirlwind tour of who's who in the financial service industry—people who could provide you with financial advice, as well as how to rate your current financial advisor and what to do if it's time to move on.

THE RANGE OF LICENSES YOU FIND

Everyone in Canada who offers financial products to the public is required to hold a license with a provincial or federal regulator. There is currently a myriad of educational requirements, courses and exams among the programs leading up the different licenses and registrations.

In the days of the four traditional pillars, if you went to your banker, you discussed banking. If you when to an insurance agent, you'd discuss life insurance. If you went to a stockbroker, you'd discuss individual stocks and bonds and if you went to an investment counsellor, you'd discuss having a privately managed portfolio or the investment of your company pension plan. As we discussed in Chapter 2, there is consolidation and convergence occurring in the financial services industry although the regulation of the people who offer products still follows the traditional four pillars, not based on the advice they provide.

The investment solution you get depends on the license the financial advisor holds—the broader the product range, the greater the number of options they can consider for your situation. An objective financial advisor will recommend the best course of action and the most appropriate investment options for you regardless of the types of investments they, themselves, have available.

Unfortunately, they might try to sell you what they have, rather than advise you to go somewhere else to get what you need.

Someone licensed as a life insurance agent can offer life insurance products, including life insurance policies and segregated funds. Someone licensed as a mutual fund salesperson can offer mutual funds and mutual fund products, such as certain asset allocation programs. A person licensed as a stockbroker can offer investment products including stocks, bonds, index stocks and mutual funds. A person who is dually licensed would be able to offer insurance products as well as mutual funds or stocks.

Let's run through the different types of licenses or registrations a person might have and then start to look at how you can find what you're looking for.

Mutual Fund Licenses

Before a person can be registered to sell mutual funds and certain managed money products, they must complete the Canadian Investment Funds Course (by correspondence) and pass a multiple-choice exam, or complete the Canadian Securities Course. In some provinces, if someone with a mutual fund license also wants to sell Labour Sponsored Venture Capital funds (LSVCF), they must pass a separate exam covering them or the Canadian Securities Course.

The day they pass the exam and become registered mutual funds salespeople, they can offer their services to the public. They don't currently have to commit to any continuing education, but those who hold a financial planning or insurance designation may complete 30 hours or more each year of ongoing education.

People registered as mutual funds salespeople are not licensed to sell stocks and bonds and cannot trade them for you. To be able to offer you life insurance products, including segregated funds, they must also hold a life insurance license.

You'll find licensed mutual fund salespeople working with the public as independent mutual fund salespeople, in financial planning firms, as employees of companies that sell direct, in mutual fund dealerships, and in banks and credit unions.

Securities Licenses

Those licensed to offer stocks, bonds, mutual funds, labour sponsored funds, managed money products, strip bonds, and other products to the public may have many titles. They might be called stockbrokers, investment counsellors, investment executives, or investment advisors, to name a few. Regardless of the title on their business card, their registration with the provincial securities regulators will either be as:

- an investment representative, which allows them to take orders, such as at a discount broker, but not to give advice
- a registered representative, which allows them to also make investment recommendations.

To be licensed as a broker, a person must take a preparatory course and pass the Canadian Securities Course exam, which consists of multiple-choice, case studies, and questions that require short answers, as well as the Conduct and Practices Handbook (CPH) exam.

Unless they work at a discounter, brokers are also required to complete a supervised 90-day training program at their firm before working with clients. They also have to complete the first part of the Certified Investment Manager (CIM) exam within 30 months. If their business is mostly fee-based, presumably that person also has financial planning expertise. If they deal in options, futures or derivative investments, they also need to be licensed to trade each of those.

You'll find people with a securities license working with the public in full-service, discount and on-line brokerage firms, as well as in financial planning firms that are registered as securities dealers with the provincial securities regulators. At some discount brokers, new staff is considered ready to deal with the public after just 30 days of training. So when you call, remember that the person on the other end of the phone may be just starting out in the business and have little more experience than you do.

It may be time for a new licensing exam that prepares those entering the industry for the real world they will work in. In addition to understanding Canadian investments and the trading side of the business, the exam should cover the full range of investment and insurance products available, including international investing. If these people are going to trade securities in international markets on the new global exchanges, they should understand the technical issues of those markets, as well as the local cultures.

Advisors who hold a securities license can now also be licensed to provide life insurance, something that was forbidden until just a few years ago. While some industry insiders state that the brokerage side of the business is becoming more fee-based (which may reduce their commission income), is it a coincidence that some brokers are now selling more insurance, including life insurance policies and segregated funds, which are still primarily commission-based?

 TREND The role of the broker is changing from someone who provides investments to someone who provides a full range of products and advice, acts as a sounding broad, and filters through the appropriate information on behalf of their clients.

Insurance Agents

To become licensed as an insurance agent in Canada, a person has to pass a three-hour multiple-choice exam (to qualify for level I license) and be sponsored into the industry by a life insurance company. As soon as they are registered, they can immediately offer life insurance products to prospective clients. Within four years of obtaining their level I exam, they must pass the level II examination if they want to continue in the business. In Alberta, individuals who hold a mutual fund and life insurance license have to write an additional exam if they want to sell segregated funds.

Life insurance agents may sell a number of products, including life insurance, segregated funds, disability insurance, critical illness coverage, long-term care, and property and casualty insurance.

You'll find people registered to sell life insurance working as:

- career life insurance agents who offer the products of a particular life insurance company
- independent life insurance brokers who offer products of a number of different life insurance companies
- stockbrokers who are also licensed to offer life insurance products and investments as well as securities and mutual funds.

Investment Counsellors

In order to be registered as an investment counsellor with the provincial securities regulators, a person has to complete certain courses that are offered by the Canadian Securities Institute, as well as part of the Chartered Financial Analyst (CFA) program, and have five or more years of experience managing money.

An investment counsellor's training prepares them for managing investments, that is, deciding what investments should be in the portfolio to give investors the best returns for their stated investment objectives. They might manage money for individual investors and/or investment portfolios for pension plans, mutual funds and segregated funds. You'll also find them working with the public as investment advisors and trust officers.

Holding the Chartered Financial Analyst (CFA) designation has long been considered one of the top qualifications an individual could have when it came to managing money. The CFA is a three-year program offered by the Association of Investment Management Research (AIMR) in the United States. The training focuses on developing the skills to select investments for the portfolios they build and manage. But the CFA is an American course, with American content and biases which contains limited material relating to Canadian tax laws and financial planning—two key aspects of wealth management important to Canadians with higher net worths.

Is a License Enough?

The training and licensing of financial advisors focuses on the product side of the business, licensing people to sell life insurance, stocks and mutual funds, or some combination of products, rather than on their ability to provide comprehensive financial advice. Having a licence and being registered with the appropriate regulatory authorities means that a person has passed an exam, but it may not prepare them for the real world of working with clients.

Most of these exams have not kept up to date with the changing nature of the financial industry and the fact that there are now more products, more sophisticated clients and more complex issues to deal with. A license to sell is not the same as being qualified to provide comprehensive financial advice. Just because you can pass a car driving test and are issued with a driver's license does not mean you are a good driver, nor does it qualify you to drive a motorcycle or transport truck. Just being licensed to sell certain products does not automatically prepare nor qualify a person for working in today's world.

TREND The educational standards for entry into the financial services industry will become more coordinated. All licensed salespeople will have to have at least a basic knowledge of all types of investments (including stocks, bonds, mutual funds, and wrap accounts) and insurance products (such as life insurance, health, disability, and segregated funds.) And if they want to hold themselves out as financial planners, they will have to demonstrate they are proficient in financial planning as well.

THE NATURE OF A PROFESSIONAL RELATIONSHIP

Integrated financial advice focuses on your personal objectives and the professional aspects of money management. It is a professional relationship, not a friendship. You don't have to work with someone you don't like, but your primary motivation is to work with someone you can trust who is knowledgeable and will put your interests first. You can have a professional relationship with an accountant and lawyer based on their ability to provide you with frank, candid, up-to-date advice. The same should be true of your financial advisor.

Some financial institutions talk about "relationship management." But what is it? Is it a professional relationship or will you end up "being managed?" Some relationship management systems seems to have more to do with cross-selling products to existing clients, such as life insurance products to an investment client, than ensuring that the client's goals and objectives are met. I've heard of situations where individuals have been invited in for their annual review and ended up receiving little more than a sales pitch for more products. While it is often more profitable for a firm to market additional products and services to existing clients than to find new ones, your review meeting should not be used just as an additional sales opportunity.

One Canadian bank announced a new service they were offering to its US clients with $2 million or more. In addition to investment management and "on-line interactive financial services" the private wealth management program came with a "relationship manager available on the client's schedule, day or night." If this is the type of service you are looking for, make sure the relationship manager has the skills and expertise you'd be looking for at 3 a.m. While any good financial advisor or other professional will be there for their top clients when they need them, particularly in an emergency, will people working the graveyard shift be the top financial advisors or someone with less experience?

Some firms are talking about providing wealth management services to their clients, others have realigned their organization along these lines. But as a professional service, integrated financial advice still often lacks many of the characteristics one would expect to exist in a mature profession or service such as:

- clear contractual obligations between the client and the advisor
- written expectations
- description of the services being provided, such as an investment policy statement and a written financial plan
- full disclosure of all the costs involved and potential conflicts of interest
- clear descriptions of who the services are best suited for.

What's Trust Got to Do with It?

It's been said that you have to trust your financial advisor for them to be able to assist you, so select someone you believe will earn your trust over time. But never put your complete trust in another person who stands to profit from what you do. Certainly, you need to determine if the financial advisor has the skill, professionalism and resources to be able to guide you. Very early in the relationship, you will need to provide the financial advisor with the details of your finances, your career situation and goals, your family dynamics and your business interests for them to have a complete picture of your financial and personal life. The advisor will ask questions to help you prioritize your goals. If you do not feel that the individual is someone you want to have these discussions with, take your business elsewhere.

But there is more to working with a qualified professional than just trust. Some people are too trusting and want their advisor to make decisions for them, but that is not their role. You should actively participate in the decisions that affect your financial well-being. Yes, you should trust the professionals you work with, but blind trust—the kind of trust based on emotion—can be detrimental to your financial health.

TREND Expect to see more wealth management services that combine professional money management with advanced financial planning advice, as well as more on-line services that will guide those with less wealth through the basics of investment management and financial planning. We already have basic on-line portfolio design and financial planning software.

If you have concerns about any of the investments or strategies the financial advisor is recommending, ask for the following information in writing:

- Why are you recommending this for me?
- How does the performance of this investment compare with similar types of investments?
- What risks are involved?
- How do the costs for this investment compare with similar investments and other options?
- What is your firm's compensation for this investment in the first year? Over five years? Over 10 years?
- Are there any potential conflicts of interest?
  You should never feel pressured.

WHAT DO ADVISORS REALLY DO?

In addition to recommending and discussing investment ideas (products), an advisor can assist you in building and managing a portfolio according to your specifications (investment advice) as well as developing your financial plan (financial planning advice). Everything is firing on all cylinders when you consider your personal situation, in conjunction with investment advice and financial planning—then you get the power of integrated financial advice.

You'll find financial advisors acting as "stock jockeys" who focus on their stock picking ability and as salespeople hawking products. Some financial advisors focus on investment management and manage the money themselves; others subcontract it to mutual fund managers and other money managers. Others focus on financial planning advice such as tax and estate planning, or provide integrated financial advice to their clients. Still others provide a second opinion on your current financial strategies.

The Disclosure Statement

Financial advisors should be able to give you a disclosure statement in writing that outlines:

- who they are
- the range of products and services they are licensed to provide
- their professional qualifications and experience in the industry
- if they have had any disciplinary action taken against them
- the names of any proprietary products their company offers and any potential conflicts of interest
- how they are compensated

- an estimate of what it will cost you to work with them and the services that are included
- what services might cost extra
- the responsibilities of the client and the advisor
- a statement regarding the confidentiality of client information
- whether or not they manage your money themselves, as part of a team, or farm out the investment management to a mutual fund or other professional money manager.

WHAT DO YOU WANT: PRODUCTS, ADVICE OR BOTH?

When choosing someone to work with, you need to decide what kind of service and advice you want. Are you looking for investment advice or do you want advice on tax, estate and retirement questions or both? At one extreme, you might meet an advisor who focuses on trading stocks or accumulating assets for the fees they would generate, where advice is only incidental to the investments. At the other, you could find an advisor who focuses on providing sound, impartial advice as their primary service, where the advice is key, not incidental, to their services.

WHAT DO YOU WANT FROM A FINANCIAL ADVISOR?

Check off all that apply.

❏ Help with a specific type of product (i.e., funds, insurance, stocks)

❏ Help selecting from wide range of products

❏ Investment advice to build a sound investment portfolio

❏ Investment management services

❏ Financial planning advice

❑ Integrated financial advice

❑ A review of what you are currently doing

❑ An independent, objective opinion

❑ Nothing

If your advisor is also selling product, it is fair to ask if that advice is independent and objective. There is nothing dishonorable about selling. The best salespeople often act more like consultants who try to understand your needs and recommend appropriate solutions. But with more and more firms providing their own line of investment products, it can be hard for the consumer to determine if these products are in their best interest or in the best interest of the financial advisor.

HOW DO ADVISORS GET PAID?

When buying a car, you know that there is good money to be made by the dealership not just by selling the car, but also from the ongoing service, especially if you come in every 5,000 kilometers for maintenance. You can even see the base price over the Internet. You know the salesperson works on commission or is paid a salary and may be receiving bonuses—cash or otherwise—for selling certain products or reaching sales targets.

It's not that different in the financial services. Selling securities, mutual funds and insurance on commission is still the most common way for financial advisors to earn their income, although salary and asset-based compensation are becoming more common. Some also charge an hourly rate for their services.

The amount your financial advisor receives depends on their arrangement with the firm they work for, but generally, the more revenue they generate for the firm, the higher their share of the fees or commissions. At some firms the payout rate ranges from 20 to 50 percent or more where the firm provides much of the services the advisor requires, such as the office equipment and support staff. At other firms, the payout rate can be from 40 to 85 percent or more, but the advisors are required to pay for more of their own expenses, such as rent and office equipment.

As advisors reach certain sales or production targets, they receive some form of bonus or credits. Their firm's compensation program will reflect the characteristics or products it wants to promote. Lately, some of these programs have focused on setting up fee-based client accounts or the selling of proprietary products. At one firm, as an example, financial advisors were receiving commissions from the sale of third party mutual funds at par and getting one-and-a-half times the credit for selling their own firm's products or more subtle pressures such as waiving trustee fees for accounts invested in those products and special education programs.

When meeting targets means you get to keep your job or take care of your family, some advisors consider what the firm wants them to do rather than what is best for their client. Although I don't believe that most financial advisors are enticed by their firm's internal compensation programs, maybe we need to see some compensation programs that factor in client retention and satisfaction.

Here's a summary of the most common ways of compensating your financial advisor.

Fee for Service

Under a fee-for-service arrangement, you pay by the hour (or by the project) for financial advice, second opinions or even acting as expert witnesses. None of compensation a fee-for-service financial advisor receives is related to product or the size of your investment portfolio.

Fees range from $50 to $250 an hour and up, depending on the service you require, the part of the country you live in and the experience and reputation of the financial advisor. Although some clients don't like the idea of having a meter running when they sit down with a financial advisors, others say it's the size of the annual fee that is important and don't mind as long as their annual fee is lower.

This compensation method is similar to what you might pay if you hired a lawyer or an accountant. If you needed a will, you would pay for it based on the time you spend with the lawyer, or a flat fee based on their fee schedule, depending on the needs of your situation. Usually the flat fee is only for fairly straightforward cases; anything more complicated would mean an hourly rate. Some financial advisors who charge by the hour will bill you for the first meeting but offer you a pre-interview over the phone and send out a financial services agreement before you start working together.

The number of strictly fee-for-service financial advisors—who don't make investments on behalf of their clients—is less than 5 percent of those calling themselves financial planners. They may not be licensed to offer or recommend products for your portfolio.

TREND Your financial advisor might become your professional financial shopper, assessing what you are paying for your banking and investment services and helping you find the services that best suit your needs at competitive prices.

Salaried Employees

Salaried employees are a mixed breed and are found at a few brokerage firms and at the banks, credit unions, and firms that sell their investments direct to the public. While you don't pay for their services directly, their compensation is paid from the fees the firm collects from the investments you hold with them, such as transaction fees for trading, trailers fees from mutual funds or monthly service fees. From a business perspective, your account and other business with the firm has to generate enough money so the firm can pay these employees. While someone on salary may appear to be more objective than someone on commission, this is not necessarily so, particularly if you do not know what sort of bonus programs they have.

Commission-Based Compensation

Commission-based compensation is based on the investments when you acquire them. You could pay directly, such as on a front-end load mutual fund or indirectly, such as for a deferred-sales-charge mutual or segregated fund or universal life insurance policy. The investment or insurance product is offered and sold; any advice (such as financial planning) was considered to have been free or paid for separately.

Some investors bought their investments on a commission basis years ago and then looked for a qualified financial advisor who could provide them with financial advice. In the commission-based compensation model, the next financial advisor would have to sell you something else to be compensated for their advice and time. Since this is not always appropriate, some commission-based financial advisors may also offer asset-based programs or financial planning on an hourly basis.

Asset-Based Compensation

Asset-based compensation, or fee-based compensation, pays for any transactions you require as well for the services and advice of a financial advisor. The on-going fees are charged based on the size of your account and could be paid directly by you or indirectly by the investments you have in your account. Many people think of these ongoing fees as payment for the financial advice they receive, rather than for any specific investment products

Indirect fee-based compensation is where the fees are based on the types of assets you hold in your account, and deducted from the investment rather than from your account statement, such as the ongoing fees for some managed money investments including mutual funds, segregated funds and wrap accounts. They are often collected as part of the management expense fees and a percentage is then paid to the financial advisor. Some financial advisors see these fees as a retainer for the services they provide on an ongoing basis; others just collect the fees because you happen to hold your account with them.

Direct fee-based compensation is sometimes referred to as fee-only. These on-going fees are based on the size of your account, not investment products, and may or may not be based on the asset mix in your account.

When the fees are based on the types of assets in the account, some financial advisors may find it difficult to hold cash in your account if it is not generating enough fees. But if it's appropriate for you to hold money in money market mutual funds or cash, do it, whether or not that investment generates any revenue for the advisor or the firm. Advisors tell stories about being taken to task by their managers for having "too much" of their clients' money in money market investments. These managers never asked why it was there or about the client's situation—the account just wasn't making the firm as much profit as it could. You want an advisor who will do what is right for you.

• tip If your financial advisor calls themselves "fee-based" or "fee-only," it means they accept no commission. But some are still accepting the healthy commissions from life insurance-related investment products, such as segregated funds and universal life policies, without offsetting the annual fee you pay.

Some financial advisors provide comprehensive financial advice on your entire situation. Some advisors base the fee for this advice on the assets you currently hold with them, rather than the time that is involved, so how are they charging you for advice that relates to assets you have with other brokers? Are they doing some sort of mental accounting of the time it takes them to do the plan or just hoping that you will bring those other assets over to them? Considering that around 70 percent of investors in the US now have at least one on-line trading account, this could create an interesting question: How long will asset-based financial advisors be willing to "throw in" advice related to your other assets, wherever they are held? Remember that financial advisors could be exposing themselves to potential liability for their advice, regardless of where your assets are located.

Performance-Based Compensation

There are some people in the industry who base a portion of their compensation on your investment performance, with the fee based on the returns they earn on your behalf, almost like a bonus. It seems simple: the more you make, the more they make.

Once your rate of return reaches the agreed-upon minimum, the excess returns are split between the investors and the financial advisor or money manager. The money manager might receive as much as 25 to 35 percent or more of this return—in addition to any management fees. Suppose the agreement you have states that once your portfolio returns more than 10 percent, net of fees, any return over that are to be split with 30 percent going to the money manager and 70 percent going to you. Suppose your investment performance for the year is 20 percent. Your statement would show a return of 17 percent (10 % + 7 %) and the money manager would have earned a bonus of 3 percent of the value of your portfolio for providing that additional return.

It's typical to see this type of fee structure increase in popularity when market returns are going through the roof. But unless you are an aggressive investor, you could end up with a much riskier portfolio than you are really comfortable with. After all, investment theory says that you should expect to be rewarded with higher returns for taking higher risks. Are you prepared to take these added risks so that you and your advisor can make more money? Some people prefer to limit the risk in their portfolio to the returns they need to achieve their financial goals. Would your financial advisor be willing to settle for that?

If you think about it, there is an element of performance-based compensation to all asset-based programs when the fees are linked to the investments in the accounts. The trailer fees for mutual funds and segregated funds, and the fees collected from fee-based investment accounts, all increase as the size of your account grows—and provide an annuity payment, of a sort, to the financial advisor and their firm.

The fee you pay often bundled together the cost of investment management, financial planning and the time you spend with a financial advisor. No one ever said that the compensation system within any business was completely fair and it is up to you—even though the industry does not make it easy—to make sure you get what you are paying for. Are you more concerned with *how* you pay for your advice, or whether or not you getting good value?

WORKING WITH A FINANCIAL ADVISOR

If you decide you would be better off working with a financial advisor than going it alone, you need someone who is knowledgeable and with whom you feel sufficiently at ease to consider establishing a long-term relationship. They should be experienced and have your best interests at the heart of every recommendation they make. You also want an advisor who has references and a good reputation as being competent, ethical and honest

> **• tip** Select a financial advisor who can provide the services and/or products you need. Don't be afraid to ask questions. Base the breadth of the advice and service they provide for you, in part, on the questions *they* ask you and the type of information they request from you.

The Initial Meeting

You will have to interview the financial advisor to find out if there is a good fit between your communication styles and personalities. Many financial advisors working on fees or commissions offer a first meeting or initial consultation at no charge so you can determine if they have the right stuff. How will you know? Ask. Here's a list of questions to help you get started.

QUESTIONS TO CONSIDER BEFORE BEGINNING A PROFESSIONAL RELATIONSHIP

These questions will help you decide if a particular financial advisor can provide the advice you need, on the basis you want to receive it. Remember that you are considering hiring them—so treat the questioning like a job interview.

LEVEL OF SERVICE AND ADVICE

1. Will you be providing comprehensive, integrated financial advice? If not, what advice will you be providing?
2. How often will I hear from you?
3. How often will we review my financial plan to make sure I am on track?
4. Do you provide a written summary of the highlights of our meetings?

5. When I call, how long will it be before I will hear back? Will you return the call yourself or will your associate?

6. If we have a problem, what steps should I take?

TYPE OF RELATIONSHIP

7. Will our conversations be treated as confidential?

8. Who besides you will have access to my information?

9. Will I be dealing with you or one of your associates?

10. Describe the profile of your typical client? Your ideal client?

11. Is a minimum account size required?

12. Is my account larger/smaller than your average account size?

THE COSTS

13. How do I pay you?

    Directly: Fee for service, commissions, fee based on the size of my account, fees based on portfolio performance

    Indirectly: Deferred sales charges and/or trailer fees, or salary paid by your firm.

14. What fees and other costs, both direct and indirect, are involved in working with you and your firm?

15. Can you give me a dollar estimate of what those fees and costs would be for someone with my needs?

16. Do you have a minimum annual fee?

17. Do I have to pay GST or HST on top of these costs?

QUALIFICATIONS

18. Are you or your firm licensed to offer investments to the public? If yes, are you registered to provide financial planning advice?

    If no, are you qualified to provide financial planning advice?

19. What is your professional training?

20. What is your experience as a financial advisor?

21. Do you carry professional liability insurance?

22. How many hours of continuing education do you complete each year?

23. Are you a member of any professional association?

24. Has the regulator or your professional association ever disciplined you?

IF YOU WANT THEM TO MANAGE YOUR INVESTMENTS

25. Will you manage the investments yourself or outsource it?

26. Is your firm registered with a major stock exchange or a member of the Investment Dealers Association?

27. What sort of investor protection is available?

28. What range of products and services do you offer?

29. What is your investment philosophy?

30. Will you be recommending any investments that would tie me to your firm? If so, which ones and why?

31. What types of investments are you currently recommending?

32. What potential conflicts of interest should I be aware of?

33. Will you be required to call me before you make any changes in my investments?

34. How often will you be reviewing my investment performance?

A good financial advisor expects you to discuss these topics and any other issues you feel would be pertinent to establishing a solid working relationship with them.

Although your personal and financial information should be kept confidential, your conversations are not considered to be privileged information, as they would be with a lawyer. Ask who else in the firm will have access to your financial information, such as their support team and the firm's compliance officer. If you will be meeting with one or more of the financial advisor's associates, you should also ask about their qualifications, competency and experience. When you hire a particular individual to be your financial advisor, he or she should not delegate the advice to associates or staff without your knowledge and permission.

You and the financial advisor also need to set expectations for the relationship, preferably in writing, that are tailored to your needs. You need to know how often you should expect to hear from your financial advisor and how often you will meet in person. Many clients meet with their advisor in person once or twice a year, receive two or three mailings, and a couple of phone calls or phone meetings. Other relationships have more frequent contact, such as quarterly meetings. It depends on your needs and the income your advisor expects to earn from your account.

The first meeting will be relatively informal and you and the advisor will have a chance to find out whether or not you have the basis for a working relationship. If you both like what you see and hear, you can set up another meeting to further discuss the details of your situation. Always remember you should not be charged for anything unless you have agreed to it in advance.

The financial advisor is not obligated to take you on as a client. As you are interviewing them, they will be interviewing you to see if they have the combination of services and advice you are interested in and that they feel they would be able to meet your expectations. If you expect unrealistic returns, some financial advisors will suggest you take your business elsewhere—no one can guarantee double-digit returns even in the best of times.

Financial advisors are becoming more selective about the clients they work with. Advisors who have built their reputations on giving integrated financial advice may not be willing to work with individuals who want advice based on incomplete information.

The Working Relationship

Once you have selected your financial advisor, the real work begins. You should meet or communicate on a regular basis. Some people prefer to meet in person. Others prefer the phone or the convenience of e-mail. Relationships are a two-way street. Your financial advisor should be receptive to your calls, questions and requests for information. They are working on your behalf and you should feel free to speak with them. Of course, your expectations should not be unreasonable. Unless the sky has just fallen, you don't need to speak with your financial advisor every day.

When you bought your home, the real estate broker probably asked you a series of questions and took you to a number of different houses to get an idea of what you were looking for. Similarly, your advisor will put forward ideas to get a better sense of your priorities. Just as you did not buy every house you looked at, it is not necessary for you to agree with every recommendation your advisor suggests.

You might want to start your relationship with the preparation of an investment policy statement, and a personal financial plan. Some financial advisors build these master plans early in the relationship. They may charge a fee for the plan or an upfront commission to cover the cost of the planning, or assume you will be working with them for several years and can recover their costs over time out of fees based on the assets they manage for you. Others will develop the financial plan over, say, three years. They might focus on investments in year one, taxes and estate planning in year two, and the remaining issues in year three, tying the actual planning they do for you to the fees they collect.

If you've hired the financial advisor for comprehensive financial advice, why not do the plan in the first year? After all, isn't one of the reasons you want to work with them to make sure everything is in order? What would the impact be to your family if you died in year one before you and your financial advisor had discussed the importance of having a will? Or why wouldn't you want to save taxes right from the start?

Rating Your Financial Advisor

Answer this question honestly: Would you seek out the services of your current financial advisor if you had to write a cheque for every hour you spent with them? Would you keep them on retainer so they would be available when you need them? There should be a relationship between the fees you are paying and the value you receive.

The 1999 Securities Industry Association Investor Survey reported that 63 percent of investors have a "very" or "somewhat favourable" view of the securities industry" and that 95 percent of investors were "very" or "somewhat satisfied" with the service and advice they receive from their broker. In this same study 81 percent indicated that their broker had an "excellent" or "good" investment track record (Source: www.sia.com/public_trust/html/inv_survey.html). I wonder if as many people would have rated their broker as highly if investment performance had been less stellar?

Here's a report card you can use to rate your financial advisor. Not all points will be applicable to your situation or your needs.

REPORT CARD FOR MY FINANCIAL ADVISOR

Is your financial advisor measuring up to your expectations? Here's a report card you can use to rate the job your financial advisor did over the last year for each item that is appropriate for your situation, from F for "failing grade" to A+ for "outstanding."

Trust

Tells me everything relevant	F	D	C	B	A	A+	n/a
I haven't felt the need to hold anything back	F	D	C	B	A	A+	n/a

Follows through on promises, on time	F	D	C	B	A	A+	n/a
Provides me with objective advice	F	D	C	B	A	A+	n/a
Discloses how much I pay each year, directly and indirectly	F	D	C	B	A	A+	n/a
Gives me no reason to question his/her integrity	F	D	C	B	A	A+	n/a
Holds my information confidential	F	D	C	B	A	A+	n/a
Knows more about me and my family than most people do	F	D	C	B	A	A+	n/a
Deals with me in a professional manner	F	D	C	B	A	A+	n/a
Is someone I can bounce ideas off	F	D	C	B	A	A+	n/a
Doesn't just agree with what I say	F	D	C	B	A	A+	n/a
If I had more money, I'd give it to him/her	F	D	C	B	A	A+	n/a
Would recommend him/her readily	F	D	C	B	A	A+	n/a

Empathy

Understands my needs	F	D	C	B	A	A+	n/a
Really listens to me	F	D	C	B	A	A+	n/a
Answers questions without making me feel uncomfortable	F	D	C	B	A	A+	n/a
Talks in a language I understand— no techno or legal babble	F	D	C	B	A	A+	n/a
Is willing to discuss more than the markets	F	D	C	B	A	A+	n/a
Provides me with the discipline to stay on course	F	D	C	B	A	A+	n/a

Personalized Service

Returns calls or e-mails within 24 hours	F	D	C	B	A	A+	n/a
Deals with a limited number of clients	F	D	C	B	A	A+	n/a
Always has time to take my call	F	D	C	B	A	A+	n/a
Meets with me in person as often as it suits my needs	F	D	C	B	A	A+	n/a
Meetings start within five minutes of the scheduled time	F	D	C	B	A	A+	n/a
Conducts my reviews personally	F	D	C	B	A	A+	n/a

Provides a written summary after each meeting	F	D	C	B	A	A+	n/a
Has financial books and other material to loan	F	D	C	B	A	A+	n/a
Errors in my account are infrequent	F	D	C	B	A	A+	n/a
Any errors are fixed to my satisfaction	F	D	C	B	A	A+	n/a
Calls me	F	D	C	B	A	A+	n/a

Knowledge

Experienced in dealing with people with concerns similar to mine	F	D	C	B	A	A+	n/a
Has good understanding of life	F	D	C	B	A	A+	n/a
Is respected by my accountant and/or lawyer	F	D	C	B	A	A+	n/a
Commits to hours of continuing education each year	F	D	C	B	A	A+	n/a
Holds a financial planning designation	F	D	C	B	A	A+	n/a
Keeps me up to date with changes that might affect my progress	F	D	C	B	A	A+	n/a

Investments

Can provide a full range of products	F	D	C	B	A	A+	n/a
Has prepared an IPS	F	D	C	B	A	A+	n/a
Recommends what is best for me	F	D	C	B	A	A+	n/a
Has recommended cost-effective investment solutions	F	D	C	B	A	A+	n/a
Is willing to discuss long-term and short-term investment ideas	F	D	C	B	A	A+	n/a
Has built a tax-effective portfolio	F	D	C	B	A	A+	n/a
Provides detailed annual tax reporting	F	D	C	B	A	A+	n/a
Provides accurate portfolio statements	F	D	C	B	A	A+	n/a
Has on-line access to my account information	F	D	C	B	A	A+	n/a
Provides me with a personalized rate of return	F	D	C	B	A	A+	n/a
Portfolio performance compares favourably	F	D	C	B	A	A+	n/a

Deals with any under performance head on	F	D	C	B	A	A+	n/a
Provides the level of investment research I'm looking for	F	D	C	B	A	A+	n/a
Has built my portfolio to weather whatever happens in the markets	F	D	C	B	A	A+	n/a
Provides more than investment advice	F	D	C	B	A	A+	n/a

Financial Planning

Has prepared a financial planning agreement	F	D	C	B	A	A+	n/a
Has prepared a financial plan that has given me focus	F	D	C	B	A	A+	n/a
Assisted me in clarifying my goals	F	D	C	B	A	A+	n/a

Has addressed my financial planning needs regarding:

Tax planning	F	D	C	B	A	A+	n/a
Estate planning	F	D	C	B	A	A+	n/a
Retirement planning	F	D	C	B	A	A+	n/a
Investment management	F	D	C	B	A	A+	n/a
Risk management and insurance	F	D	C	B	A	A+	n/a
Increasing my net worth	F	D	C	B	A	A+	n/a
Cash flow and debt management	F	D	C	B	A	A+	n/a
Has demonstrated the value of the plan	F	D	C	B	A	A+	n/a
Updates the plan every one or two years	F	D	C	B	A	A+	n/a

Overall Evaluation

Review the ratings you've circled and use them to come up with an overall rating for your advisor.

Overall rating	F	D	C	B	A	A+	n/a

A+ Couldn't ask for more!

A Looking good.

B Would you be better off working with someone else?

C Time for a talk with your financial advisor about what you expect and whether or not he or she is willing and able to provide it.

D Why are you still trying to work with this advisor?

F You know what you need to do.

You might want to discuss any item you've rated as a B or lower with your financial advisor. You are never excused from the responsibility of determining who you will work with and monitoring the relationship.

If things do not work out as you had hoped, or you are unhappy for any reason, speak with your advisor. If they don't know there is a problem, they can't address your concerns. Most likely, they will be able to. If not, you know what you have to do. (See "Firing Your Financial Advisor," below.)

When Your Financial Advisor Retires

Financial advisors are people too. They can and do leave the business for many reasons, including not making a significant enough contribution to their firm's profitability. Even those who love what they do, expect, much like their clients, to retire some day. They might also die, move on, or be promoted to a position where they can no longer be your personal financial advisor. Even Martha Stewart, yes The Martha Stewart, was a broker for a number of years before she set out to become the conglomerate she is now.

If you move from one province to another and your advisor is not licensed in that province, you will have to find a new financial advisor. Even though on-line technology lets you communicate with someone on the other side of the world, securities regulation is provincial. This creates a good old-fashioned trade barrier for those working in the industry and hampers their ability to continue to serve their clients. How different can conditions really be from province to province?

 TREND Regulations will become standardized across the country so client/advisor relationships can continue, despite geographic distance.

The financial advisor who looks after your needs today will be interested in making sure you are taken care of when they move on. Succession planning is as important in the financial advisory business as it is in the boardroom. Ideally their successor shares the values regarding investment management and advice, and if they have been handpicked, the transition will be as seamless as it can be.

If you have been working with your current advisor for a number of years, and have established a long, trusting relationship with him or her, it may be hard for you to accept a change. Do you have to? In a word, no. Someone called me after the advisor he had selected moved. He had been reassigned to another advisor at the firm and didn't feel that the relationship was working out. He wanted to know how to go about finding a new advisor. Just into the conversation, it was obvious he didn't realize that he could try to find a better fit within the same firm. I recommended he call up the branch manager and ask for the names of at least three other advisors he could interview. You don't have to accept just any advisor. It is your prerogative to work with one you select. Unless you are a problem client, the firm would rather keep your assets than see them transfer out.

If your advisor dies or quits suddenly without a succession plan, your account will be reassigned to another financial advisor within the firm to ensure you continue to be served. If you are not pleased with the new arrangement, you are free to find your own advisor.

When Your Financial Advisor Changes Firms

Advisors change firms for many different reasons. Maybe the new firm offers them a better range of services or products for their clients, better back office support, educational programs or just a better pay package. You'll need to decide what you want to do. You have two choices: follow that individual to their new firm or stay and be reassigned to another financial advisor.

The firm may attempt to prevent the advisor from soliciting your business away from them or they may contact you to remind you of all their services and the reasons you should consider staying with them. If you stay, they'll transfer your accounts to another advisor within the firm at no cost to you.

Some firms are attempting to lock in the loyalties of their advisors with non-competition and/or non-solicitation agreements. If your advisor has signed one of these, it is highly unlikely he or she will leave the firm unless they are ready to leave the business.

There is a belief in the industry that you are "owned" by a financial advisor or their firm, but when the dust settles, it's only you who owns you. It's up to you to decide:

- the advisor you would like to work with
- the types of investments you want
- the level of advice and service you require
- the cost structure that works best for what you need
- the firm that will hold your accounts.

Not Getting What You Expected?

You and your financial advisor may not always agree—two people rarely do—but you should feel you are free to ask questions and are getting the information you need to make informed decisions. But don't confuse the advice you need with what you want to hear. One might be much more valuable than the other. Your financial advisor should be willing to give you a reality check and make recommendations on what they think you need to do. The advice should be appropriate for someone in your circumstances and with your experience.

FIRING YOUR FINANCIAL ADVISOR

Changing advisors is not easy, particularly if you like them personally. But don't confuse your personal feelings for them with the job you have hired them to do. If you are not getting what you are paying for, you deserve better. Are they too aggressive with your money? Did they make a recommendation you didn't feel was in your best interest? Did they fail to return your calls? Are you unsure they have the expertise you require? Maybe you just don't like them. If they have done something they shouldn't have, report the problem or file a complaint. Don't just walk away quietly.

If you can't work through the issues, it may be time to find someone you have more confidence in. It takes time and energy to decide to make a change. It might be helpful to assess why are you leaving them since it could give you some ideas of what you should look for. It might even be time to consider another type of service or investment program. Take another look at the above report card and highlight the items you "must" receive from an advisor.

There are many reasons you might stay "loyal" to your investments, the firm or your financial advisor, even if you are unhappy. Here's just a few:

1. You're a capital gains hostage. You have profits on investments that are exclusive to that firm and would have to be sold if your transfer to another firm. Suppose the value of your investments has increased from $50,000 to $110,000. If you sell them, the capital gains of $60,000 would have a significant impact on your tax bill for that year!

2. You're held hostage by redemption fees or surrender charges on mutual funds, segregated funds or managed money products. A DSC redemption fee schedule makes it less likely you will move out of the mutual fund family as long as that schedule lasts— from three to nine years. Suppose you put $10,000 in a DSC

mutual fund that two years later you want to sell. If the redemption fee in the second year is 5 percent, you'd have to pay up to $500 to get out of that fund family. You can call your financial advisor or the mutual fund company to find out the dollar amount of any redemption fees.

A surrender charge (such as is found on insurance products or redeemable GICs) means you are less likely to redeem the investment early because it eats into your returns. As an example, you may have a five-year interest rate on a GIC, but cashing in early might mean you'd lose the higher interest rate and end up with one closer to the rate paid on a daily interest savings account.

3. You're held hostage by the guarantee on a segregated fund. If your investment has gone down in value and you sell before the 10-year guarantee period is up or market value goes back up, you will lose the guarantee and some of your capital. Suppose you invest $10,000 in a segregated fund that falls to $9,000. If you sold it before the end of the 10-year guarantee period, you'd be out $1,000 and any redemption fees that might be charged.

4. The investment is non-redeemable. Some fixed income and index-linked GICs, and other investments are simply non-redeemable before maturity.

5. Inertia. It's sometimes just easier to stay put, but you owe it to yourself to be loyal to your own needs.

Transferring Your Investment Account

There are other reasons for transferring your account than just the advice you receive. You might want to consolidate your assets under one umbrella to make it easier to track and manage your portfolio or to access a lower fee schedule that is only available for larger accounts. Or your portfolio may have grown and you are now interested in a different level of service. Many firms now offer a full range of services so that as the value of your assets grows, you don't have to leave to "graduate" to services that were previously only available elsewhere. For example, you might have a mutual fund portfolio, and later want to have a pooled investment account or a discretionary investment program.

When you've decided to move your account, you might consider phoning or writing your former advisor to tell him or her why you are changing, so that they can understand what didn't work out. If your former advisor has already seen the transfer papers you've signed, they will know you are leaving. They might even call you to see if they can convince you to stay.

If you transfer an investment account to an advisor at another firm you may have to deal with:

- transfer out fees
- redemption fees
- changes that would affect the foreign content of your RRSP/RRIF or the timing of a RRIF withdrawal
- income taxes, if you sell your investments that are held in a non-registered account (that is not an RRSP, RRIF or RESP) before you move your account

Transfer Fees

Some brokerage firms charge a transfer fee of up to $125 plus GST when an RRSP/RRIF/RESP is transferred to another financial firm and $75 to $100 plus GST for a cash or margin (a non-registered) account. When a firm is looking to attract new clients, they may cover all or a portion of the transfer fee on your behalf either by reimbursing the fees or by paying you a "signing bonus" large enough to cover the fee.

Redemption Fees

If the redemption fee you have to pay is more than 1.5 percent, you may want to postpone selling your investments unless the financial advisor taking over your account is able to rebate the amount of that redemption fee. But watch out. Sometimes they are only willing to rebate the fees if they are able to collect commission to cover the amount to be rebated.

Suppose you have $10,000 invested in a DSC mutual fund that you want to get out of, but selling it would trigger a redemption fee of $300. If the advisor offers to rebate this fee and recommends investing in another DSC mutual fund where the commission is, say, 5 percent, here's how it works. The $10,000 would be invested and out of that $500 commission, they would rebate the $300 to you and keep the difference.

For this privilege, you would now be locked into the new fund company for the length of the new redemption fee schedule. Alternatively, if you are unhappy with the mutual fund you are in, you might consider transferring to another investment within the same mutual fund company—some have over 100 to choose from—until the redemption schedule is completed.

TREND Now that investors have access to on-line research and rating services, financial advisors and fund companies can no longer rely on a redemption fee schedule to help retain the assets.

Foreign Content Limit for RRSPs and RRIFs

When a RRSP or RRIF is transferred from one firm to another, the book value—the value used to calculate your foreign content limit—is often reset to the current market values. Suppose the original book value of your account is $80,000, and that of your foreign investment $16,000, you are well within the foreign content limit.

But if, at the time of the transfer, the market value of your account is $100,000 and your foreign investments $35,000, the new foreign content would have to be adjusted to bring it down from 35 percent.

• tip Prior to transferring a registered account, find out how the foreign content will be handled. If appropriate, ask if the foreign content can be taken from the statement of the firm transferring your account, rather than being reset, and then keep an eye on your foreign content to make sure you don't face penalties for exceeding the allowable limit.

Tax Implications

If you transfer your existing investments from one advisor or firm to another (sometimes called a change of dealer and account transfer), there are no tax implications. If the investments are propriety products—only available through that firm and cannot be held in an account at another firm—they would likely have to be sold at their current market value prior to the account being transferred. Outside a registered plan, this would result in taxable capital gains if you sold them at a profit to start a new investment program.

If you transfer your registered assets (RRSP, RRIF or RESP), there should be no tax implications either, since these investments are taxed only when you make a withdrawal. However, the financial institution holding your RRIF is responsible for paying the minimum withdrawal for the year. If you initiate a RRIF transfer early in the year, expect to receive an early payout of the balance of the year's withdrawal. Suppose your minimum required withdrawal for the year is $12,000—$1,000 a month. If you transfer your RRIF to another institution at the end of June, you would receive a cheque for $6,000 for the remaining six withdrawals of the year, and the balance of the RRIF would transfer to the new firm.

Timeliness

According to the standards of the Investment Dealers Association (IDA), accounts must be transferred within 10 days of the appropriate paperwork being received, although it may take longer to transfer mutual funds held at firms that do not transfer their investments electronically and to transfer foreign stocks.

If you don't see signs of your account transfer being initiated within 10 days after you have signed all the papers, contact the firm you are transferring to and make sure they have sent out the paperwork and then call the relinquishing firm to make sure they have received it. If nothing is happening, call the IDA at 416-364-6133 to complain. Brokerage firms who do not comply with a transfer out request in a timely manner can face fines ranging from $2,000 to $50,000 for repeat offenders.

 TREND Brokerage firms, or a third-party firm, will develop and implement a clearing house system to transfer investment, RRSPs, RRIFs, and other types of accounts, from firm to firm. This type of system would improve the accuracy and timeliness of transfers.

Transferring Life Insurance Policies and Segregated Funds

Your life insurance policy may be paying renewal premiums—sometimes only a minuscule amount each year—to the agent on record. If the person who sold you the policy is not staying in touch, some people believe it makes sense to have the person who is currently providing you with financial advice receive them. Sometimes this can be done, sometimes not. It depends on the agreement the agent has with the life insurance company.

SUMMARY

Working with the right financial advisor can add value to your financial life, but as with any professional relationships you enter, you have certain responsibilities, including making sure the professional knows your priorities. You do this by asking questions you need the answers to, monitoring the relationship and speaking up when something is bothering you.

CHAPTER NINE

Are You Getting Your Money's Worth?

"A prudent person profits from personal experience, a wise one from the experience of others."

Joseph Collins

"I intended to give you some advice, but now I remember how much is left over from last year unused."

George Harris

We all know the old adage, you get what you pay for. Investors often don't know what to expect or the price they are paying, which is why it's been difficult for them to know if they are getting their money's worth. Mistakenly, much of the "value" of financial advice has been based on performance and while that is important, it is just one aspect of the entire picture, and something that can come and go depending on overall market conditions.

While the industry debates whether fees or commissions are the best way for consumers to pay for advice, the real issue is about getting value.

BEST PRODUCT, BEST ADVICE, LOWEST PRICE

A signed posted on the wall of a printing shop read, "Fast, good, cheap. Pick two." The shop owner was tired of customers who thought they could have it all. Unrealistically, some consumers of financial services want the best product and the best advice, for the lowest possible price. While you can now get investment products for a low transaction fee or acquisition fee, they don't come with advice. Since you can't have all three, you have to decide what you are willing to give up to get the other two.

You are paying for your financial services, products and advice either directly or indirectly. Just because you may have never written a cheque for advice nor had any fees or charges deducted from your statement, doesn't mean that it didn't cost anything. Your bank may claim it offers you "free" chequing privileges, but you may be paying for them through a monthly service fee or by accepting a lower rate of interest on your account. The same is true with a financial advisor. Fees may be hidden and indirect, but make no mistake, you are paying them. Maybe it was deferred sales charges or the way management fees were collected that created the misconception. Maybe bundling product and advice together lulled investors into believing they could get financial advice for free. There is no free lunch.

The wide range of services and products and the competition for your business will lead to lower fees, but the lowest-price product may not come with the level of advice you may be looking for—then again, neither might the most expensive. What you get depends, in part, on the level of experience and service provided by your financial advisor, which could range from full-service financial advice to simple order taking. You could deal with a real financial advisor who provides integrated quality financial advice or a sales person. Some people get very little in the way of service and advice, while others have been known to exclaim to their financial advisor, "whatever I'm paying you is not enough."

There are a number of signs that more attention is being paid to the fees and costs of minding your money. Some firms have even attempted to made pre-emptive strikes to compete for new business based on cost rather than advice. Here are five examples.

1. Discount Brokers Rebating Commissions

In 1998, some discount brokers "rebated" a portion of the mutual fund DSC commissions back to the investor's account. If the deferred sales commission was 5 percent and the rebate was 2 percent of the amount invested, then $2 of every $100 invested went back to the investor. If the discount brokerage firm is really just taking an investor's order, why should they keep the same amount of commission that a full-service advisor does?

2. Discount Brokers Rebating Trailer Fees

Some brokers were rebating a portion of the annual trailer or service fees they collected or waiving the trustee fees. If you had $100,000 invested in equity mutual funds, the trailer fees could be more than $1,000 a year. The least discounters could do was to waive the $125 trustee fee for your RRSP/RRIF if they are not providing you with any service.

Actually, I think that the trailer fee should be renamed a "service fee" and the dollar amount appear on investors' statements. If the dollar amount of the service fees were printed on your statement, it would be harder for you to ignore what you are paying. Many financial advisors already see the service fee as compensation for the ongoing service and advice they provide their clients.

Investments and advice will be sold both separately or bundled together. We will see products introduced that pay no commission and no trailer fees—the closest we have today are low-fee index investments. Then Canadians could separate the cost of advice from the cost of the investments.

3. Elimination of Commission on Front-End Load Funds

No advice, no sales commission—provided your purchase is large enough to meet the firm's minimum for 0 percent front-end load investments. But they are not doing it for free. They still collect the trailer or service fees just from holding your mutual or segregated funds—and the management fee if the investment is the firm's own proprietary product.

4. Preferred Pricing for Large Mutual Fund Investors

The cost to administer for one account worth $500,000 is less than for 10 accounts each worth $50,000. After all, it's cheaper to mail one envelope than 10. For larger accounts—$500,000 or more— some mutual fund companies rebate a portion of the management fees back to the investor, and some are introducing separate investment services with preferred pricing for investors. Other firms have set up separate classes of investments with lower fees that require a larger minimum account size.

5. Costs Are the Next Big Thing

A number of industry professionals have commented that costs and pricing will be the next area of competition in the investment industry. Consumers are already asking if what they pay is fair and reasonable. We are continually looking south of the border and wondering why prices seem so much higher here. When and if performance lags, consumers will ask this question even louder.

WHAT IS VALUE?

Professional financial advice should provide more than peace of mind to help you feel good (especially if you find out later that you've been "taken for a ride"). While feeling good about your financial decisions is a goal in itself, working with a financial advisor, professional money manager or receiving financial advice from another source should provide you with results that you would not be able to easily achieve on your own. After all, if you could do the same thing yourself, why would you pay someone else to do it?

There are two ways to look at value for financial advice. One is, does your investment program and/or the relationship you have with your financial advisor generate enough benefits to you to help you achieve your financial goals? And two is, are you paying a competitive price for the products and advice you are receiving or is there something else that would do the same job for less money? If you're paying 2 1/2 percent a year for the same set of financial products and advice you could be getting somewhere else for less, that's not value.

We'll be considering these questions in this chapter.

WHAT IS ADVICE?

So just what is advice anyway? Financial advice means different things to different people, ranging from stock picking to estate planning and it is time we had a working definition. Here's one from the Canadian Oxford dictionary. Advice is "words offered as an opinion or recommendation about future action; counsel." Financial advice consists of options and recommendations about what you can do to achieve your financial objectives, whether it relates to a short-term financial goal or a longer-term one. But before any professional can give you their opinion or recommendations—their advice—they need to understand what you want.

Don't Confuse Advice and Service

Are you looking for advice or service? There is a difference. While it depends on how you use the words, advice implies more than service. I take my car in to a mechanic for service; when dealing with a professional advisor, I want advice. Lawyers advise their clients, they don't just service them.

Service keeps everything moving along. Advice is what helps to achieve your financial goals. If you want your financial advisor to advise you, then you'll want them to offer opinions or recommendations as to what you should do. Service, on the other hand, does not require someone to put his or her opinions or recommendations on the line. What are you receiving from your current financial advisor or broker—service, advice or something in between?

THE SERVICE/ADVICE CONTINUUM	
Service ◄--► Advice	
Assistance, maintenance	Opinions, recommendations
Superficial	Deep, complex
Service Rep	Expert, Professional

The advice you receive could range from superficial to deep. Some on-line advice is relatively superficial and certainly not very personal. The more complex your situation, the deeper and more personal the advice and guidance should be.

• tip Put your money on the expertise your financial advisor offers, not just on the number of phone calls you receive a year. Look for written job descriptions of what you expect your financial advisor to do—a financial plan and/or investment policy statement—and hold regular "performance" reviews of your progress and the job you've hired them to do, not just your investment performance.

COST-BENEFIT ANALYSIS

When I was in the computer industry, we used the cost-benefit analysis to assess the cost of implementing a project, including salaries for programmers, hardware and software, and compared that to the benefits the organization could reasonably expect to receive. Not only did the benefits have to outweigh the costs, but also the project itself also had to generate enough value—in this case return on investment (ROI)—to achieve the corporate objectives.

To consider the value of the services and/or the financial advice you receive, you start by adding up the initial and ongoing costs and compare them to the tangible and intangible benefits you receive. Refer to Chapter 6 for more details on costs.

The Benefits

The benefits of professional investment and financial planning advice might be tangible or intangible. With tangible benefits you can see the cost-benefit, or dollar value of the advice or service. When you know how much you are paying for the advice and the actual dollar value of the benefits you receive, you can calculate how much further ahead you are because of that advice. An intangible benefit is sometimes called a "soft" benefit. With a soft benefit, you know the advice is to your advantage, but you cannot attach a dollar value to it. For example, simplifying the investments in your portfolio makes them easier to manage, but doesn't necessarily bring you any extra returns.

There are numerous ideas that have the potential to provide tangible and/or intangible benefits. The benefits may result in a one-time savings opportunity or may provide ongoing savings. Sometimes a strategy will produce both tangible and intangible benefits. We're only going to consider a few in this chapter.

TREND Expect to see your financial advisor providing you with a report of the financial and non-financial benefits you receive from working together.

The Tangible Benefits of Investment Advice and Service

There are some basic mechanical costs associated with all investing. Many of these costs are built in, but others are either charged to you directly or built into other fees you might pay. These costs include such things as opening and setting up your account, printing and mailing your statements, compliance with the required rules and securities regulations, posting information on the Web site, and training of the staff.

These costs are part of what the economists call "frictional costs," expenses that reduce the income you might have made from your investments. But not all costs are bad, particularly if they enable you to do better than you would have done on your own. Suppose you were holding GICs earning 5 percent and move some of that money into an investment portfolio that ends up earning 8 percent. Even if the expenses related to those security investments were 1.5 percent, you would still be 1 1/2 percent ahead.

Tangible benefits might include:

- dollars saved by not buying a losing stock.

- increased long-term returns by improving your asset mix, or reduced risk of significant losses.
- Improving the tax efficiency of your portfolio. This might include holding assets that attract the highest tax rate inside your RRSP or holding those investments most at risk for potential capital losses outside your RRSP.

The Tangible Benefits of Financial Planning

The slogan of the Financial Planners Association (FPA) is "Planning pays off." But how does it pay off, and how much? The value of the financial advice an individual receives depends on its quality. The value of advice could range from the peace of mind you get from knowing you are doing everything possible to reach your financial goals, including managing your investment portfolio to increase your potential investment returns without significantly increasing your investment risk, and implementing any appropriate strategic financial planning, As well, working with someone with experience means you don't have to learn the hard way.

Here's how just a few financial planning ideas could pay off if they are appropriate for your situation:

- Making contributions to a spousal RRSP rather than your own can save taxes of up to $11,000 a year in retirement.
- Negotiating a 20-year instead of a 25-year mortgage will save you money. At 8 percent, the difference in the monthly payments on a $100,000 mortgage would be $828 vs. $763, but the potential amount of interest saved is $128,963—98,804 = $30,159.
- Setting up a testamentary trust for a minor beneficiary, saving taxes and government interference. Every year the testamentary trust exists, up to $11,000 in taxes could be saved.
- Setting up a spousal testamentary trust might allow your spouse to save up to $11,000 a year in taxes when compared to receiving the inheritance outright.

- Converting some of your RRSP to a RRIF or annuity to generate $1,000 of pension income from age 65 to 70 could generate an additional tax credit of $850— $170 for 5 years.

- Contributing $2,000 for your grandchild's RESP allows him or her to receive the maximum Canadian Education Savings Grant (CESG) of $7,200 plus interest—$400 a year for 18 years.

- Providing detailed tax reporting so you don't have to pay an accountant to do the calculations for you—$300 or more a year.

Some of these strategies could save money over a number of years, others just money in the first year. Can they add value to your financial bottom line? Yes, but their savings don't necessarily show up in your returns on your statement. For example, the tax dollars you save might be reinvested or even just spent on other things. The added benefits might even make enough of a difference so you could retire earlier, leave more to your beneficiaries or even create enough so you don't have to take as much risk in the markets.

Could you implement all of these items yourself? Probably. Would you take the time to implement them all? That's an entirely different question.

Intangible Benefits

Just because it may not be possible to attach a dollar value to the benefit doesn't mean it doesn't have value, it could be just intangible. An intangible benefit may result from the relationship you have with your financial advisor. Maybe it's something they helped you or a member of your family with that made a difference. Maybe they asked you a question that started you thinking about what you wanted to do with the rest of your life or sent one of your children in the right career direction. Maybe they were just there when you needed them or help you know you're being responsible with your money.

There may be other strategies the financial advisor helped you with that don't show up on your investment statement such as:

- hiring a good lawyer to implement your estate plan
- recommending an accountant to keep you on the straight and narrow
- helping you find a solution to a family need
- keeping you from making mistakes that you might have made out of your own fear or greed

Lawyers on retainer are there when you need them. Is your financial advisor receiving adequate compensation to be there for you when you need them? What is it worth to you to meet with a full-service financial advisor two or three times a year and know they are just a phone call away?

ARE YOU GETTING YOUR MONEY'S WORTH?

While ongoing fees may provide the financial firm with a steady predictable income, you need to make sure you are not paying for services you don't need or won't use. This section will look at value from the following perspectives:

1. Is there a comparable product at a better price?
2. Is there a cheaper way to build your portfolio?
3. Are you getting the advice you are paying for?
4. Is your portfolio taking on more risk than you need?
5. Are your fees increasing but not your services?
6. Is your fee structure tied to your asset allocation?

1. Is There a Comparable Product at a Better Price?

One test of value is to make sure you are not paying more than you have to. When buying a car, you do some comparison shopping and look at the sticker prices of similar models. Why not do the same for investment services and products?

Suppose that your portfolio is worth $100,000 and you are looking at two similar investments where the fees are 2 and 2 1/2 percent and the manager of both investments is able to earn 8 1/2 before fees. (We'll make the assumption that the investments were purchased with no-load so the full amount was invested.) If your annual fees were 2 1/2 percent, after 10 years your balance would be $179,084. But if your annual fees were 2 percent, your balance would be $187,713 or $8,629 more. If both investment programs provide the same type of products and advice, which one would you rather be dealing with? Obviously, you'll get more value from the one with the lower fees when the return before fees is the same.

One other point. If your financial plan indicates that you need to earn a return of 6.5 percent (after all fees) and one investment program charges fees that are higher, you'd need to assume a higher level of investment risk in that portfolio to pay their fees and meet your return targets.

2. Is There a Cheaper Way to Build Your Portfolio?

Building and holding a portfolio of individual stocks and bonds is the cheapest way to build your portfolio, as long as it meets your investment objectives and risk tolerance and you don't need any ongoing financial advice. But not everyone has enough savings to buy sufficient individual securities to provide adequate diversification, which is one reason why people invest in indexes or mutual funds. Every once in a while it makes good consumer sense to see if there's a better way to achieve your investment objectives.

Suppose you have fixed income investments in your portfolio. Compare buying individual bonds, a bond mutual fund or holding them in a fee-based account. If you buy bonds and plan to hold them, certainly it's cheaper to buy them directly, if you have enough money in your portfolio. When you buy the bond, you pay the spread (usually somewhere between 1 to 3 percent or more) once but then you pay nothing more to maintain the investment in your account until maturity. Suppose the spread is 1 percent and you hold the bond until it matures in five years. Over five years, the cost of acquiring and maintaining that investment averages out to 1/5th of 1 percent. If you have to sell the bond prior to maturity, that will add to your costs.

If you buy bonds as part of a mutual fund or other managed money program, or inside a fee-based account, you will be paying ongoing fees for the product as well as on-going advice. The current average MER on Canadian bond funds is around 1.61 percent. The annual charge for a fee-based account might be 1 percent or more.

 TREND Many people believe the ongoing fees on fixed income investments are too high given today's yields—and that the fees will come down.

Compared to the 10-year returns on bond funds, these fees seem relatively modest. But if today's fixed income investments are earning 5 1/2 to 7 percent, even the best portfolio manager will find it challenging to boost the returns on these fixed income investments enough to offset an annual fees.

 Recently, there has been a lot of interest in foreign clone funds, funds that enable an investor to hold more than the

25% foreign content limit in their RRSP or RRIF. Most of the clone funds have higher fees than direct foreign mutual funds, so to lower your fees, hold up to 25% in direct foreign investments, before using the foreign clone funds.

3. Are You Getting the Advice You Are Paying For?

There is a wide range of approaches to financial advice and level of advice provided by different financial advisors. You could work with two financial advisors and receive very different products, advice and services—some good, some not so good.

There are three distinct types of advice:

- product advice, related specifically to the product being discussed
- investment advice regarding investment management which we discussed in Chapter 4.
- financial planning advice regarding your overall financial plan which we discussed in Chapter 5.

In an ideal world, the cost of obtaining financial advice would be less than the value you receive from following that advice. Suppose you wrote a cheque for $10,000 for financial strategies that clearly increased your portfolio value by $25,000 over five years. You'd end up with a net financial benefit of $15,000. The benefits might show up as less tax paid or only on your net worth statement (and how often do you really do one of these?)

Should you pay the $10,000 upfront or $2,000 for five years? Given the choice, the five-year interest-free plan would be the most advantageous for you, but can you expect the financial advisor to give you full-service advice without being paid for it upfront or without any assurance that you will continue to be their client for five years? Unfortunately, this is the way many Canadians expect to "pay" for their financial planning. They expect a full financial plan from their financial advisor but expect them to be compensated either in instalments, through mutual or segregated fund trailer services fees (assuming you remain a client for long enough) or, by selling investment products to you—without any assurance they will ever be paid for the work they do. Would you be willing to work on that basis? For example, would anyone be willing to do a renovation on your kitchen for nothing down, and know they would only be paid if you continue to live in that house? I don't think so. Maybe this is one reason we don't see more financial plans being done today.

So what method would be fairest to you and the professional you hire? Should the fee for the advice be tied to the amount of time the advisor spends on your situation, the way a lawyer might be compensated? Or should it be tied to the amount of money the advice "saves" you? For example, if the advisor recommends a prudent strategy that saves you $2,000 in tax each year or recommends a strategy that reduces the cost of probate your estate would otherwise pay, what should the cost of that advice be? If your financial advisor or their firm recommends a stock that triples in value in three months, should you be expected to share some of your profits with them? Should the fee be tied to the size of the account, the amount of activity in it or the number of minutes you speak with a live person? Sometimes the larger the account, the more work involved, but sometimes a larger account requires no more work than a smaller account or even much less.

While some people believe that your advisor's goals will be better aligned with yours when the fees are based on the size of your account and that you are less likely to have potential conflicts of interest than a traditional commission-based account might, there are still a few things you should consider.

4. Is Your Portfolio Taking on More Risk Than You Need?

When fees are charged based on the size of your account, the compensation your financial advisor receives increases when your value of your account increases, even though the general direction of the financial markets is not under the control of any money manager.

Historically, equities earn more than the other asset categories and generate higher fees over time.

• tip Beware of the financial advisor who over-weights your portfolio in equities with their higher risk and higher fees, unless your financial plan shows you need to try to earn a higher return to achieve your financial goals.

5. Are Your Fees Increasing But Not Your Services?

If you pay a fee based on the size of your account (either a fee-based percentage or a management fee such as for managed money or mutual funds), will the services and advice you receive increase along with your fees?

Suppose your account is worth $100,000 today. At 2 percent a year, you'd be paying $2,000 a year in fees, but when your account grows to $250,000, you'd be paying $5,000 a year, and at $350,000, the fees would be $7,000. Would you expect to receive more value or attention in return for paying the higher fee? I would. But some higher end clients pay fees that end up subsidizing the services the smaller clients in a financial advisor's practice—rather than receiving full-value themselves.

The financial services industry seems to want fees to be the preferred method of compensation—but this movement is coming from within the industry, not from its clients. How can a program that pays the advisor annual recurring revenue—which means you are paying annual recurring fees that increase as the value of your account increases—be better for investors?

The scope of the job done by the financial advisor is not the same every year. In the first year, there is a lot of upfront work , for example, preparing the IPS and the initial financial plan. In subsequent years, these need to be updated, but that does not take the same amount of time and effort as the original, unless there are significant changes to your personal circumstances.

A good financial advisor will be a good advisor regardless of the method of compensation. Conversely, I believe consumers will be willing to pay fair compensation as long as the job being done provides them with value.

 TREND Once portfolios reach a certain size, we will see more flat-fee, or fee-based investment programs that have a maximum fee.

6. Are Your Fees Tied to Your Asset Allocation?

Some fee-based accounts charge a flat percentage for the account you hold with them, regardless of your asset mix. Suppose the fee is 1.5 percent a year, and you have $200,000 in your portfolio. Your annual fee would be $3,000, regardless of whether you held 80 percent in equities and 20 percent in fixed income or 80 percent in cash and fixed income investments and 20 percent in equities. Most people would argue that it is not as difficult to manage a cash or fixed income portfolio, so maybe it shouldn't cost as much as one invested primarily in equities.

How high is too high? Certainly, a higher fee is considered appropriate for a portfolio that is invested in equities, particularly if it is actively managed. But apart from the fees for portfolio design or financial advice, the fees for a portfolio that is managed passively or invests in indexes should be quite low.

TREND Consumers will increasingly want to pay annual fees related to the advice they receive and not just how much money they have.

How Much Is Too Much?

Regardless of what its value might actually be, the perceived value of investment advice has fallen to almost zero for those who are willing to do it themselves. The bull stock market, the ability to access quality research and the low cost of trading on-line has undermined the value of traditional investment research and service.

But for those who want to work with a qualified financial advisor, there should be some relationship between the price paid and the amount of work done. It used to be that executors settling an estate could charge the standard 5 percent fee regardless of the work that was involved. Today, trends indicate that there must be some relationship between the work involved in settling an estate and the fee charged.

Some lawyers who see the amount their clients are spending on financial advice and money management are both jealous and concerned. One client with a portfolio worth $2 million was upset with the $60,000 in fees that he was paying each year for wealth management. While this 3 percent annual fee is within the range charged by many managed money services, the dollar amount was starting to look excessive to the client and his lawyer.

As long as the fee is small relative to the overall returns they receive, most people don't give their fees a second thought. Currently, the price for having your money managed professionally ranges from less than 1 percent to over 3 percent per year, of the value of the portfolio (plus GST). These fees are charged regardless of whether you earn double-digit returns or have a losing year. When your return is 10 percent and your costs are 2%, they represent one-fifth of your total returns which may seem satisfactory. But if your return is 6 percent, an annual cost of 2 percent represents a full one-third of your returns and takes a significant bite out of what you get to keep.

Although I can usually tell when my car needs help, I'm not really interested in what goes on under the hood. I know I could learn how to fix my car—at least deal with the basics, but I have no desire to spend my weekends tinkering on it. I will probably always spend more than I want to on my car, but is it more than I should? That's a tougher question to answer.

As with cars, when it comes to financial services, you have to decide whether you want to do it yourself, let the pros take over or something in between. Do you have the time, inclination or knowledge to do it yourself, or are you willing to pay an expert to advise you? There are many Canadians who don't feel they know enough to do it themselves and are willing to hire someone for guidance and direction. As Red Adair, the professional oil-rig firefighter has been attributed as saying, "if you think hiring a professional is expensive, try hiring an amateur."

DO IT YOURSELF OR FULLY ASSEMBLED?

In the early '90s, manufacturers proposed that a personal computer could be sold for under $1,000. But retailers, anxious to maintain their revenue streams, didn't lower prices. Instead, they added more services and bundled them in with the price of the computer, or differentiated their product by aligning them with some sort of service. It took almost 10 more years for the price to fall below $1,000. Something similar is going on in the financial services. Even though we can trade on-line for less than $30, at the other end of the spectrum we have more services—or solutions as the business sometimes refers to them—being bundled in with the price of the investments.

When buying a personal computer, you have four main options:

1. Buy the individual components and put them together yourself

2. Mix and match the hardware and software to get a fully customized system to meet your needs

3. Buy it right out of the box, where you get a pre-packaged combination of hardware with software

4. Hire someone else to assess your needs, get your specifications, and set it all up and maintain it for you

While not to belabour the analogy, when buying investments today you can:

- Buy individual stocks and bonds for your portfolio
- Mix and match your investments and investment management services to build a customized portfolio
- Buy pre-packaged investments, such as mutual funds and segregated funds, that include some level of investment management and advice
- Hire a financial advisor or investment counsellor to assess your needs, spec out your requirements and build and manage your portfolio on an ongoing basis

Just like you do when looking for cell phone package that suits you needs, you will be able to select a trading account or investment program that fits the bill. If you're concerned about costs (and if you've flipped through a book on index investing you probably are), you'll need to match your account package to the level of trading activity in your account and then monitor what you are doing, as well as the markets. Similar to finding the right bank service package, you'll need to find the right package of investments, services and advice. For traders, the packages will range from a basic set of services to the "pro" version.

Financial firms will model the fee packages for investment services along the lines of those for banking services, and introduce several pre-set packages offering a range of services, for a fixed monthly fee.

Currently, most financial advisors offer advice as a value-added service to an investment product or program. Over time, providing advice will become the primary function of a financial advisor, and offering the investments will be the service. But for now, the investments are much more lucrative.

As the price for basic investment services is pushed lower, you may start to see fees charged for advice over and above any basic transaction fees or commissions. If may even cost money to see a real person. Of course, the fee would be waived if your account is large enough or you use enough of the financial firm's services. Charging additional fees for advice or the personal touch is not isolated to the financial services industry. Not too long ago I received a letter from my travel agent informing me that because of further commission cuts, they would be providing me with certain services on a fee-for-service basis. These service charges applied to car and hotel reservations, issuing and changing airline tickets, as well as for consultations regarding vacation planning.

There was a notation in the letter that read, "as all travel vendors struggle to compete in an increasingly oversupplied and price-sensitive market, you will benefit significantly by using the services of a professional travel agent who is able to search out the best possible travel values for your particular travel needs." How closely this applies to the financial services industry. Substitute financial advisor for travel agent: "as all financial advisors struggle to compete in an

increasingly oversupplied and price-sensitive market, you will benefit significantly by using the services of a professional financial advisor who is able to search out the best possible value for your
particular financial needs."

INVESTMENT SERVICES
AND PROGRAMS SHOPPING LIST

There are no hard-and-fast rules to define all the investment services
and programs that bring the money management process to your
portfolio. Some investment products specialize in investment selection and management. Others have features or processes that give
them a look and feel somewhat like an investment counselling program. Active investors who like to pick and trade their own portfolio investments might consider them for their serious money.

The Labelling of Investment Products

Similar products come with slightly different names, slightly different marketing spins and different pricing which, instead of clarifying
what the products are and do, often confuses consumers. For example, a mutual fund and a segregated fund have some similar features
and some unique differences. Not too long ago I saw an ad for a
"Market Mix RRSP GIC," a mouthful by any stretch. This investment
turned out to be an index-linked GIC that could be held inside an
RRSP where returns would be based on stock and bond performance. Consider something called the "American Growth Value
Fund." Is it a value fund, a growth fund, or what?

When products start to look alike and sound alike, it's important
that you be able to distinguish what features are suitable for your
needs and how much they will cost, both now and over the total
period of the time you intend to hold them. In many industries, the

terms they use to describe their products are restricted. For example, in the food industry terms like "fat-free" and "cholesterol-free" are restricted so consumers are not easily misled. Even the computer industry has standardized its products. The financial services industry is running a little behind.

Investments products are marketed and advertised much like any other consumer product. Just a few years ago, advertising for investment products was based primarily on performance, much the way cars used to be marketed, when all that was talked about was horsepower and acceleration. Today, ads for consumer products often sell lifestyle. When it comes to money, they talk about what you might do in retirement, how you can educate your children or just live a more comfortable life. What do the ups and downs of the stock market really have to do with what you see marketed in these ads?

Consider how powerful advertising and marketing can be. A lottery commercial stated that there was a "1 in 25 chance you will win." Doesn't that sound better than there is a "24 in 25 chance you will lose?"

TREND In the interests of better disclosure to the consumer, the financial services industry will end up restricting the terms that can be used when labeling products and services. These terms might include no-load, wrap, pool, segregated funds, equity-linked GICs, fee-for-service, fee-only, fee-based to just name a few.

You Can't Always Tell By the Name

So where do you start to figure out the level of advice and services you need and how much it will cost? There are no industry standards for what level of service or advice is included in the fees you pay. To get what you want or need, you have to compare the features based on those that interest *you*. When you go grocery shopping, you don't want to pay for items you don't need nor do you want to come home without everything you do. The following shopping list will help you define the services you want.

INVESTMENT SERVICES AND PROGRAMS SHOPPING LIST

Using the first column, identify all the features and services you want your ideal investment program to provide. Then work through the features that your current program has to see if it matches your most important needs. If there is not a strong match between your current and your ideal, you can then use the remaining columns to compare the options you are most seriously considering and look beyond the sales brochures. When you have defined the parameters for your search, you may be able to find the investment option you need, rather than settle for the one being sold.

You may not be able to find the perfect match but this checklist should help you compare the different options side by side and determine which one(s) most closely match what you are looking for. Feel free to add any additional features you want to compare.

	IDEAL	CURRENT	OPTION 1	OPTION 2	OPTION 3
Features					
Needs assessment	❑	❑	❑	❑	❑
Personalized IPS	❑	❑	❑	❑	❑
Written financial plan	❑	❑	❑	❑	❑
Minimum account size	$___	$___	$___	$___	$___
Programs and Services Offered					
Stock and bond trading	❑	❑	❑	❑	❑

	IDEAL	CURRENT	OPTION 1	OPTION 2	OPTION 3
Pension plan management	❏	❏	❏	❏	❏
Mutual funds	❏	❏	❏	❏	❏
Segregated funds	❏	❏	❏	❏	❏
Fund-of-funds	❏	❏	❏	❏	❏
Wrap account	❏	❏	❏	❏	❏
Privately managed pool accounts	❏	❏	❏	❏	❏
Private money management program	❏	❏	❏	❏	❏
Universal life policies	❏	❏	❏	❏	❏

Financial Considerations

	IDEAL	CURRENT	OPTION 1	OPTION 2	OPTION 3
Commission-based	❏	❏	❏	❏	❏
No acquisition/sales fee	❏	❏	❏	❏	❏
Deferred sales charge	____%	____%	____%	____%	____%
Load/sales fee	____%	____%	____%	____%	____%
Fees based on size of account	❏	❏	❏	❏	❏
Fees charged by asset type	❏	❏	❏	❏	❏
Fees based on performance	❏	❏	❏	❏	❏

Fees Collected

	IDEAL	CURRENT	OPTION 1	OPTION 2	OPTION 3
in advance	❏	❏	❏	❏	❏
in arrears	❏	❏	❏	❏	❏
Minimum annual fee required	$____	$____	$____	$____	$____
Fees that fall as account size grows	❏	❏	❏	❏	❏
If yes, what are the thresholds?	$____	$____	$____	$____	$____
	$____	$____	$____	$____	$____
	$____	$____	$____	$____	$____

Estimated Annual Fees for My Portfolio

	IDEAL	CURRENT	OPTION 1	OPTION 2	OPTION 3
Percentage	____%	____%	____%	____%	____%

	IDEAL	CURRENT	OPTION 1	OPTION 2	OPTION 3
Dollars (estimate)	$____	$____	$____	$____	$____

Account Types

	IDEAL	CURRENT	OPTION 1	OPTION 2	OPTION 3
Segregated/pooled	❏	❏	❏	❏	❏
Open	❏	❏	❏	❏	❏
Registered (RRSP/RRIF/RESP)	❏	❏	❏	❏	❏
Discretionary	❏	❏	❏	❏	❏
Insurance (Universal Life)	❏	❏	❏	❏	❏
Trustee or custodian	❏	❏	❏	❏	❏
Chequing	❏	❏	❏	❏	❏

Performance

	IDEAL	CURRENT	OPTION 1	OPTION 2	OPTION 3
Results are audited independently	❏	❏	❏	❏	❏

1-year returns ending December 31st

	IDEAL	CURRENT	OPTION 1	OPTION 2	OPTION 3
1996	____%	____%	____%	____%	____%
1997	____%	____%	____%	____%	____%
1998	____%	____%	____%	____%	____%
1999	____%	____%	____%	____%	____%
2000	____%	____%	____%	____%	____%
2001	____%	____%	____%	____%	____%
_____	____%	____%	____%	____%	____%
_____	____%	____%	____%	____%	____%
For the most recent quarter	____%	____%	____%	____%	____%

To End the Relationship

	IDEAL	CURRENT	OPTION 1	OPTION 2	OPTION 3
Investments are portable	❏	❏	❏	❏	❏
Redemption fees	❏	❏	❏	❏	❏
Transfer out fees	❏	❏	❏	❏	❏

	IDEAL	CURRENT	OPTION 1	OPTION 2	OPTION 3
Other					
Trading Services (see Chapter 3)	❑	❑	❑	❑	❑
Investment Management Services (see Chapter 4)	❑	❑	❑	❑	❑
Financial Planning Services (see Chapter 5)	❑	❑	❑	❑	❑
Full range of banking services	❑	❑	❑	❑	❑
Detailed tax reporting	❑	❑	❑	❑	❑
_____	❑	❑	❑	❑	❑
_____	❑	❑	❑	❑	❑

SUMMARY

When it comes to managing their money, some people think that if they have to ask *how much* it costs, they probably can't afford it. Not so. Getting your money's worth comes from the three Ps: people, planning and your portfolio. It comes from working with the people with the right stuff, applying the financial planning process and building a sound portfolio.

Paying too much for services or advice you don't need or aren't getting, just isn't right. But in real life, the level of service and advice an investor receives varies from nothing to high and the irony is that the financial advisor gets paid regardless of the quality or the amount of work they do for their clients.

Though much of the financial services industry is commission-based, it is trying to move to a fee-based business. While this may be good for consumers, you should know that it is very good for the industry since it creates an annual income they can count on.

The financial services industry is itself trying to figure out the right amount to charge for their services and this could create some opportunities for investors. The cost of any service should bear a relationship to the monetary benefits it delivers, as well as the intangible benefits investors receive from the relationship. When you know how much it costs, directly or indirectly, you'll be able to be more a discerning consumer.

In the next chapter, we'll look at the role of the regulators.

CHAPTER TEN

The Regulators:
WHO'S PROTECTING YOUR MONEY?

"A verbal contract isn't worth the paper it's written on."

Samuel Goldwyn

The regulation of the financial services industry continues to reflect the historical roots of the traditional product lines, not today's increasingly seamless financial marketplace. That's why we have separate regulations for each type of investment product—securities, mutual funds and segregated funds, etc.—as well as the people licensed to offer them.

TREND The regulators and regulations are moving from being fragmented along product lines to a streamlined regulatory environment where all providers of products and financial advice are required to follow one common set of regulations.

FRAUD AND OTHER WRONGDOINGS

An investor may find they have become involved with a financial advisor who is dishonest or provides inappropriate advice. Within any profession there are a few bad apples. If you have had the misfortune to find yourself dealing with an unscrupulous individual, you owe it to yourself and other investors to report him or her to the authorities through which they hold their license(s). They will investigate, and where appropriate, lay charges to fit the situation. To see who's been made an example of lately, visit www.ida.ca.

With all the regulations the security industry has developed over the years, you might wonder how this could still happen. Financial advisors deal with hundreds and thousands of dollars, a great deal of trust, and sometimes opportunity. So situations can occur. Some of the wrongdoings include:

- trading activity in your account without your authorization (unless it is a discretionary account)
- delaying the transfer of your account over to another financial institution
- misappropriating or withdrawing money from your account without your knowledge
- manipulating the price of a stock, such as paying more for a stock than it's current price to make the portfolio performance look better than it is
- churning (frequent, unnecessary trading in your account) to generate extra commissions

- improper redemptions of investments or replacement of life insurance policies
- recommending an investment that is not suitable for your objectives
- recommending a strategy not suitable for your objectives or level of risk, such as unnecessary leveraging
- misrepresenting the details of an investment
- lending clients' money, either personally or through a business
- borrowing money from clients' or their accounts
- undisclosed conflicts of interest
- receiving undisclosed compensation, such as sales incentives, that may cloud their objectivity
- pressuring clients to make decisions
- breach of fiduciary responsibilities, where the financial advisor puts his or her own interests above those of the client
- using fake credentials or dealing in securities for which they are not licensed
- fraud and outright theft
- mismanaging your investments.

If you believe you are being treated unfairly, been the victim of bad advice or professional negligence, you need to stand up for yourself. If you want to feel confident that what you have experienced is not normal; you might pay to get a second opinion from a financial advisor at another firm before logging a formal complaint, although it is not required.

TREND Disappointed investors will increasingly challenge their advisors, the fees they pay, and the advice they receive for a number of reasons, including undisclosed conflicts of interest, disappointing investment returns and incomplete advice.

THE PUNISHMENT

The securities regulators place sanctions on firms and advisors who are found to have broken the law. These could include:

- paying fines or administrative penalties to the regulators
- repaying any commissions they received
- paying for the cost of investigation
- reimbursing the client for losses or damages
- suspending advisors for a period of time, and placing them under the direct supervision of senior management when they are allowed to return
- limiting the activities they can perform, such as keeping them from dealing directly with the public
- permanently banning individuals from working in any aspect of the securities or insurance industry where the public's trust would be involved
- criminal prosecution including jail time.

 TREND There will eventually be a central database listing who is licensed to sell products in Canada. Once the securities and insurance regulators operate from the same regulation pages, it will no longer be possible for someone who was banned from the securities side of the business to work on the insurance side.

Although the regulators have been very pro-industry and stood by their own members whenever possible, I have seen a shift. More advisors and their firms are being made examples of for issues that range from relatively minor administrative problems to the most serious ones. Early in 2000, over $2 million in damages and losses was awarded by the Supreme Court of Canada to a Quebec investor when it ruled that his portfolio had been mismanaged by his stock-broker. In the summer of 2000, John Cleghorn, chairman of Royal Bank Financial Group, publicly apologized for "inappropriate trading activities at our pension and institutional investment unit, RT Capital Management Inc." RT Capital was fined $3 million by the Ontario Securities Commission and nine of their staff were sanctioned for acting inappropriately.

It is important to the Canadian securities industry that it be seen as a safe, reliable place to do business.

HOW TO COMPLAIN EFFECTIVELY

1. *Talk to your financial advisor.* Bring the problem to the attention of your financial advisor or their firm as soon as you identify it.
2. *Put it in writing.* Document the problem, how it developed and when you noticed it. Be as specific as you can about the dates and details of conversations and meetings related to the situation.
3. *Take it to the top.* If no one seems to be paying attention to your concerns or if the situation is not being addressed within a reasonable amount of time, take your problem to the next level.
4. *Act professionally.* It is better to keep your cool and discuss the problem as impersonally as possible, than to lose your temper.
5. *Be specific.* Tell them what you want done to fix the problem.

SEVEN STEPS TO MAKE IT RIGHT

So what do you do if you need to log a formal complaint? Like most people, you probably do not like to complain, but you need to speak up for yourself if the situation calls for it. At one extreme, you might just need to point out an error to have it corrected if the problem resulted from a simple misunderstanding. Mistakes do happen. At the other extreme, if you received inappropriate advice or believe you have been the victim of something illegal, pointing it out could save yourself and others, money and further headaches.

Here are seven steps you might take to try to make it right, starting with your advisor and ending with the courts.

1. Start with Your Financial Advisor and/or the Compliance Department

As difficult as it might be to do, the first step is to speak directly to your financial advisor, particularly if the problem looks like an error that needs to be corrected. If this does not solve the problem, or the problem is more serious, contact the financial advisor's manager (you can get the person's name by speaking to the receptionist in the office), or speak directly to the company's compliance officer, who is usually found at the head office. If you are dealing direct and don't have a financial advisor, contact the compliance officer, whose job it is to make sure the firm and its people comply with securities regulations.

You could also provide the financial advisor and the firm with written instructions to freeze all trading in your account, or even close it, if that seems warranted.

 TREND All financial firms will establish complaint resolution systems and will be required to tell you who to contact if you have a problem or concern.

The Consumer Assistance Centre of the Canadian Life and Health Insurance Association Inc. also acts as a liaison for consumer complaints and the life and health insurance industry. To contact the Consumer Assistance Centre or CompCorp, call 1-800-268-8099 or in Toronto 416- 777-2344.

2. File a Compliant with the Government Regulator

If the firm is not responding to your concerns, the provincial regulators would be the next step. Unfortunately, you currently need to take your complaint to the regulators based on the type of license your advisor holds. You'll find contact information in the Appendix. If the financial advisor is registered:

- to provide life insurance products including segregated funds, go to the provincial superintendent of insurance and then the Office of the Superintendent of Financial Institutions (OSFI) as necessary

- for stocks, bonds, mutual funds or as an investment counsellor, file your complaint with the provincial regulatory organization, such as the Investment Dealers Association and/or the provincial stock exchange

- to offer mutual funds but not stocks and bonds, you'll eventually be able to take your complaint to the newly formed Mutual Fund Dealers Association (MFDA)

TREND The provincial regulators for securities and insurance will move to consolidate, reducing the duplication in their administrations, streamlining the regulation of the people who offer investment and insurance products and better align the regulations and disclosure requirements for those products, including mutual funds and segregated funds.

Here's a sample of the costs, taken from the Manitoba Securities Web site, that illustrate what might be involved when a commission is conducting an investigation, audit or hearing:

- $600 for each half day for the commission, regardless of the number of members involved
- $400 per day for any counsel, auditor or other person on the commission staff
- the costs for any counsel, auditor or person not on the commission staff, hired under contract
- witness' expenses, including travelling fees

These costs are charged to the broker or their firm if they are found to have been in the wrong.

3. File a Complaint with the Member's Professional Association

Not all financial advisors are members of a professional organization, but if yours is a member of a one, such as the Canadian Financial Planners Association (CAFP), Investment Counsel of Canada (ICAC), the Financial Planners Standards Council (FPSC), or the Canadian Association of Insurance and Financial Advisors (CAIFA), you can also file a complaint with them. You can find the complaint procedures on their Web site or by calling the national office. You'll find contact information in the Appendix.

4. Appeal to the Office of the Ombudsman

If your account is with a bank and a bank-owned brokerage firm, your place of last resort is the Canadian Banking Ombudsman. Their job is to help resolve problems that have exhausted all other channels. Before you contact them, you are expected to have worked through all the channels of the bank, starting with the local manager. If that person is unable to resolve your problem to your satisfaction, then you have to take your problem to one of the bank's vice-presidents. If that doesn't work, write or send an e-mail directly to that bank's president. Then, if your problem is still not resolved, you can take it to the bank's own ombudsman whose role is to help to resolve problems with its own customers. Then, if necessary, you can approach the Office of the Canadian Banking Ombudsman. For more information see www.bankingombudsman.com or contact them at 1-888-451-4519 or 416-287-2877 in Toronto.

If the financial reforms tabled by Paul Martin in June 2000 are passed, they will create a Financial Consumer Agency which will have the mandate of looking out for the interests of consumers and setting up the Canadian Financial Services Ombudsman to handle complaints for banks and any other financial services institution that wishes to participate.

TREND There will eventually be one centralized office or agency where people can go if they have a complaint, regardless of the type of financial problem, financial institution or investment product.

5. Appeal to the Media

If no one seems to be paying attention to your problem, you could pick up the phone and call a reporter at your local paper, radio or TV station who might do a story that could publicly embarrass the financial firm, or get them to pay attention to your concerns. Some media outlets have full-time consumer advocates. You could start with the business or a financial reporter to see if they think your story is newsworthy.

Media stories work because no one wants to receive bad publicity. Of course, you must be willing to make public the details of your situation.

6. Consider Arbitration

Arbitration is a process that attempts to resolve disputes without having to go to court. It is process that is used to resolve many types of problems ranging from divorce and estate issues to disputes between an investment dealer and clients. A neutral third party is hired as an independent arbitrator to decide in private how the dispute should be resolved after hearing the facts and arguments of both parties. In the securities industry, if the client requests that an arbitrator deal with the dispute, the investment dealer has to participate in the process and the arbitrator's decision is binding. Mandatory programs currently exist in all provinces except Newfoundland.

Arbitration is generally less expensive and faster than asking the courts to deal with the issue—it can sometimes be concluded in less than 90 days. The cost depends on the time it takes to resolve the dispute and any outside legal advice you hire. The minimum cost involves a three or four hour arbitration hearing, costing between $775 and $1,350, and then an hourly charge for the additional time that may be required.

The Investment Dealers Association of Canada (IDA) has set up arbitration processes for those that qualify as follows, although there may be exceptions:

- the dealer is a member of the Investment Dealers Association of Canada (IDA)

- an attempt has already been made to solve the problem through the securities dealer's own firm

- the claim, not including costs, must be more than $6,000 but no more than $100,000

- the dispute occurred after the following dates:

     January 1, 1992   BC
     January 1, 1996   Quebec

| June 30, 1998 | Ontario |
| July 1, 1999 | Alberta, Manitoba, New Brunswick, Nova Scotia, PEI, Saskatchewan |

Before making a request for alternative dispute resolution, you might want to consult with a securities lawyer to determine if it could be reasonably expected to provide the solution you are looking for. If you decide to proceed with this process, register your request for Alternative Dispute Resolution with the ADR chambers in your province and provide written details of the dispute, the dollar amount in question and how you have attempted to resolve the issue with the investment dealer (or their representative). For more information about your province's arbitration process, call 1-800-856-5154 or 416-362-8555 in Toronto.

7. Consider Court Action

For relatively small claims (for example, in Ontario under $6,000), you could consider taking your issue to Small Claims Court, which is relatively inexpensive. For larger amounts, you could initiate a court case either individually, or if a number of people are involved, as a class action suit, depending on the province you live in. If you are considering this route, you'll need to deal with a lawyer who specializes in securities law and has experience in resolving complaints. They will be able to review and assess your situation and tell you if it warrants court action.

TREND More lawyers will be willing to take on lawsuits on a contingency basis (where they take no fee upfront, but will take a percentage of any settlement), particularly where there is a potentially large settlement.

PROTECTION FOR YOUR DEPOSITS AND INVESTMENTS

Protection exists for investors in the event the financial institution they deal with goes bankrupt, but not if you lose money in the stock market. The amount of coverage depends on what financial institution you deal with and the types of investments you have. Here's a brief summary of what's available. Ask your financial firm for the details of the protection they have for your deposits and investments.

Canadian Deposit Insurance Corporation (CDIC)

The Canadian Deposit Insurance Corporation (CDIC), or for residents of Quebec, the Quebec Deposit Insurance Board, provides insurance coverage of up to $60,000 cash and GIC deposits held in cash accounts, RRSPs, RRIFs, and joint accounts that mature in five years or less at those firms covered by CDIC. Mutual funds, including money market funds, segregated funds, managed money products, and individual stocks and bonds are not covered under CDIC, since they are classified as investments, not deposits.

Suppose you have $55,000 in an RRSP and $50,000 in a GIC. The full amount would be protected because the money is held in different types of accounts. But if you have $70,000 in an RRIF account *in* GIC investments, only $60,000 would be protected if the company went under. The $60,000 limit applies to your principal *and* interest per depositor and account type. If you deposit $60,000 and it earns $5,000 in interest, that $5,000 is not covered.

• tip To get as much protection as possible under CDIC, some Canadians:

- deposit up to $60,000 in their own name and $60,000 in joint names at the same financial institution to have protection for up to $120,000
- will have their financial institution split their deposits between the bank/trust company and their related mortgage company

To determine how much insurance you have on your deposits, the CDIC Web site www.cdic.ca has a deposit insurance calculator.

There is currently over $400 million in the CDIC contingency fund. Each financial institution that is a member of CDIC pays an annual premium for its coverage based on its financial situation. Unfortunately, information related to their financial situation is not made public. Would it make sense to let consumers know who's doing well so they can make a more informed decision about who they are going to let mind their money?

Provincial Deposit Insurance Agencies

Deposits at credit unions are covered by the provincial deposit insurance agencies. The amount can vary from $60,000 to 100 percent of the funds on deposit depending on the coverage they have. In Quebec, deposits at caisses populaires, loan companies and provincial trust companies are covered by the Quebec Deposit Insurance Board. Contact your local credit union or caisses populaires for details.

Canadian Investors Protection Fund (CIPF)

CIPF offers protection against losses if the firm suffers a financial failure to investors who hold their accounts with a brokerage firm registered with one of the major exchanges or the Investment Dealers Association (IDA). These firms are required to meet minimum standards for internal controls, accounting, reporting, and record keeping, as well maintaining adequate capital and cash flow to ensure their financial stability. Clients of mutual fund dealer firms are not protected by the CIPF unless the firm is registered with a major exchange or the IDA.

Coverage of up to a total of $1 million exists for cash and investment accounts, and up to $1 million for registered accounts (RRSP, RRIF, etc.) in accounts at each securities firm you deal with, for losses after September 1, 1999. These are covered as follows:

- The value of your registered accounts—RRSPs and RRIFs, LIFs, LIRAs, etc.—are combined and treated as one account. Suppose you have an RRSP valued at $550,000 and a RRIF valued at $600,000. Only the first $1 million would be covered under the basic CIPF coverage.

- The value of all your own open accounts is combined with your share of any jointly registered open accounts. Suppose you have an open account valued at $500,000 and own 50 percent of an account valued at $800,000. Your total CIPF coverage would be $900,000.

The firm pays fees into the fund based on the risk it potentially represents. The fund, which is overseen by the Canadian Securities Administrators (CSA), is currently over $200 million. For more information about the Canadian Investor Protection Fund and a current listing of all the members of the CIPF, see www.cipf.ca or call the CIPF at 416-866-8366.

Some investment firms also carry additional investor coverage.

Provincial Investor Protection Plans

Ontario, BC, Quebec, and Nova Scotia have plans that provide investor protection ranging from $2,500 to $10,000. For example, the Ontario Contingency Trust Fund (OCTF) currently provides up to $5,000 of coverage for Ontario clients that hold their mutual fund accounts with mutual fund dealers who are not covered under CIPF (because they are not a member of a major stock exchange or the IDA).

The Mutual Fund Dealers Association of Canada has a proposed Investor Protection Plan that will be modelled after the CIPF. It will be designed to protect investors who hold their accounts with mutual funds dealers from loss in the event the firm fails financially or ends up insolvent. When this MFDA Investor Protection Plan is implemented, Canadian investors will have similar protection, regardless of whether they purchase and hold their investments through a mutual fund dealer or a brokerage firm.

CompCorp

CompCorp, operated by the Canadian Life and Health Insurance Compensation Plan, offers protection for policyholders that have annuities or life insurance policies issued by member Canadian life insurance companies. CompCorp guarantees up to $200,000 death benefits under life insurance policies and annuity payments of up to $2,000 a month for each annuitant, from each insurer. For joint and survivor annuities, the limit is $2,000 a month for *each* annuitant covered. CompCorp also guarantees deposits of up to $60,000 held in RRSP, RRIF and non-registered savings accounts.

HOW TO PROTECT YOURSELF

It's often easier to prevent something going wrong beforehand, than it is to try to fix a problem after it happens. Here are nine things you can do to protect yourself and your investments:

1. Get it in writing. Always insist on a written agreement on how your account will be managed, such as a letter of understanding

or an investment policy statement that includes a statement of your financial situation and your investment objectives. Keep copies of all forms you sign including your application form and other agreements, and keep this information up to date. Never sign anything that makes you uncomfortable.

TREND More advisors will be using an investment policy statement and a written financial plan to clarify the terms of the relationship, your needs and what you can expect.

2. Check references. Contact the regulators and the professional associations to find out if any complaints have been registered against the advisor and what licenses they hold. Also consider contacting other clients to see how their relationship is working out.

TREND Look for an on-line directory of financial advisors registered in Canada in the near future. It would include the types of products each is licensed to sell, the protection offered to the investor and any disciplinary judgments logged against the advisor.

3. Read everything. Before signing any documents, read them and ask questions about anything that is unclear. If you are provided with documentation, such as a simplified prospectus for mutual funds, information folder for segregated funds or preliminary prospectus for a new stock issue, read it before proceeding. It can't help if you don't read it. If you have purchased life insurance and the policy has been delivered to you, read it during the 10-day examination period to make sure the terms are acceptable to you

4. Don't sign blank forms. Just don't do it.

5. Make sure it's needed. A power of attorney, for example, is a powerful document that gives the person named the authority to make investments for you without contacting you. Don't underestimate the power you are giving over when you sign this document.

   The power of attorney document is mainly used for discretionary money management relationships, or investments in limited partnerships, not just because it's more "convenient." It is best to discuss the potential need for this document with your lawyer or someone you trust.

6. Know what to do. Find out what to do in case something goes wrong in the future.

7. Keep records. Keep written records of all your activities with your financial advisor, including the dates and topic(s) of conversation, outlining exactly what was discussed and what was agreed to.

8. Check your statements. Review all your statements as soon as they arrive to ensure that all the activity and holdings in your account are accurate—and that there are no surprises. If you deal with a brokerage firm, the statements must be sent to you at least quarterly, or every month if there is activity in your account. Mutual fund companies send out statements semi-annually for accounts held directly with them and life insurance companies are recognizing that clients who hold investments, such as segregated funds or universal life policies, are looking to see a statement more than once a year.

   Soon you may be able to print your own statement on-line whenever you want. Having access to more timely information will help you review the information for accuracy and use it to confirm all the activity for the time period. But reporting and checking your statements is not the same as managing your investments.

9. Just ask. If you have any questions or concerns about the activity in your account, raise them with your financial advisor, their firm, and if necessary, the appropriate authorities.

 TREND More information will be provided in plain English, free of legal, technical, and investment jargon. Rule number one of disclosure: Write the material so people can understand it.

SUMMARY

While there is a trend in the financial services industry to disclose more information to help protect the investing public, don't rely too heavily on disclosure information to protect you when that information comes from within the industry itself. Often disclosure rules are put into place after a problem, or potential problem, has surfaced— closing the barn door after the horse has already left! Disclosure rules require that a *minimum* amount of information be communicated to investors, but you should ask enough questions so that you get all the information you need to know. You have to keep asking (and reading and researching) until you are comfortable with what is being discussed, or move on until you do find what you need.

Increasing your financial knowledge is the route to financial success, which is why financial intelligence is the topic of the next chapter.

Financial Intelligence Shouldn't Be An Oxymoron

"Experience does not err; only your judgments err
by expecting from her what is not in her power."

Leonardo Da Vinci

Investment success depends, in part, on knowing the rules of the
game and the type of investor you are, and then figuring out what
will work for your situation, not just doing what you think everyone else is doing. Here's some profiles of some investors I've met.
(Any resemblance to someone you might know is strictly coinci-
dental.)

INVESTOR PROFILES

Bull	Sees nothing but a market that goes straight up. Doesn't want any of that "negative talk." Risk is something he's just "not going to worry about."
Bear	"Oh dear, oh dear." Sees nothing but the potential for the market to go straight down and take all his money with it. Better described as a saver than an investor.
(Card) Shark	Or rather, the gambler. Loves the rush. Willing to step right up and give the wheel a spin. Lady Luck is on his side. Wins some and loses some. But never adds it up to see if he's getting ahead.
Lamb	The investing version of a "babe in the woods." Has lots to learn and follows those who are making the most noise. Needs to learn how to keep from being slaughtered.
Pig	"What do you mean, I earned only 20 percent?!!" Just plain greedy. Focused more on returns than achieving financial goals.
Ostrich	"Just don't tell me about it." Wants his financial advisor to do what they think needs to be done. Sometimes mistaken for a "lamb."
Monkey	"You can't catch me. Look at me." Jumps from investment to investment, or broker to broker. May or may not spend hours doing research.
Dolphin	The thinker and decision maker. Considers the information and makes decisions he is prepared to live with, regardless of the way the current is going.

SEX IS TAUGHT IN SCHOOL.
WHY NOT MONEY?

I guess more properly, the title of this section should be *"sex education* is taught in schools. Why not money?" Isn't the ability to be self-sufficient and not have to depend on government support a model that every government want us to buy into?

Why then can we teach sex education in our schools and not financial literacy? In Toronto, sex education has been part of the health and life skills curriculum since the early '70s (I was in one of the very first classes and remember how controversial it was). It seems that money is treated as if it is even a more taboo topic, but knowing how money works is an essential life skill that students shouldn't leave high school without.

Graduating students are sent unsolicited credit cards without detailed instructions outlining their prudent care and management and for some—even some of our brightest—it is a one-way street to the dark side of debt. Money management concepts and investing should not be something only those students who take business or economics get a taste of. Nor do the investing simulation games they may play provide them with the essential skills they need, unless we want them to become day traders.

To be fair, educators could not have imagined that investing would become something that any one with a computer would be able to access directly. Not too long ago, investing was the exclusive preserve of the rich and professionals, but times have changed and it's time the government took steps to ensure that every student graduating from high school in this country knows how to navigate their way through the financial services industry. Everyone needs to know how to mind their money and how be a good consumer of financial services, not just how to invest.

THE KNOWLEDGE GAP

In her "Investment Funds in Canada and Consumer Protection" report published in October 1998, Glorianne Stromberg referred to the "knowledge gap" that exists between the consumer and the investment professional. But that gap may be even wider, since a knowledge gap exists between the consumer and almost all financial services professionals, and for more than just investment funds—it includes life insurance, taxation, all managed money products, and dealing with debt, to name just a few topics.

In the '70s and '80s, the banks and trust companies made large profits from lending Canadians money to buy homes or consumer products. Often, those borrowers had little idea of how much interest they paid, but eventually, every new loan application was required to disclose the total cost of borrowing, in actual dollars, not just expressed as a percentage. It took until 2000 for mutual funds, just one of the many managed products, to offer estimates of their costs in dollars, not just in percentages.

You don't have to know anything about the economy, businesses, prudent financial management, and the risks in the financial markets before you can click your way to financial success or financial ruin. Poor investments, either in terms of their performance or high costs, could add stress to our social safety net, including CPP and OAS. Now, I'm not suggesting that people *have* to have a license before they can do their own investing, but investors would be better off if they had basic training and understood the rules, because it's *not* a game. Everyone should assess how equipped he or she is.

HOW WELL EQUIPPED ARE YOU?

While this list is not extensive, here are 10 questions you can use to assess whether or not you are on the right track. Answer them as honestly as you can.

Yes No Don't know

❑ ❑ ❑ Would you be able to pass the Canadian Securities Course?

❑ ❑ ❑ Would you be able to pass the new Financial Planning Proficiency Exam?

❑ ❑ ❑ Are you confident about the investment decisions you make?

❑ ❑ ❑ Do you know the difference between a market order and a limit order?

❑ ❑ ❑ Do you have any experience making money in a losing market?

❑ ❑ ❑ Do you know how much risk you have in your portfolio?

❑ ❑ ❑ Are you using any strategies to protect your money from extreme losses?

❑ ❑ ❑ Is your portfolio doing better than the appropriate benchmark?

❑ ❑ ❑ Do you know how much you paid (in dollars) in fees, commissions and other expenses over the last 12 months?

❑ ❑ ❑ Is your portfolio making the return you need to achieve your financial goals?

If you didn't answer yes to most of the above questions, you have some work to do. Managing your money is not like a computer game. What you don't know could have adverse effect on your net worth. Mistakes are an expensive way to learn.

DO YOU NEED TO PAY MORE ATTENTION TO YOUR PENSION PLAN?

It's not just the money you have in your registered plans and investment accounts that you may need to pay attention to. Your employer pension plan could end up being worth more than anything else you own—and you could be responsible for minding it.

Company Pension Plans

About 45 percent of working Canadians expect to receive a company pension from their employer. Pension plans are not mandatory and are not created equally, nor are they well understood by those who have them.

There are two main types of employer-sponsored pension plans:

- The defined benefit plan, where the income in retirement is guaranteed and based on a defined formula. The employer administers the plan, makes the investment decisions and backs the guarantee. You may or may not be required to make contributions.

- The defined contribution plan that does *not* guarantee any specific benefit at retirement. The money contributed and the money it earns determine what you'll get in retirement. *You* need to make sure the investments work so your money grows to provide you with enough income in retirement.

Defined Benefit Plan

Under a defined benefit plan, the employer is responsible (with the help of an actuary) for ensuring there is enough money to pay the pensions of all retirees. The benefit at retirement is based on some sort of formula, such as the number of years of service and a percentage of your salary. It is the fiduciary responsibility of the employer and trustees of the defined pension benefit plan to manage the money in it prudently on behalf of the employees. They establish performance benchmarks for the pension fund manager(s) who is expected to produce competitive investment returns. They also set strict investment guidelines for the pension plan, sometimes referred to as an investment policy statement, and an appropriate asset allocation. Every three years or so, the pension plan is reviewed by an actuary who determines whether the funds in the defined pension plan, combined with future contributions and earnings, will be adequate to provide the guaranteed retirement benefits. If the plan is considered to be underfunded, the employer is required to add money to it.

If the actuary determines that the current amount in the plan, plus projected earnings and contributions are more than necessary to pay the current and future pension liabilities to the employees, the fund is said to have developed a "surplus." This "extra" money can become the source of a legal and political battle since there is no legislation that clarifies who the surplus belongs to: the employees or the employer.

Defined Contribution Plan

A defined contribution pension plan (DCP)—also known as a money purchase plan (MPP)—only specifies how much the employee and employer have to contribute each year. There is no guarantee as to how much retirement income you will get. The amount you put in and how much it earns determines your retirement income. The term "money purchase" came from the time when the money that had accumulated in your account had to be used to purchase an annuity at retirement.

Your income in retirement will be the result of the decisions you make or didn't make, so it is up to you to ensure your money is managed wisely. If there is a shortfall in the income your savings will provide, you are the one who ends up having to live on less. Your employer is not responsible for funding any shortfall.

Do You Know Enough to Make the Right Decisions?

Does your defined contribution plan require you to make decisions about something you know very little about? If you don't know how to make good investment decisions, how well are you going to be able to manage your own pension money? It is ironic that pension funds that are held in a defined benefit plan, are professionally managed by money managers who must adhere to a strict investment program and are overseen by the trustees of the pension plan and/or the employer. But pension funds that are held in a defined contribution plan are left to the individual employee who may have very limited financial intelligence—through no fault of their own. Does it seem right to you that two employees who contribute the same amount to their defined contribution plan would receive very different incomes in retirement just because they selected different investment options based on their investment expertise, or lack of it?

If employers expect their employees to manage their own pension money, then they need to ensure those employers are prepared to make good decisions or provide them with financial education and the tools the need to make informed decisions.

TREND Financial education and independent financial advice will become a standard employee benefit that is paid for by the employer, much like dental or prescription drug coverage.

Changing from a Defined Benefit to a Defined Contribution Plan

Because the final liability for funding a defined benefit plan lies with the employer, some companies want to change their defined benefit plan to a defined contribution plan. That would improve the corporation's bottom line by reducing their own future obligations and shift the risk of there not being enough money in the plan for retirement—*from* the employer *to* the employee. If the portfolio underperforms, the employee could end up with less in retirement than they would have as a member of a defined benefit plan.

The defined contribution plan gives the employee the opportunity to make their own investment decisions, but some may underestimate the responsibility they will be taking on for their own retirement income. If your employer wants to change from a defined benefit to a defined contribution plan, you should seriously examine whether or not you know enough to successfully manage your own pension fund. If you don't, then your employer should also be willing to provide an extensive financial education program, not just financial incentives.

Before you make your final decision, you should get independent advice from a lawyer or financial advisor. Making this major a financial decision without such advice would be like a spouse requesting that their partner (soon to be ex-partner) sign divorce papers without independent legal advice.

TREND Employees considering moving from a defined benefit to a defined contribution plan will be required to get their own independent advice, or will have to waive their right to that independent financial advice, before signing any official papers.

STEPS YOU CAN TAKE NOW

There is a lot of information available on investment products, financial strategies, and market conditions. This information, while interesting, can provide more stress and anxiety and lead to information over-load as you try to make sense of it all.

So what steps can you take to increase your financial intelligence? There are courses you can take, seminars you can attend, educational material on the Web, and books filling the shelves at libraries and bookstores. Whether you are managing your own investments or working with a financial advisor, you can be more successful if you take the time to learn the ropes.

Take Some Courses

It's not too late for you to go back to school. In fact, your investment in financial education could give you a bigger return than what you've made on your investments so far. Some of the courses just require your time. Others require an investment of both time and money.

Investor Learning Centre

The Investor Learning Centre, funded in part by the Canadian Securities Institute, has developed some great educational material for the investing public focusing on investment literacy. It holds numerous educational programs that highlight the basics of investing, covers investing products as well as how to analyze stocks. Their Web site is www.investorlearning.ca and they can also be reached at 1-888-452-5566.

Canadian Securities Institute (CSI)

If you want to take the course brokers are required to take before they can become licensed, you could take the Canadian Securities Course offered through the Canadian Securities Institute (CSI) as a private (rather than an industry) student. You can take any of their courses including the ones on investment management, personal financial planning and wealth management techniques. You can get their complete list of courses at 1-800-274-8355 or www.csi.ca.

Financial Planning Courses

A number of colleges offer programs in personal financial planning, courses that are recognized as being preparatory to the Certified Financial Planning (CFP) designation. The Canadian Institute of

Financial Planning (CIFP) also offers a six-part course on personal financial planning.

You may also find night courses offered at your local college or high school. These are educational in content, but some may be taught by salespeople looking for new clients.

Public Seminars

You may have attended a public seminar, hoping to learn about an investment or a financial strategy that would make a difference to your financial situation. Some seminars are little more than one-hour commercials for the latest investment product, delivered by a paid speaker designed to round up and wind up an audience. Others contain a lot of good educational material that may or may not apply to your specific situation.

As a good consumer, you need to know to whom you are listening, what their qualifications and biases are, as well as the purpose of the seminar. While you may pick up some good tips, it's wise not to believe everything you hear. Use the seminar as a starting point for exploring a financial idea, not the end point.

Canadian Shareowners Association

The Canadian Shareowners Association is also a good place to look if you are just starting out. If you want to learn the basics of investing in stocks, you can become a member and receive their newsletter and guides, and invest in their preselected list of stocks on a monthly basis without spending a lot of money. You'll find them at www.shareowner.ca

Investment Clubs

Investment clubs can be a good way to learn about investing in stocks. You and a group of investors, some you know and some you don't, pool some dollars and then get together on a regular basis to discuss the ins and outs of investing and decide which stocks to buy and sell. Today, you can even find clubs on the Internet, although you can't see who you are dealing with so it can be harder to know their motivation.

Educational Material on the Web

If you haven't looked lately, there's lots of information on the Web at sites hosted by major financial and educational institutions—and some that is hosted by individuals working out of their basement. However, there is so much duplication of information that you really have to sift through the sites to find something unique.

The information is there, for everything from basic concepts, frequently asked questions to financial calculators. Unfortunately, not all the information is up-to-date and it does not provide you with everything you need to know.

 TREND Now you can invest without the guidance of a financial advisor, brokerage Web sites are building libraries of educational material. Providing this information for you, even it you don't use it, may lighten some of the brokerage's liability, or reduce the number of questions you need to ask their staff.

Investors will eventually be able to use on-line quizzes to assess their investment knowledge, as well as how to use the on-line software. Some on-line brokers may want their investors to take an on-line "test-drive" before they allow them to use certain features of the site. For example, you might not be able to trade in options unless you can prove you know what you are doing.

On-Line Investment Simulations

Another way to test your skill in the stock market is to try one of the on-line investing simulation games. What better way to learn how to invest without having to risk any of your own money? A number of sites offer on-line simulation games. Here's are a couple of the more regular ones:

www.tse.com   Toronto Stock Exchange "Investment Challenge"

www.tradersplay.com   Hosted by E*trade

However, these games can be a mixed blessing. You'll get a feel for what it's like to trade, but you may not get a real sense of how you would react if you ended up with less money than you started with. It's one thing to lose imaginary money, but it's entirely different to lose the real thing.

To imagine how you might feel if you lost money, pretend you have $100,000 to invest. Use the following personal rating system to record what your reaction might be if that $100,000 suffered real losses and your account went down to $90,000, $80,000 or even $60,000.

PERSONAL LOSS RATING SYSTEM	
If my $100,000 turned into:	Personal Rating *(Use the rating system below)*
$ 90,000	_____
$ 80,000	_____
$ 60,000	_____
$120,000	I'm a genius!
Rating System	
C	Comfortable. I'm not concerned.
H	How could I be so stupid!
M	My spouse/partner will think I'm stupid.

| S | Stop! I can't stand to lose any more. |
| E | Enough is enough. Now I have to work longer at my day job to earn it back. |

You might have seen newspaper articles where experienced professional money managers are pitted against novices in investment games and the novice investor outperforms the experienced money managers. How is that possible? One of the key differences between them is that the professional is used to investing with real money and being responsible for "other people's money." They know how much risk is involved in the investments they select and probably have difficulty thinking of investing as a game. They have developed a professional aversion to unnecessary investment risk and plan for the worst. On the other hand, the novice has nothing to lose and just goes for the highest potential profits in the spirit of the game.

Books to Read

About a decade ago, financial books started to become hot sellers and there is no scarcity of books about investing and financial planning. Not all of them will be right for you, but there are a number of good books that many people have found to be worth their time. I've been asked many times over for a list of good books on investment and financial planning strategies. Here are just a few suggestions.

GETTING STARTED	
Chilton, David	*The Wealthy Barber: Everyone's Common-Sense Guide to Becoming Financially Independent*
Cooper, Sherry	*The Cooper Files: A Practical Guide to Your Financial Future*

Croft, Richard
  & Kirzer, Eric   *The Beginner's Guide to Investing: A Practical Guide To Putting Your Money to Work for You*

INVESTMENT CLASSICS

Graham, Benjamin   *The Intelligent Investor*

Seigel, Jeremy   *Stocks for the Long-Run: The Definitive Guide to Financial Market Returns and Long-Term Investment Strategies*

Schwed, Jr, Fred   *Where Are the Customers' Yachts? or A Good Hard Look at Wall Street*

Stanley, T.
  & Danko, W.   *The Millionaire Next Door: The Surprising Secrets of America's Wealthy*

ASPECTS OF FINANCIAL PLANNING

Cohen, Bruce   *The Money Advisor: The Canadian Guide to Successful Financial Planning*

Foster, Sandra   *You Can't Take It With You: The Common-Sense Guide to Estate Planning for Canadians*

Foster, Sandra   *Make the Most of What You've Got: The Canadian Guide to Managing Retirement Income*

Hartman, George   *Risk is Still a Four Letter Word: The Asset Allocation Approach to Investing*

KPMG   *Tax Planning for You and Your Family, 2000*

Jacks, Evelyn   *201 Easy Ways to Reduce your Taxes*

Jacks, Evelyn   *Make Sure It's Deductible: Little-Known Tax Tips for Your Small Business*

Pape, Gordon   *Gordon Pape's 2000 Buyer's Guide to RRSPs*

FOR WOMEN ONLY

While I don't believe that money cares what your gender is, if you prefer to read a book for women by a woman, here are a couple to consider.

Thomas-Yaccato,
Joanne   *The Balancing Act: A Canadian Woman's Finan-
                    cial Success Guide*
Vax-Oxlade, Gail   *A Woman of Independent Means: A Woman's
                    Guide to Full Financial Security*

SUMMARY

The stock market doesn't care who you are, how much money you have or what you know. In golf, you get a handicap if you are not as good as the people you are playing with, but in the stock market you don't. You are playing for real. Remember, some people spend a lot of time learning how to invest or selecting a financial advisor or professional money managers to do it for them, because they don't want to play against people who are more experienced. Remember, it takes financial intelligence to make good financial decisions.

No One Cares About Your Money As Much As You Do

"Knowledge doesn't pay. It is what you do with it."
Arnold Glasow

If investing and managing money were easy, there'd be more millionaires in Canada. It takes know-how, discipline, research, and time to grow a portfolio and manage your finances.

Behavioural finance is a relatively new area of study that examines why investors do what they do. There seem to be a number of ways investors inadvertently set themselves up for disappointment. Here are seven of the leading ones:

1. Investors become overconfident and believe they understand more than they really do. The Internet gives access to a multitude of information, and as E*Trade Canada says, provides "you with the most current tools that make it easy to feel confident about your trades."

   Terrance Odean, an assistant professor at the University of California, with Brad Barber, studied investors who switched from phone-based trading to on-line trading. In their September 1999 report entitled "On-line Investors: Do The Slow Die First?" they found that when investors go on-line, "they trade more actively, more speculatively and less profitably than before—lagging the market by more than three percent annually." They concluded that investors become overconfident and attributed this to the "illusion of knowledge and the illusion of control." Maybe the cost of the trade isn't the most important factor.

2. Some investors like to buy what everyone is buying, believing that everyone can't be wrong. It's easier to be wrong with friends than to be right alone.

3. There are people who tend to do too much trading. This is no surprise, what with all the information they receive through newspapers, financial TV and radio shows, magazines, and on-line sites.

4. Too many investors focus on the short-term rather than the long-term trends. Maybe this is because delayed gratification is, well, so delayed.

5. They become emotionally attached to their investments and find it hard to sell them, even when they are losing money. Rather than selling them when their research indicates they should, they want to hold them until they can get back at least as much as they paid for it.

6. Some investors, and their advisors, become overly optimistic or pessimistic. When markets are good, they invest like the market will only go up and don't take enough steps to protect their capital. When markets are difficult, they invest as if market will always go down.

7. When making choices, investors tend to pick something from each option offered. Richard Thaler, a professor of economics and behavioural science at the University of Chicago stated, that if an investor is offered a certain number of investment options, he or she will chose that number of investments for their portfolio. Suppose your company pension plan offers you two investment options, a bond fund and an equity fund. Based on his study of 401(k)—sort of like an RRSP—investors, you'd likely put half your portfolio in the bond fund and the half in the equity fund. And what happens when there are four choices? Investors tend to put 25% of their money in each investment option.

When your investment portfolio is based on the number of choices offered rather than the potential returns these investments might make toward helping you achieve your financial goals, there is a disconnect between what you need to do and what you actually do.

DON'T CONFUSE
A BULL MARKET FOR BRAINS

Investors have been lulled into a false sense of security about how easy it is to make money. The continually rising stock market makes us feel as if we are more in control, but don't confuse access to trading and research with being able to control the markets. The stock markets are not something you can ever control. At best, you might learn how to manage your investments wisely. But it's not your fault. Much of the information you now see and hear related to investing is really some form of advertising or marketing. We even call equities, those stocks that go up and down, "growth" investments because investors seem to like that term better. "Past performance is not indicative of future returns" is more than a slogan.

Be honest. Do you want to be a serious investor, or is it trading in a bull market that you find exciting? If it's trading, you are not the only one. But despite the thrill of trading, it's having enough stocks in your portfolio that makes the difference.

THE INTERNET: THE GREAT EQUALIZER?

It's been said that the Internet is a great equalizer, but it is only a tool and you have to know both how to use it and how to apply it. Inexperienced investors are now going head-to-head with the best in the industry. Some may have beginners' luck and others will just ride the bull market for as long as it lasts, but it takes more than picking a few good stocks to be a successful long-term investor. It's only when you know how to apply the information that is available that the Internet becomes a great equalizer. Even though it's cheap to place a trade on-line, the wrong decision can still be costly.

Investment management and financial planning can help you make sure you don't take on more risk than you need to. A written investment policy statement and financial plan, may provide you with more protection than the suitability rules ever did and help you be clear about what you want to accomplish.

MORE CHOICES THAN EVER BEFORE

For some people, buying financial products and advice is like buying clothes—for some, off the rack is fine, while others will settle for nothing less than made-to-measure. There are financial products available off-the-rack, off-the-rack but with alterations, ready-made with alterations, and those that are totally made-to-measure. When it comes to selecting investment products and advice, you don't have to settle for something that is "almost" right, but just a little too tight on the budget, a little too loose in the approach or not quite the right style. You shouldn't pay for financial advice you don't need, accept less than you are paying for, or pay too much. And never confuse sales ability with professional financial advice.

There isn't anything wrong with paying fees for work you want done. If you want someone to paint your house, cut the grass or fix your car, you pay to have it done. If you need a lawyer to represent you or an accountant to do your books, you're going to pay for their services. But is it not uncommon to ask for an estimate of what it will cost and to do some comparison shopping to find out if the price is competitive and receive a detailed itemized statement. If mechanics are required to provide you with a quote and an itemized invoice for all the work they do on your car, why not financial advisors and brokerage firms? Investment products and services are often priced at what people are willing to pay, rather than whether or not they provide real value. Although you can't control the financial markets, you can manage your costs and make sure you are getting value for the dollars you pay. After all, it is your money.

KNOW WHO YOU ARE DEALING WITH

The financial services industry is very profitable—whether the firm sells, distributes or manufactures investment or insurance products or offers banking services. These firms are looking not just to have more assets to administer, but for more assets to manage—for fees. You'll find firms that do it all, manufacturing, distributing and selling their own proprietary products along with the products of other firms. Now many banks are offering their own investment products as well as the mutual funds of third-party companies such as AGF and Fidelity.

While this vertical integration is good for the financial firms, how do you make sure your interests are foremost in the advice or recommendations you receive?

VERTICAL INTEGRATION WITHIN THE FINANCIAL SERVICES INDUSTRY

Manufacturers	builds and brings investment products to market and wants greater market share—more money under management
The Dealer Firm	distributes products manufactured by their own firm or by others
Financial Advisor	works with clients and distributes products that may or may not be manufactured by a related company
Client/Consumer	may rely on a financial advisor for advice and product selection or deal direct

Financial services regulations set out only the minimum standards for proficiency and disclosure. As it stands now, you have to rely on the very people who stand to profit from the services and products they provide you with for information. While these disclosure requirements attempt to protect consumers from unscrupulous advisors, they are not designed to help protect you from yourself.

Can you do it yourself? Most people can learn how to manage their own finances—given enough time, education and experience—if they are willing to make the commitment. If you aren't, you would be better off partnering with a qualified financial advisor who has the experience and perspective to help you avoid making expensive investment mistakes or missing key planning opportunities. But even in this type of partnership, you are still responsible for acting in your own best interests so make sure you don't abdicate your responsibility for the decisions that affect your future.

It's up to you to decide the level of service you need, how much you will pay, the types of investments you want for your account, and the depth of advice you need. Throughout the book, I've given you some of the questions you can ask to help you get the information you need to help you make the right decisions for you and your family. Don't be afraid to use them.

You are the one who has to live with the consequences of your decisions. When it comes to "who's minding your money," you'd better be a big part of it. After all, no one cares about your money as much as *you* do!

In a time when we have access to more information than we ever had before, author Henry David Thoreau's words of advice still ring true:

> *To know that we know what we know, and*
> *that we do not know what we do not know,*
> *that is true knowledge.*

Appendix A

CONTACT NUMBERS

Here's a list of contact phone numbers and Web site addresses (where they exist) for various industry organizations, associations and regulators.

PROVINCIAL REGULATORS

Alberta

Alberta Securities Commission	780-427-5201	www.gov.ab.ca
Alberta Insurance Council	780-422-1592	

British Columbia

BC Securities Commission	604-899-6597	www.gov.bc.ca
Insurance Council of British Columbia	604-660-2947	

Manitoba

The Manitoba Securities Commission	204-945-2548	www.gov.mb.ca
Superintendent of Insurance	204-945-2542	

New Brunswick

Office of the Administrator 506-658-3060 www.gov.nb.ca
Superintendent of Insurance 506-453-2541

Newfoundland and Labrador

Securities Division 709-729-4189 www.gov.nf.ca
Insurance Division 709-729-2571

Nova Scotia

Nova Scotia Securities Commission 902-424-6859 www.gov.ns.ca
Superintendent of Insurance 902-424-7742

Ontario

Ontario Securities Commission 416-597-0681 www.osc.gov.on.ca
Financial Services Commission 416-590-7000 www.fsco.gov.on.ca

NWT

Securities Registry 867-873-0243

Nunavut

Legal Registries 867-873-0586

Quebec

Securities Division 514-940-2150 www.gov.qc.ca
Insurance Division 418-528-9140

PEI

Registrar of Securities 902-368-4550 www.gov.pe.ca
Superintendent of Insurance 902-368-4550

Saskatchewan

Saskatchewan Securities
Commission 306-787-5645 www.gov.sk.ca
Superintendent of Insurance 306-787-7881

Yukon Territory

Registrar of Securities 867-393-6251 www.gov.yk.ca
Superintendent of Insurance 867-667-5111

OTHER USEFUL FINANCIAL SERVICES CONTACTS

Canadian Association of
  Financial Planners (CAFP)   416-593-6592 www.cafp.org

Canadian Association of Insurance
  and Financial Advisors (CAIFA)   1-800-563-5822 www.caifa.com
                                       416-444-5251

Canadian Banking Ombudsman
  (CBO)   1-888-451-4519
                                       www.bankingombudsman.com
                                       416-287-2877

Canadian Institute of Chartered
  Accountants   416-977- 3222 www.cica.ca

Canadian Institute of Financial
  Planning   416-865-1237 www.cifp.ca

Canadian Securities Institute (CSI)   1-800-274-8355 www.csi.ca

Canadian Venture Exchange
  (CNDX)   1-877-884-CNDX www.cdnx.ca

Certified General Accountants
  Association of Canada   1-800-663-1529
                                       www.cga-canada.org

Consumer Assistance Centre,
  Canada Life and Health
  Insurance Association Inc.   English
                                       1-800-268-8099 www.clhia.ca
                                       416-777-2344
                                       French
                                       1-800-361-8070
                                       514-845-6173

Credit Union Institute of Canada   1-800-267-CDIC www.ciuc.com

Deposit Insurance Corporation
  of Ontario   1-800-268-6653 www.dico.com

Financial Planners Standards
  Council (FPSC)   416-593-8586 www.cfp-ca.org

Institute of Canadian Bankers   1-800-361-7339 www.icb.org

Insurance Brokers Association
  of Canada   1-800-387-2880 www.ibc.ca

Investment Counsel of Canada	416-504-1118
	www.investmentcounsel.org
Investment Dealers Association (IDA)	416-364-6133 www.ida.ca
Investment Funds Institute of Canada	1-888-865-4342 www.ific.ca
Investor Learning Centre	1-888-452-5566
	www.investorlearning.ca
Montreal Exchange (ME)	1-800-361-5353 www.me.org
Mutual Fund Dealers Association (MFDA)	416-943-5827 www.mfda.ca
Office of the Superintendent of Financial Institutions (OSFI)	1-800-385-8647
	www.osfi-bsif.gc.ca
	614-990-7788
Quebec Deposit Insurance Board	1-800-463-5662
	www.igif.gouv.qc.ca
	418-528 9728
Society of Management Accountants of Canada	905-949-3106
	www.cam-canada.org
Toronto Stock Exchange (TSE)	1-888-TSE-8392 www.tse.com
	416-947-4670

Appendix B

COST TABLES

The fees and other costs you pay each year erode the dollars you get to keep. These tables can be used to calculate how much you might be paying over the years for any type of investment program where an ongoing fee is charged—mutual funds, segregated funds, wraps, pooled, and discretionary accounts, other managed money products, fee-based accounts or investments inside a universal life policy.

Here's how to use the tables.

Locate the table for the long-term rate of return, before fees, you assume your portfolio will earn. Find the column for the annual percent you are being charged in fees or expenses. Go down to the row for the number of years you expect to hold that investment to get your personal cost factor. Then multiply the value of your account today by this cost factor. The result estimates the amount you can expect to pay to have your money managed.

Suppose you have a target return of 9 percent before expenses and your annual fees are 2.5 percent. If the current market value of your account is $100,000 and you intend to be invested for 20 years, your cost factor is 1.0326. Your total cost would be approximately $103,260 ($100,000 x 1.0326), in this case more than the amount you originally invested.

These tables assume that the expenses are collected in arrears, that is, at the end of each 12-month period. In reality, they are collected throughout the year and will be charged daily or monthly against the value of your account. As well, your returns will fluctuate throughout the year.

6% RETURNS BEFORE EXPENSES

	1.0%	1.5%	2.0%	2.5%	3.0%	3.5%	4.0%
1	0.0106	0.0159	0.0212	0.0265	0.0318	0.0371	0.0424
2	0.0217	0.0325	0.0432	0.0539	0.0645	0.0750	0.0855
3	0.0334	0.0498	0.0661	0.0822	0.0981	0.1139	0.1295
4	0.0456	0.0679	0.0899	0.1114	0.1327	0.1536	0.1741
5	0.0585	0.0868	0.1146	0.1417	0.1682	0.1942	0.2196
6	0.0720	0.1066	0.1402	0.1729	0.2048	0.2357	0.2659
7	0.0861	0.1272	0.1668	0.2052	0.2423	0.2782	0.3129
8	0.1010	0.1487	0.1945	0.2386	0.2810	0.3217	0.3608
9	0.1166	0.1711	0.2233	0.2731	0.3207	0.3662	0.4096
10	0.1330	0.1946	0.2531	0.3087	0.3615	0.4117	0.4592
11	0.1501	0.2190	0.2841	0.3456	0.4035	0.4582	0.5097
12	0.1681	0.2446	0.3164	0.3837	0.4467	0.5058	0.5611
13	0.1870	0.2713	0.3498	0.4230	0.4911	0.5545	0.6133
14	0.2069	0.2992	0.3846	0.4637	0.5368	0.6043	0.6665
15	0.2277	0.3283	0.4207	0.5057	0.5837	0.6552	0.7207
16	0.2496	0.3586	0.4583	0.5492	0.6320	0.7073	0.7757
17	0.2725	0.3903	0.4972	0.5940	0.6816	0.7606	0.8318
18	0.2965	0.4235	0.5377	0.6405	0.7326	0.8151	0.8888
19	0.3218	0.4580	0.5798	0.6884	0.7851	0.8709	0.9469
20	0.3483	0.4941	0.6235	0.7380	0.8390	0.9279	1.0059
21	0.3761	0.5318	0.6689	0.7892	0.8945	0.9863	
22	0.4053	0.5712	0.7160	0.8421	0.9515	1.0460	

6% RETURNS CONT'D

	1.0%	1.5%	2.0%	2.5%	3.0%	3.5%	4.0%
23	0.4359	0.6123	0.7650	0.8968	1.0101		
24	0.4680	0.6552	0.8159	0.9534			
25	0.5017	0.7000	0.8688	1.0118			
26	0.5371	0.7467	0.9237				
27	0.5743	0.7956	0.9807				
28	0.6132	0.8465	1.0400				
29	0.6541	0.8998					
30	0.6970	0.9554					
31	0.7421	1.0134					
32	0.7787						
33	0.8172						
34	0.8576						
35	0.8999						
36	0.9444						
37	0.9910						
38	1.0400						

7% RETURNS BEFORE EXPENSES

	1.0%	1.5%	2.0%	2.5%	3.0%	3.5%	4.0%
1	0.0107	0.0161	0.0214	0.0268	0.0321	0.0375	0.0428
2	0.0220	0.0330	0.0438	0.0547	0.0654	0.0761	0.0868
3	0.0340	0.0508	0.0674	0.0838	0.1000	0.1160	0.1319
4	0.0468	0.0696	0.0920	0.1141	0.1359	0.1573	0.1783
5	0.0602	0.0894	0.1179	0.1458	0.1731	0.1998	0.2260
6	0.0745	0.1103	0.1450	0.1789	0.2118	0.2438	0.2749
7	0.0896	0.1323	0.1735	0.2134	0.2519	0.2892	0.3252
8	0.1056	0.1554	0.2033	0.2494	0.2936	0.3360	0.3768
9	0.1226	0.1799	0.2346	0.2869	0.3368	0.3844	0.4299
10	0.1406	0.2056	0.2674	0.3260	0.3817	0.4344	0.4844
11	0.1596	0.2328	0.3018	0.3669	0.4282	0.4860	0.5403
12	0.1798	0.2614	0.3379	0.4095	0.4766	0.5393	0.5978
13	0.2011	0.2915	0.3757	0.4540	0.5267	0.5943	0.6569
14	0.2238	0.3233	0.4154	0.5004	0.5788	0.6511	0.7176
15	0.2477	0.3568	0.4569	0.5488	0.6328	0.7097	0.7799

7% RETURNS CONT'D

	1.0%	1.5%	2.0%	2.5%	3.0%	3.5%	4.0%
16	0.2731	0.3921	0.5006	0.5992	0.6889	0.7702	0.8439
17	0.3000	0.4293	0.5463	0.6519	0.7471	0.8328	0.9097
18	0.3285	0.4685	0.5942	0.7068	0.8075	0.8973	0.9772
19	0.3587	0.5099	0.6445	0.7642	0.8702	0.9640	1.0466
20	0.3907	0.5534	0.6972	0.8240	0.9353	1.0328	
21	0.4245	0.5993	0.7525	0.8864	1.0029		
22	0.4604	0.6477	0.8105	0.9514			
23	0.4984	0.6987	0.8713	1.0193			
24	0.5387	0.7524	0.9350				
25	0.5813	0.8091	1.0019				
26	0.6265	0.8688					
27	0.6743	0.9317					
28	0.7250	0.9980					
29	0.7787	1.0679					
30	0.8356						
31	0.8958						
32	0.9596						
33	1.0273						

8% RETURNS BEFORE EXPENSES

	1.0%	1.5%	2.0%	2.5%	3.0%	3.5%	4.0%
1	0.0108	0.0162	0.0216	0.0270	0.0324	0.0378	0.0432
2	0.0223	0.0334	0.0445	0.0554	0.0663	0.0772	0.0880
3	0.0347	0.0518	0.0687	0.0854	0.1019	0.1183	0.1344
4	0.0479	0.0713	0.0943	0.1169	0.1392	0.1610	0.1826
5	0.0620	0.0920	0.1214	0.1501	0.1782	0.2056	0.2325
6	0.0771	0.1141	0.1501	0.1850	0.2191	0.2521	0.2842
7	0.0932	0.1376	0.1804	0.2219	0.2619	0.3006	0.3379
8	0.1105	0.1625	0.2126	0.2606	0.3067	0.3510	0.3935
9	0.1289	0.1891	0.2466	0.3014	0.3537	0.4037	0.4512
10	0.1487	0.2174	0.2826	0.3444	0.4030	0.4585	0.5110
11	0.1697	0.2474	0.3207	0.3896	0.4546	0.5156	0.5730
12	0.1923	0.2794	0.3610	0.4373	0.5086	0.5752	0.6373
13	0.2164	0.3135	0.4037	0.4875	0.5652	0.6373	0.7040

8% RETURNS CONT'D

	1.0%	1.5%	2.0%	2.5%	3.0%	3.5%	4.0%
14	0.2422	0.3497	0.4489	0.5403	0.6245	0.7020	0.7731
15	0.2697	0.3882	0.4967	0.5960	0.6866	0.7694	0.8447
16	0.2992	0.4291	0.5473	0.6545	0.7517	0.8397	0.9190
17	0.3307	0.4727	0.6008	0.7162	0.8199	0.9129	0.9960
18	0.3644	0.5191	0.6575	0.7812	0.8913	0.9892	1.0759
19	0.4004	0.5684	0.7175	0.8496	0.9662	1.0688	
20	0.4389	0.6209	0.7810	0.9216	1.0446		
21	0.4801	0.6767	0.8482	0.9975			
22	0.5241	0.7360	0.9194	1.0773			
23	0.5712	0.7992	0.9947				
24	0.6215	0.8664	1.0744				
25	0.6753	0.9379					
26	0.7328	1.0139					
27	0.7943						
28	0.8601						
29	0.9304						
30	1.0056						

9% RETURNS BEFORE EXPENSES

	1.0%	1.5%	2.0%	2.5%	3.0%	3.5%	4.0%
1	0.0109	0.0164	0.0218	0.0273	0.0327	0.0382	0.0436
2	0.0227	0.0339	0.0451	0.0562	0.0673	0.0783	0.0892
3	0.0354	0.0528	0.0700	0.0870	0.1038	0.1205	0.1370
4	0.0491	0.0730	0.0965	0.1197	0.1425	0.1649	0.1869
5	0.0638	0.0947	0.1249	0.1545	0.1833	0.2116	0.2392
6	0.0798	0.1180	0.1552	0.1914	0.2265	0.2607	0.2939
7	0.0970	0.1431	0.1876	0.2307	0.2722	0.3124	0.2503
8	0.1156	0.1700	0.2222	0.2724	0.3205	0.3667	0.4110
9	0.1356	0.1988	0.2592	0.3167	0.3716	0.4239	0.4737
10	0.1572	0.2298	0.2986	0.3638	0.4256	0.4840	0.5393
11	0.1806	0.2631	0.3408	0.4139	0.4827	0.5473	0.6079
12	0.2058	0.2988	0.3859	0.4672	0.5430	0.6138	0.6797
13	0.2329	0.3372	0.4340	0.5237	0.6068	0.6838	0.7548
14	0.2622	0.3784	0.4854	0.5838	0.6743	0.7574	0.8335

9% RETURNS CONT'D

	1.0%	1.5%	2.0%	2.5%	3.0%	3.5%	4.0%
15	0.2939	0.4226	0.5403	0.6477	0.7457	0.8348	0.9157
16	0.3280	0.4701	0.5989	0.7156	0.8211	0.9162	1.0018
17	0.3649	0.5210	0.6616	0.7878	0.9008	1.0019	
18	0.4047	0.5758	0.7285	0.8644	0.9851		
19	0.4476	0.6345	0.8000	0.9459	1.0743		
20	0.4939	0.6976	0.8763	1.0326			
21	0.5438	0.7653	0.9579				
22	0.5977	0.8381	1.0450				
23	0.6559	0.9161					
24	0.7187	0.9999					
25	0.7865	1.0899					
26	0.8596						
27	0.9385						
28	1.0236						

10% RETURNS BEFORE EXPENSES

	1.0%	1.5%	2.0%	2.5%	3.0%	3.5%	4.0%
1	0.0110	0.0165	0.0220	0.0275	0.0330	0.0385	0.0440
2	0.0230	0.0344	0.0457	0.0570	0.0682	0.0794	0.0905
3	0.0360	0.0537	0.0713	0.0886	0.1058	0.1227	0.1395
4	0.0502	0.0747	0.0988	0.1226	0.1459	0.1688	0.1913
5	0.0657	0.0975	0.1286	0.1589	0.1886	0.2177	0.2461
6	0.0825	0.1221	0.1606	0.1980	0.2343	0.2696	0.3038
7	0.1009	0.1488	0.1951	0.2398	0.2830	0.3246	0.3649
8	0.1209	0.1777	0.2323	0.2847	0.3349	0.3831	0.4293
9	0.1426	0.2091	0.2724	0.3328	0.3904	0.4452	0.4973
10	0.1663	0.2430	0.3157	0.3845	0.4495	0.5110	0.5692
11	0.1921	0.2798	0.3623	0.4398	0.5127	0.5810	0.6450
12	0.2202	0.3197	0.4126	0.4992	0.5800	0.6552	0.7252
13	0.2508	0.3629	0.4668	0.5629	0.6519	0.7340	0.8098
14	0.2842	0.4097	0.5252	0.6312	0.7285	0.8176	0.8991
15	0.3204	0.4604	0.5881	0.7045	0.8103	0.9064	0.9935

10% RETURNS CONT'D

	1.0%	1.5%	2.0%	2.5%	3.0%	3.5%	4.0%
16	0.3600	0.5153	0.6560	0.7831	0.8976	1.0007	1.0931
17	0.4030	0.5749	0.7292	0.8674	0.9908		
18	0.4499	0.6394	0.8080	0.9577	1.0902		
19	0.5009	0.7093	0.8931	1.0547			
20	0.5565	0.7850	0.9847				
21	0.6170	0.8670	1.0835				
22	0.6829	0.9559					
23	0.7547	1.0523					
24	0.8329						
25	0.9180						
26	1.0107						

12% RETURNS BEFORE EXPENSES

	1.0%	1.5%	2.0%	2.5%	3.0%	3.5%	4.0%
1	0.0112	0.0168	0.0224	0.0280	0.0336	0.0392	0.0448
2	0.0236	0.0353	0.0470	0.0586	0.0701	0.0816	0.0930
3	0.0374	0.0558	0.0740	0.0920	0.1098	0.1274	0.1448
4	0.0527	0.0783	0.1036	0.1284	0.1528	0.1768	0.2004
5	0.0696	0.1032	0.1361	0.1682	0.1996	0.2303	0.2603
6	0.0884	0.1307	0.1718	0.2117	0.2505	0.2881	0.3247
7	0.1092	0.1610	0.2110	0.2592	0.3057	0.3506	0.3939
8	0.1322	0.1944	0.2539	0.3110	0.3658	0.4182	0.4683
9	0.1578	0.2312	0.3011	0.3677	0.4310	0.4912	0.5484
10	0.1862	0.2719	0.3529	0.4295	0.5018	0.5700	0.6344
11	0.2177	0.3168	0.4098	0.4970	0.5787	0.6553	0.7269
12	0.2525	0.3662	0.4722	0.5707	0.6624	0.7474	0.8264
13	0.2912	0.4208	0.5406	0.6512	0.7532	0.8470	0.9333
14	0.3341	0.4811	0.6158	0.7391	0.8519	0.9547	1.0483
15	0.3817	0.5475	0.6983	0.8351	0.9591	1.0710	1.1719
16	0.4344	0.6208	0.7889	0.9400	1.0755	1.1968	1.3048
17	0.4928	0.7017	0.8883	1.0545	1.2020	1.3326	1.4478
18	0.5577	0.7909	0.9973	1.1795	1.3395	1.4795	1.6014
19	0.6295	0.8893	1.1171	1.3160	1.4888	1.6383	1.7667

12% RETURNS CONT'D

	1.0%	1.5%	2.0%	2.5%	3.0%	3.5%	4.0%
20	0.7092	0.9979	1.2485	1.4650	1.6511	1.8098	1.9443
21	0.7976	1.1177	1.3928	1.6278	1.8273	1.9953	2.1353
22	0.8956	1.2498	1.5511	1.8056	2.0188	2.1957	
23	1.0042	1.3956	1.7249	1.9997	2.2268		
24	1.1247	1.5564	1.9156	2.2117	2.4528		
25	1.2583	1.7339	2.1250	2.4431	2.6983		
26	1.4063	1.9296	2.3548	2.6959	2.9651		
27	1.5706	2.1455	2.6070	2.9719	3.2549		
28	1.7526	2.3837	2.8839	3.2734			
29	1.9545	2.6465	3.1877				
30	2.1784	2.9365					
31	2.4266	3.2563					
32	2.7018						
33	3.0070						

15% RETURNS BEFORE EXPENSES

	1.0%	1.5%	2.0%	2.5%	3.0%	3.5%	4.0%
1	0.0115	0.0173	0.0200	0.0288	0.0345	0.0403	0.0460
2	0.0246	0.0368	0.0489	0.0610	0.0730	0.0849	0.0968
3	0.0395	0.0589	0.0781	0.0971	0.1159	0.1345	0.1528
4	0.0565	0.0840	0.1111	0.1377	0.1638	0.1895	0.2147
5	0.0758	0.1124	0.1482	0.1831	0.2172	0.2505	0.2831
6	0.0978	0.1446	0.1900	0.2340	0.2768	0.3183	0.3585
7	0.1228	0.1810	0.2371	0.2912	0.3433	0.3935	0.4418
8	0.1513	0.2223	0.2902	0.3552	0.4174	0.4769	0.5338
9	0.1838	0.2690	0.3501	0.4271	0.5001	0.5695	0.6353
10	0.2208	0.3220	0.4175	0.5076	0.5924	0.6723	0.7473
11	0.2628	0.3820	0.4936	0.0000	0.6953	0.7863	0.8711
12	0.3107	0.4500	0.5792	0.6991	0.8101	0.9128	1.0076
13	0.3653	0.5270	0.6758	0.8126	0.9382	1.0533	1.1584

15% **RETURNS** CONT'D

	1.0%	1.5%	2.0%	2.5%	3.0%	3.5%	4.0%
14	0.4274	0.6142	0.7846	0.9399	1.0811	1.2091	1.3249
15	0.4981	0.7129	0.9073	1.0826	1.2404	1.3821	1.5087
16	0.5785	0.8248	1.0455		1.4182	1.5740	1.7116
17	0.6702	0.9516			1.6165	1.7870	1.9356
18	0.7745	1.0951			1.8377	2.0233	2.1829
19	0.8933				2.0845	2.2857	2.4559
20	1.0285				2.3597	2.5768	2.7574

Index

SUGGESTIONS AND SEMINARS

Founded by Sandra Foster, CaratConnect's mandate is to provide quality, independent advice and expertise to the financial services industry and financial education to Canadians.

SERVICES INCLUDE:

- Consumer education through books and presentations.
- Expertise to the Canadian media.
- The 24-Carat Professional development programs. Products and services include consulting on a corporate and individual basis, customized workshops, written materials and tools.
- Strategic advice regarding organizational change, including business structure, acquiring a business, reputation management, business planning, human resources, regulations and communications.

If you have comments, opinions or are interested in having a seminar or workshop for your group or association, please contact us through one of the methods below:

By fax:	(416) 494-9530
Through the publisher:	John Wiley & Sons, Canada, Ltd. 5353 Dundas St. West, 4th Floor Etobicoke, Ontario, M9B 6H8
Or through	CaratConnect 4936 Yonge Street, Suite 252 North York, Ontario M2N 6S3
By email:	fosters@idirect.com